In the mornings we found ice on our water buckets and our milk a chunky slush.

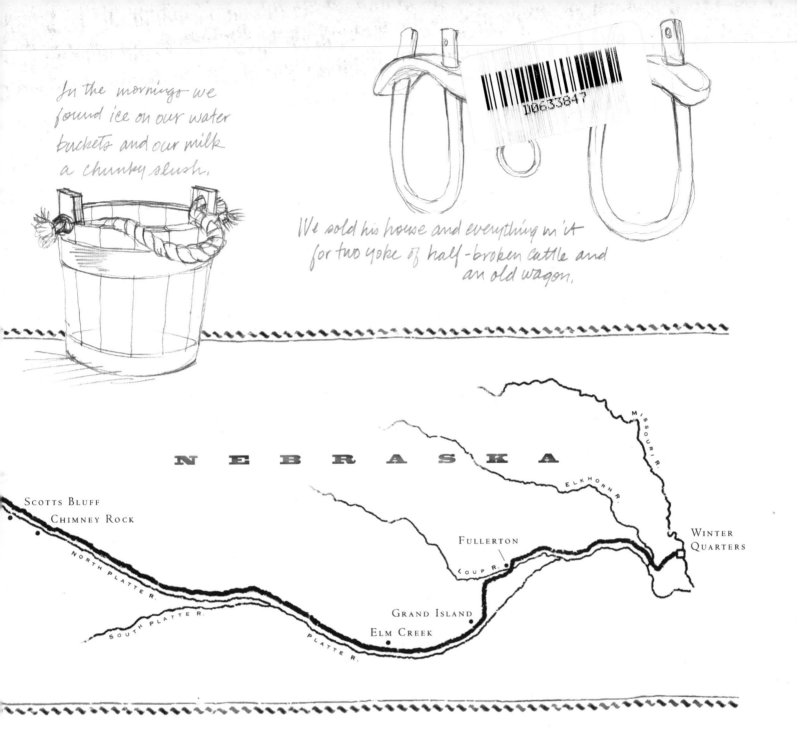

We sold his house and everything in it for two yoke of half-broken cattle and an old wagon.

N E B R A S K A

MISSOURI R.

ELKHORN R.

Scotts Bluff
CHIMNEY ROCK

NORTH PLATTER R.

FULLERTON

LOUP R.

WINTER QUARTERS

SOUTH PLATTER R.

PLATTER R.

GRAND ISLAND

ELM CREEK

Chimney Rock still grows plainer to our view. We have seen it for at least forty-two miles.

Where timber was scarce, we used buffalo chips to make a fire and boil water.

The men in their clean hickory shirts and the women and children in their clean starched sunbonnets and dresses looked pure and neat though humble and primitive.

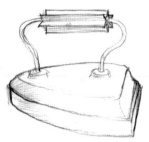

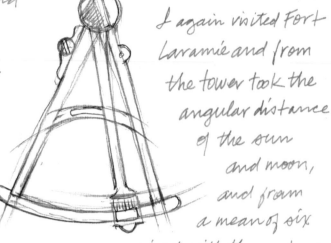

I again visited Fort Laramie and from the tower took the angular distance of the sun and moon, and from a mean of six sights with the sextant, determined the longitude to be 104 deg., 11 min., 53 sec.

When the Indians got too close, we fired the cannon as a warning.

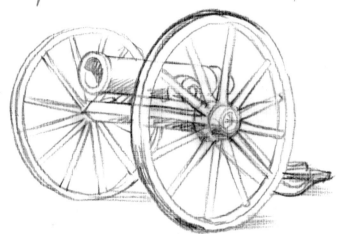

Key to Carthage Jail

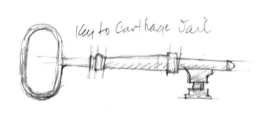

I urged would-be emigrants not to bring so many chests of clothing which would have to be discarded at Mormon Grove anyway. Far better, I said, to use the money to pay the passage for another soul.

We were hungry all day long and into the night. Potato peelings and rawhide off old handcarts were good if we could get it. I, myself set by the campfire and scraped

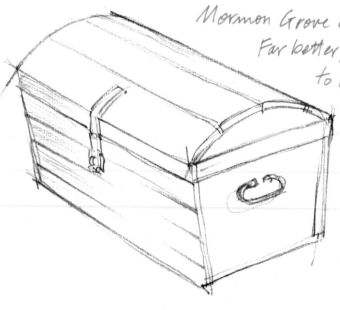

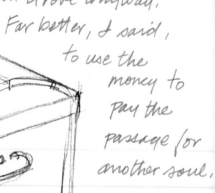

and singed the hair off a piece of hide.

THE GATHERING

MORMON PIONEERS ON THE TRAIL TO ZION

MAURINE JENSEN PROCTOR
SCOT FACER PROCTOR

Designed by Scott Eggers

DESERET BOOK COMPANY
SALT LAKE CITY, UTAH

Library of Congress Cataloging-in-Publication Data

Proctor, Maurine Jensen.
    The gathering : Mormon pioneers on the trail to Zion / Maurine
Jensen Proctor and Scot Facer Proctor.
        p. cm.
    Includes bibliographical references.
    ISBN 1-57345-087-1
    1. Mormon converts—Biography. 2. Church of Jesus Christ of
Latter-day Saints—History—19th century. 3. Mormon Church—United
States—History—19th century. 4. Mormon Trail—History—19th century.
I. Proctor, Scot Facer, 1956- .
II. Title.
BX8693.P76 1996
289.3'09'034-dc20   95-49742
                                                                 CIP

Printed in China

10   9   8   7   6   5   4   3   2   1

Contents

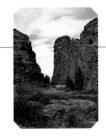

THE ANCIENT MAN WITH THE HOARY BEARD IN THE photograph is Robert Sweeten, who was just two months shy of his seventh birthday when he walked barefoot across the plains in 1847. On the way he stepped on a prickly pear, and his mother had to pull out the needles; he played "I Spy" in the grass; and he was only dimly aware of what Zion meant. He could not know that he would outlive all the pioneers of that year and be honored for years as the oldest living pioneer in parades on the streets of a city that was not yet built.

This picture intrigued us, not just because Robert Sweeten is Scot's great-great-grandfather and not just because it is a moment when four generations were caught in time—Robert, his daughter Martha Holbrook, her daughter Amanda Facer, and her baby Bill Facer, all looking at us as if tomorrow had never come. What we marvel at is that the story we tell in this book—the gathering to Zion—did not happen that long ago. It is not some far-off tale of distant faith and suffering that intrigues us like a vivid, historical novel. The baby, Bill Facer, would leave on his mission before Robert Sweeten died, and he grew up to be a man still living today. From our world of computers, microchips, and space travel, we just have to reach out to hold hands with those who came in creaking, covered wagons across the plains. Bill knew his great-grandfather, who knew Brigham Young.

In the past few years, we have made several spiritual journeys. Our purpose has been to capture photographs of significant spiritual sights, to make them vivid for readers. We have climbed the stairs of the Carthage jail, hearing in our hearts the shots that killed Joseph and Hyrum Smith. We have waited for the light to change at the Garden Tomb, whose door says, "He is not here, for he is risen." We have followed Lehi's trail through the Arabian peninsula and wondered how he and his family endured the heat and the sand. These journeys have all been more than physical. Though we packed our bags and made sure we had the proper visas, it was not merely a moving through space and time. These were journeys of our souls, experiences that moved us from one place in our hearts irrevocably to another.

Yet no journey has been more profound than the one taken for this book as we began to sense the blood of our ancestors flowing in our veins. Each step of our journey brought us closer to them. Never have we felt more keenly the loss of our grandmothers, Eveline Golden and Lydia Owen, who slithered in the mud across Iowa only to sicken, shiver, and die at Winter Quarters and be buried in unmarked graves. Lydia's husband Seely came on in the 1847 vanguard company to the Salt Lake Valley. Rarely have we felt such excitement as when we discovered that our own great-great-grandmother, Margaret Davis Rees, was the first woman baptized in Wales and came across the plains with aching hands from pulling a handcart. Our people came in the gallows of pitched ships, braved storms on the Atlantic, and faced raging cholera on the Missouri River. We both have grandmothers whose feet bled on the plains, grandfathers whose hands blistered on their way to Zion.

All of us who share this kind of heritage are marked by it, especially in a modern, comfort-seeking world that pounds us to believe that nothing really matters that much. We can't believe this. We will never believe this. As one writer said, cut us open and there is the trail. It's a monument to something so precious that no matter what it cost, the price was willingly paid. We, the remnants of the pioneers, who live in this casual twentieth-century world, can see how remarkable it is to hold something that precious.

It was a dismal, gray day as we went through the gate into the cemetery of the abandoned church at Old Langho in Lancashire, England. An abandoned church, dust thick on its benches, the grass overgrown outside, is a sorry sight. It means a dead, abandoned faith. We knew that the Proctors had come from this village, so our eyes were trained on the tombstones, looking for names. There, right in front of the massive, wooden door, was one that piqued our interest. "Henry Proctor," it read.

Henry was a four-greats uncle. He was not much different in age from our own great-great-grandfather James Bertwistle Proctor. They had grown up in the same place, had played on the same farm, must have known the same friends. Yet when the Mormon missionaries came to the area, James heard and obeyed the call, and Henry did not. Every tombstone we came to seemed in some way connected to Henry, and we scribbled names down frantically for genealogical purposes—frantically because the mist that shrouded the cemetery and clung to our hair was about to turn into rain.

Just then a man called over the slate-gray stone fence to ask what we were doing. We told him we were just looking for relatives. "What's your name?" he called out. "Proctor," we said. "Oh, everyone around here's a Proctor or related to them." We marveled: these Proctors who

farm the green fields and live in thatched cottages, these Proctors who watched their four-centuries old church become abandoned, could have been us if it had not been for James. What distinguished him from his brothers, from his Uncle Henry, that his blood should have run faster at the missionaries' word? What courage and conviction so animated his soul that he could turn his back on a church his family had attended for generations? Was he frightened when he packed up what he could take and gave the rest away? Did he weep when he said good-bye to his family, whom he would never see again? Did he take one last, long look at the fertility of the River Ribble

Billowing clouds gather at the Old Langho Church in Lancashire, England. The large, weathered tombstone of Henry Proctor can be seen in the center symbolically marking the resting place of generations of Proctors who did not hear the gospel of Jesus Christ. Who could ever calculate the effect of one's decision to join the kingdom of God?

in bondage, those who laid the foundations of this great work. This book is a tribute to memory, a reaffirmation that as a people we have something worth remembering.

In taking the photographs for this book, we traveled portions of the trail in every season. We hunted down the important historical sights in Great Britain, watching for the fleeting moments of sunlight every day. One morning we hiked early up to the top of the Herefordshire Beacon where Brigham Young had prayed about publishing the Book of Mormon in England. We waited two hours for some light, but the skies only grew thicker and darker. A few hours later, we returned again, this time with our daughter. Weighed down with the camera equipment, we hiked again. Clearly the clouds were going to break any minute. They didn't break. We finally descended again and ordered ice cream cones; just as we were about to indulge, the sun came out in full measure. This time Scot took the camera with three lenses and the tripod and ran all the way to the top. Breathless, he set up the camera and caught the light with seconds to spare before the clouds rolled in again. Such were our days in merry old England.

We would have liked to include all of Europe and the islands of the sea in this story of the gathering, but the emerald beacons of the British Isles became a type for the rest. Preston, England, is an anchor for the story of the gathering. John and Jane Benbow's farm near Ledbury still glows with the Spirit. Looking upon Edinburgh, Scotland, from Arthur's Seat is breathtaking.

We extend heartfelt thanks to the many who helped with this labor of love. We have experienced firsthand that the cooperative spirit that marked the pioneers still motivates their children. So many have sacrificed that we might work. We are indebted to Robert Scott Lorimer, John Kitchen Jr., and Kim McKinnon, the Riverton Wyoming Stake presidency, who opened their hearts and their library to share with us the pathos of the Willie and Martin handcart companies. We will never forget our time with them. Lloyd Larsen of the Riverton Stake high council volunteered at 11:00 one evening to take us into

valley and wonder how he would scratch out a living in a desert? Did his throat catch as he said, "Farewell my home"? These things we cannot know. All we can be sure of is the effect his choice has had on us. Because of him, we have the gospel. Because of him, we have scriptures that open our souls to eternity. Because of him, we pray to a personal Father. Because of him, we can be sealed in the temple. If he hadn't heard the missionaries and taken the trail to Zion, we would be strangers to the gospel. Oh, thank you, grandfather.

We got a key to the Old Langho church and went in to take a picture, a long, time exposure. While we waited, we sang our joy in the restoration, "We Thank Thee, O God, for a Prophet."

Remember is one of the most important words in the gospel, appearing in 337 verses in the Standard Works. It is one of the key attributes of Deity. The Lord promises that he will remember the covenant he has made with his people: "Can a woman forget her sucking child, that she should not have compassion on the son of her womb?" asks the Lord. "Yea, they may forget, yet will I not forget thee, O house of Israel." (1 Nephi 21:15.) He asks us, in turn, to always remember him. We are asked in type to remember those who have gone before us, those who were

Rocky Ridge at 5:00 the next morning. We have seldom seen a more tender, kind man, and his feelings for Theophilus Cox, a handcart pioneer who died there in the Wyoming highlands, influenced the way we came to feel about all the handcart pioneers. We were thunderstruck at the kindness of Glenn Williams, who, learning that Scot, a total stranger to him, was having car trouble in Lander, volunteered to drive him the six hours home to Salt Lake City and did so.

We are deeply indebted to our parents Paul and Martha Proctor and Maurine Jensen for their untiring devotion to us. They are ever here for us physically and spiritually. Our daughter, Julie Ann, traveled with us to the British Isles and, though she learned that our work trips really are work trips, never complained. She was a delightful and helpful traveling companion. When we got to our frenzied last weeks before the book was due and our ten-month-old Michaela wanted nothing but to be held, we were grateful for the rescue from Tina Van Wagoner, who not only volunteered to take our baby every day until the book was finished but also claimed that she loved doing it—a true Saint. We are also grateful for Sandy Atkin, who also took our baby so we could write and who wallpapered our office so it would be a more cheerful place to work. She is an example of Christ-like love.

We are indebted to Bill Slaughter of the Church Archives for his good-natured assistance and to the staff of the Church Historian's Library, who tirelessly help us locate sources. A very special thanks goes to Scott Eggers, who designed this book and brought to the task not only a remarkable talent but also a spirit to match. His humility and skill are a wonderful combination. Our many sessions together have been laced with emotion as we have discovered our roots.

As always, we are indebted to Ronald Millett, Sheri Dew, and Jack Lyon of Deseret Book Company, all of whom played an integral role in publishing this work. We must say that without our dear friend Sheri Dew, none of our pictorial books would have been published. Thanks to her for her continuing vision and enthusiasm, not only for our work but also for the work of the kingdom. Our gratitude goes beyond words to the Lord for our strength, health, talents, and testimonies. Without him we can do nothing.

We dedicate this book to our youngest daughter, Michaela Maurine Proctor, born February 23, 1995, a wonderful interruption to our work. We've written most of the book while we bounced her on one knee or watched her empty our desk drawers. We hope she will grow up with a sense of legacy, that remembering will transform her life.

Last light glows upon the waters of the Des Moines River along the Mormon Trail in Iowa. The suffering of the pioneers would etch deep-rooted faith into the souls of those who remembered their ancestors.

L E F T   Interior of John and Jane Benbow's home in Herefordshire, England, has not changed much in fifteen decades. The strength and sturdiness of giant wooden posts and beams throughout are reminiscent of those who wholeheartedly accepted the gospel of Jesus Christ here.

One

I REMEMBER THOSE WHO ARE UPON THE ISLES OF THE SEA

*I*T WAS A SEPTEMBER DAY IN 1842 WHEN GEORGE AND ANN Quayle Cannon stood with their six children on the windswept dock at Liverpool ready to board the great ship *Sidney* for America. Crowds of emigrants thronged the gangplank, worried over details, and clutched a few remnants of the home they were about to leave behind. They carried boxes, beds, and assorted bundles. Some had cabbages, some cheese, some bread and butter stored in tins. Like so many others, the Cannons were uprooting themselves and leaving England, but not for the bounties of America. In fact, George had written his sister in America, asking, "Please let us know what are the most necessary things to take to America in respect to clothing and utensils. . . . You have never mentioned what sort of a country it is, or how people are employed there, and how land is sold (whether high-priced or cheap)."[1] Even without this knowledge, the Cannons would go—go even though they "got nothing" for their furniture, not even their clock or "drawers," which had long belonged to their family; go even though Ann's brother did not bother to come and see them off; go even though Ann was in the midst of a sickly pregnancy and had the premonition that, should they leave then, she would not make it to America.

Yet for a long time she had kept a secret savings, skimmed from their household accounts and squirreled away to surprise her husband that they might emigrate. They had waited so long while they had helped pay for other Saints to sail, counted while months turned into years, and Ann felt it intolerable to wait any longer. What was worth all this fuss, this price, and finally, for Ann, the ultimate sacrifice? Too weak and seasick to hold anything down, she died on board ship and was buried somewhere in the vast Atlantic Ocean. George and Ann were coming to help build Zion.

"Oh Zion, dear Zion." Creating Zion was the burden of the prayers of the early Saints. They yearned for it, carried it like a fire in their hearts, longed for that society away from the oppressions of the world where a celestial order prevails. It was a heavenly homesickness they carried with them, a sense that "the world we have made and are making is not the world God meant us to have."[2] God has far better designs and happier ways for his children. So, from the earliest times of the Restoration, new converts left their fields and fortunes, coming "one from the bed, the other from the grinding,"[3] and bade farewell to all they had known to *gather.* They came first to Kirtland, then Missouri, then Nauvoo, and finally rumbled across fourteen hundred miles of plains and mountains, breaking their carts and wagons but not their spirits in pursuit of Zion. "Thy kingdom come,"[4] they prayed, and they were willing to shoulder their part to make it happen even if they left a heartbreaking string of graves across the prairies and their backs were bowed under the weight of what they had given up.

Historians who see the great western movement of the Mormon pioneers merely as an escape from persecution miss the point. Much more than escape, the pioneers were involved in a monumental creative effort. They felt themselves called out of the world because they wanted Zion. "Go ye out from Babylon. Be ye clean."[5] They were to gather to Zion for "a refuge from the storm" that would soon be poured out upon the whole earth.[6] They would gather because, according to the parable of the wheat and the tares, "the time of harvest is come."[7] They would gather in one place "to prepare their hearts and be prepared in all things"[8] for the second coming of the Lord. With particularly poignant meaning for those who had been forced from their sacred temples in Kirtland

M*orning light touches the arched doorway of a home in Downham, Lancashire, England. Preachers had steered clear of the villages of Chatburn and Downham because of their reputation of having no listening ears. A majority of the citizens of these villages were gathered into the gospel net.*

PAGES 8–9 *Looking across rolling fields to John and Jane Benbow's Hill Farm near Ledbury, Herefordshire, England. In this place the harvest would be great.*

and Nauvoo, they would gather to build a temple to God where they could make eternal covenants to be his people.

The Bible gives a fairly detailed description of Zion, but the Saints are distinctive in their response to the message. For them Zion is not a promise of a faraway, impossible tomorrow. They believe "that Zion is possible on this earth, that men possess the capacity to receive it right here and are therefore under obligation to waste no time moving in the direction of Zion."[9]

Still, when the Saints were driven from Missouri and there was no gathering place, Joseph Smith instructed the missionaries in England not to teach the doctrine of gathering. But, according to John Taylor, they "could not keep the spirit of it from the people."[10] Heber C. Kimball had not told George D. Watt anything about the doctrine of the gathering, but just ten days after George became the first man in England to be baptized, he came to Heber, "his face shining like that of an angel, and, said he, just as sure as the Lord lives the Saints will gather to America."[11]

John Taylor told of a sister in Liverpool, England, who said to him, "Brother Taylor, I had a very remarkable dream or vision. I don't know which, and it went something like this: I thought that the Saints were gathered together on the Pier Head—and there was a ship about to sail. The people said they were going to Zion, and they were singing what they called the songs of Zion, and rejoicing exceedingly; you were among them, and you were

going also. Now I want to know if you can tell what that means?"[12] Clearly, Zion swells in the hearts of her citizens.

The Saints felt the urge to gather because "the Spirit of the Lord rested upon them, and they could not stay themselves."[13] John Taylor told the British Saints, "[When the elders laid their hands] upon your heads, among other things you received the Holy Ghost and the spirit of the gathering. But you did not know what it was that was working in you, like yeast sometimes under certain conditions, producing an influence causing you to come to Zion. Yet you could not help it. If you had wanted to help it, you could not while you were living your religion."[14] Brigham Young said of the pioneers, "the spirit of the Lord was all the time prompting them. . . . They could not do anything else, because God would not let them do anything else. The brethren and sisters came across the plains because they could not stay; that is the secret of the movement."[15]

Though that silent, inner stirring is sometimes unnamed, the spiritually inclined feel a longing, almost a memory, of a former, better state, and they wish to regain it. Zion is the answer to that longing, designed on God's principles, where every institution and relationship promotes joy. It is a place of beauty, whose standard in all things is a light to the world. It is a place of peace and unity, where the false pride, follies, and selfishness of the world are forgotten. The buildings, walls, streets, and gates, the throngs in shining robes are not the essence of Zion. When all else is stripped away, Zion is the pure in heart.

Those who wanted to build Zion, then, had to begin by looking to their own hearts. "We are trying to be in the image of those who live in heaven; we are trying to pattern after them . . . to walk and talk like them, to deal like them, and build up the kingdom of heaven as they have done,"[16] said Brigham Young. Yet it is hard for those who have so long lived in the world, immersed in Babylon, to envision Zion; hard to be a Zion people when one cannot yet conceive it, can only catch glimpses of its beauty from a distant shore.

Thus, a pattern emerges in the scriptures. Those who would go to the promised land, those who are longing for Zion, must first learn its principles in the wilderness journey.

It is a difficult journey whose tests are to be endured,

Street scene early morning in Hillsborough, Ireland.
In this ancient village the first branch of the
Church in Ireland was organized, on October 1, 1840.
John Taylor was the first to preach the gospel in
Ireland and did so in the town of Newry in July 1840.

LEFT Beautiful swan on a lakeshore
in Hillsborough, Ireland. The "forty shades of green"
in Ireland were not enough to hold back
thousands from coming into the Church and making
the arduous voyage from Ireland to the
gathering place of the Saints in the Rocky Mountains.

Clouds gather around the beautiful Strathearn Hills of Scotland north of Stirling. As the Lord had said, "The harvest truly is plenteous, but the labourers are few."[1] So it was in Scotland—from the efforts of a relatively small number, thousands would be gathered.

a necessary labor to be performed in order to find the safety and joy of the promised land. The children of Israel trudged through the desert for forty years. Nephi and his family trekked the most foreboding desert of the world. At some future time, there will be another com-

ing out of Babylon, which is the world, to build Zion. In every case, the promised land is reached only after the tedious and difficult journey, and the heart is transformed in the process. Priorities became clear to converts who shed every precious keepsake along the trail, who dragged on when their bodies cried out in utter exhaustion. They came to know and prove the Lord when human strength was gone and He was there to compensate, when their faith, like gold, was seven times purified. They learned to give freely to each other and bear one another's burdens in the furnace of affliction. These are Zion lessons that the world cannot offer.

Brigham Young, who said he had Zion constantly in his view, put it simply: "I want hard times, so that every person that does not wish to stay, for the sake of religion, will leave."[17] Zion could not be built by those who would come on false premises. Though it didn't always succeed, the trail was to strip Babylon from the heart of one who wanted to build Zion.

So they came from Vermont and Kentucky, from England and Wales, came in a growing swell to build their beloved Zion and then be driven from it again. Finally, weary of being a driven people, they sought refuge in the mountains in an arid valley that nobody else wanted and formed a city called Great Salt Lake. By some estimates, nearly seventy thousand people brought rickety wagons and carts and tramped those plains; six thousand of them died along the way, their dreams of Zion buried in a trailside grave. For the rest it was "Carry on, carry on"—and they did, leaving a legacy that burns in every Mormon heart.

Though the gathering of Israel from the four corners of the earth was a much-prophesied event in the scriptures, it was Moses who gave the keys for the modern-day gathering to the Prophet Joseph Smith in the Kirtland Temple on April 3, 1836. Since the Lord works in absolute precision, it is not surprising that later in that same month, as Parley P. Pratt sat pondering his deep debt and the seeming impossibility of going on yet another mission, Heber C. Kimball knocked at his door ready to give him a blessing. "Thou shalt go to Upper Canada," he prophesied, "even to the city of Toronto, the capital, and there thou shalt find a people prepared for the fulness of

the gospel . . . and from the things growing out of this mission, shall the fulness of the gospel spread into England, and cause a great work to be done in that land."[18]

With empty pockets, Parley took a long, tiresome road to Lake Ontario, where a stranger offered him ten dollars and a letter of introduction to one John Taylor of Toronto.

John had been regularly meeting with others to search the scriptures. He later said, "When Brother Pratt came to me I was, perhaps, as well read in the letter of the Bible as I am today, and as soon as he commenced to talk about Prophets, I said, Yes, we believe in them. And he talked about Apostles and I remarked, Yes, we have been looking for such men, but we cannot find them."[19] Parley testified that the ancient church they were seeking had been restored; his message was received with great joy. They were certain he had come because of their ceaseless prayers.

Among the converts in John's circle was Joseph Fielding, a native of England, whose brother, James, and brother-in-law, Timothy Matthews, were ministers in Britain's beautiful Lancashire. It immediately became Joseph Fielding's earnest prayer that "the Lord would prepare my brethren to receive the truth in its fullness as I had received it."[20] News of the restored gospel began to lace every letter Joseph sent to England.

The next year, 1837, Kirtland was in a turmoil as apostasy raged and, not immune from the national economic crisis, the Saints' banking institution crashed. Even some of Joseph Smith's immediate friends and closest advisors were turning against him, calling him a fallen prophet. It seemed an unlikely time for Joseph to choose one of his most loyal lieutenants to leave on a mission. Yet in June while Heber C. Kimball was sitting in the Kirtland Temple, the Prophet came to him and said quietly, "The Spirit of the Lord has whispered to me, 'Let my servant Heber go to England and proclaim my Gospel, and open the door of salvation to that nation.'"[21]

Heber, who would have spared no sacrifice for the restored gospel, was staggered by the weight of the call and his own weakness. "O Lord," he prayed, "I am a man of stammering tongue, and altogether unfit for such a work; how can I go to preach in that land, which is so famed throughout Christendom for learning, knowledge and piety; the nursery of religion; and a people whose intelligence is proverbial!" He later wrote, "The idea of such a mission was almost more than I could bear up under. I was almost ready to sink under the burden which was placed upon me." However, these considerations would not deter him: "For the moment, I understood the will of my Heavenly Father, I felt a determination to go at all hazards, believing that He would support me by His almighty power."[22]

Heber would be leaving his family destitute, and the parting scene was described by Robert B. Thompson, who happened by the Kimballs' partly opened door. Heber "was pouring out his soul [to God] that he would . . . make him useful wherever his lot should be cast . . . that He . . . would supply the wants of his wife and little ones in his absence. . . . He then . . . laid his hands upon their heads individually, leaving a father's blessing upon them, and . . . while thus engaged his voice was almost lost in the sobs of those around, who tried in vain to suppress them. The idea of being separated from their protector and father for so long a time was indeed painful. He proceeded, but his heart was too much affected to do so regularly. His emotions were great, and he was obliged to stop at intervals, while the big tears rolled down his cheeks."[23]

Heber was joined on this mission by Orson Hyde, Willard Richards, Joseph Fielding, and three other converts from Parley's Canadian mission who had British roots. They made the crossing to England under July's fair skies in a quick eighteen

days on the packet ship *Garrick*, perhaps not aware that the mission they undertook would turn a throng of people with British accents into American pioneers. When the missionaries were within six or seven feet of the shore, Heber, feeling the joy and urgency of his mission, leaped onto the pier. His impressions of that nineteenth-century England were profound. Being without purse or scrip, the missionaries wandered in the streets of Liverpool, where wealth and luxury abounded side by side with penury and want. Heber recorded, "I there met the rich attired in the most costly dresses, and the next minute was saluted with the cries of the poor with scarce covering sufficient to screen them from the weather. Such a wide distinction I never saw before."[24]

The social conditions in England would continue to appall the American missionaries. England was in the midst of the Industrial Revolution, which had thrust many former agrarian and cottage industry workers into the miserable conditions of early factories. The elders would write home of the pitiful beggars who lined the

S*mall Church of Wales building in Llantrithyd dates to A.D. 1100. The original church that burned on this site was here at the end of the eighth century A.D. The strength of tradition was hard to break in many people's hearts, yet the gospel took root in Wales.*

Crowds thronged the marketplace (left) at the square in Preston, Lancashire, England, to hear the first missionaries preach on Sunday afternoon, July 30, 1837. Heber C. Kimball, who led the group, is shown above.

streets, the crime and drunkenness, the stark class division that kept a handful of wealthy at the top and ground the faces of the poor and working class, who had to send their children to bed at night still hungry. They winced at textile mills and coal factories filled with children who would never be educated, who would die young of overwork. Heber said, "I was asking some of my brethren what made the people look so bad. They said because they were famished for the wont of food."[25]

THE GOVERNMENT DID ITS part to squeeze the people. The apostles noted there were "taxes of every kind, we might say, for smoke must not go up the chimney in England without a tax, light must not come in at the window without paying duties. There are taxes for living and taxes for dying, insomuch that it is very difficult for the poor to get buried any how, and a man may emigrate to American and find a grave, for less money than he can get a decent burial for in Old England. We scarce recollect an article without tax except cats, mice and fleas."[26]

Insignificant as the apostles felt, the magnitude of their mission was simply overwhelming. As they cried to the Lord for wisdom and support, they felt to begin thirty-one miles to the north in Preston, where Joseph Fielding's brother James lived and preached.

Preston was an industrial center on the River Ribble,

whose waters wound through the woodlands and villages of the long, green valley beyond. The missionaries arrived there on Saturday, July 22, the holiday before a Monday parliamentary election. Released from labor at the textile mills and breweries for the day, people crowded the streets, bearing the colorful ribbons of the candidates they supported. Bands played, and political banners flew with an air of gaiety. Just as the missionaries' coach arrived, a flag was unfurled over their heads reading "Truth Will Prevail" in large, gilt letters. Seeing this, the missionaries cried aloud as if in one voice, "Amen! Thanks be to God, *Truth will prevail!*"[27]

The other missionaries took lodgings in the city, but Joseph Fielding went to stay with his brother James, for whom he had been fervently praying. At this time, Britain churned with religious ideas and movements of which James was a representative. The Church of England was, of course, the principal church, enjoying immense power and prestige, but in this time of social upheaval, dissenting churches such as the Presbyterians and Methodists had attracted their own large followings. It was from these dissenting groups that the Church would draw most of its converts, people already isolated from the religious mainstream and already searching. Thus, James had read his brother Joseph's letters about this new American religion, with its angels and gold plates, to his congregation, and they were primed for his visit.

James Fielding's Vauxhall Chapel was packed the next

day to hear the Mormon elders preach first in the afternoon and then in the evening. Heber C. Kimball told an eager audience about the Restoration, and Orson Hyde bore testimony. That night John Goodson and Joseph Fielding preached and received the same response. Heber said of the congregation that "they cried 'glory to God,' and rejoiced that the Lord had sent His servants unto them."[28] Another appointment was made for the following Wednesday at the Vauxhall chapel, but James Fielding was rankled. He "did not fall in with us, he did not wish his people should, and he could see it had taken hold of them,"[29] wrote Joseph. It seemed to James that he had let the wolves into the sheepfold. That Wednesday would be the last time he would open his chapel to the missionaries, and his heart would close just as surely against his brother, much to Joseph's surprise and deep sorrow. Joseph wrote, "As we were sitting down to breakfast, James began to say very hard things of us and the Book of Mormon. I was much grieved . . . and I could not eat. I got up from the table, took the book in my hand and declared to all . . . that what we had told them was the truth." Joseph then left his brother's house, and from that time, he wrote, "I have not been much in his company."[30] In his fury, James even went to the elders' lodgings, saying he forbade Elder Kimball to baptize any of his flock. "They are of age," answered Heber. "I shall baptize all who come unto me."[31]

The Reverend Fielding would rue the day he invited the Mormon missionaries to preach, seeing it as the ruin of his flock. He lamented, "Kimball bored the holes, Goodson drove the nails, and Hyde clinched them."[32] A year later James complained to his brother, "I do not believe at all that you were sent of God to rend my little church to pieces."[33]

The room where Elders Heber C. Kimball, John Goodson, and Orson Hyde were attacked by legions of devils in Preston, England. The attack came on the day of the first baptisms in England.

R I G H T *Boyhood home of John Taylor, located in the lake district near Milnthorpe, Cumbria, England. John Taylor would be in the Carthage jail at the martyrdom of Joseph and Hyrum Smith and later would become the third president of the Church.*

F A R R I G H T *Their "First Lodgings" were in the upper right of this white building on the corner of Fox and St. Wilfred Streets in Preston, England.*

Baptism for nine people, including some of the leading men of Fielding's congregation, was set for the next Sunday, July 30, 1837. Yet just as there had been an outpouring of light, so the forces of darkness conspired against the work. That morning at the elders' lodgings, Isaac Russell came upstairs from his room to ask for a blessing because he said he was tormented by devils. Heber knew Russell had complained of such troubles before and was not certain he fully believed him, yet he began to give a blessing. He later wrote of the experience, "I was struck with a great force by some invisible power and fell senseless on the floor as if I had been shot, and the first thing that I recollected was, that I was supported by Brothers Hyde and Russell, who were beseeching the throne of grace in my behalf. They then laid me on the bed, but my agony was so great that I could not endure, and I was obliged to get out, and fell on my knees and began to pray. I then sat on the bed and could distinctly see the evil spirits, who foamed and gnashed their teeth upon us." "We saw the devils coming in legions, with their leaders. . . . They came towards us like armies rushing to battle."[34]

Years later when Heber told the Prophet Joseph about this experience and asked if something was wrong that he should have such an encounter, the Prophet answered, "No, Brother Heber. . . . When I heard of it, it gave me great joy, for I then knew that the work of God had taken root in that land."[35]

The crowds of Preston taking their Sunday morning strolls in Avenham Park paused to watch the excitement that morning as George D. Watt and Henry Clegg raced to the River Ribble to see which of them would be the first to be baptized in England. This exuberant run was a moment in history not lost on its participants. They ran because the silence of centuries when humanity concocted their own religions had ended and God had spoken again. They ran because the priesthood and power and pattern of the ancient church had been restored. They ran because even if their minister scowled, they had felt the Spirit whispering to them that God knew them intimately and loved them. Watt, who was twenty-two years younger than Clegg and had youth on his side, won the race. He had grown up thinking more about survival than salvation, a street urchin who had food only if kind strangers should toss him a crust of bread. For shelter at night he had huddled in dark corners; in bad weather he simply endured, the relentless rains drenching his ragged clothing. One day while taking a bath in a river, someone stole his only clothes, and he was left helpless and naked until a woman found him, gave him something to wear, and turned him in to the poor house. He had finally been apprenticed to a brick maker and had made something of himself—but it was the gospel and the sure knowledge that God loved him that would transform his life. He would immigrate to the Salt Lake Valley and become the recorder of the talks at general conference, his name appearing regularly in the *Journal of Discourses.*

The last of the nine baptized that day was Elizabeth Ann Walmsley, a sickly consumptive, who was not expected to live and was frail enough that she had to be carried to the water by her husband. Yet Heber promised her that if she would believe, repent, and be baptized, she would be healed of her sickness. Her improvement began immediately; she eventually immigrated to Utah, raised a large family; and died at eighty-two in Bear Lake County, Idaho.

*I*T WAS A SEASON OF SUCH TRANS-forming miracles. In Preston the missionaries baptized eight on Monday, three on Thursday, one on Friday and again on Saturday, and another six the following Sunday. Beginning that week, too, they began to preach in the hamlets nestled in the River Ribble Valley with similar success. In Bedford, the Reverend Timothy Matthews, Joseph Fielding's brother-in-law, allowed missionaries to preach at his church several times, and their message was accepted by many, including Matthews, who bore testimony of its truthfulness. Forty stepped forward to be baptized. During one four-week period, Heber baptized a hundred people.

The missionaries couldn't begin to respond to the numbers clamoring for the message. Heber said, "Calls from all quarters to come and preach were constantly sounding in our ears, and we labored night and day to satisfy the people, who manifested such a desire for the truth as I never saw before. We had to speak in small and very crowded houses, and to large assemblies in the open air. Consequently our lungs were often very sore and our bodies worn down with fatigue."[36] Heber's gift was an unwavering ability to hear and follow the Spirit. Ironically, the unschooled, down-to-earth manner he had so worried about was an advantage to him in teaching. "Brother Kimball would say, 'Come my friend, sit down; do not be in a hurry;' and he would begin and preach the Gospel in

a plain, familiar manner, and make his hearers believe everything he said, and make them testify to its truth . . . asking them, 'Now, ain't that so?' and they would say, 'Yes.' And he would make scripture as he needed it, out of his own Bible, and ask, 'Now ain't that so?' and the reply would be 'Yes.' He would say, 'You see how plain the Gospel is?' . . . The people would want to come to see him

Peaceful banks of the River Ribble near Avenham Park in Preston, England. Here is where the first baptisms in England were performed in this dispensation. According to local tradition, the race of George Watt and Henry Clegg to be the first baptized in England was across the footbridge seen here.

early in the morning and stay with him until noon, and from that until night; and he would put his arm around their necks, and say, 'Come, let us go down to the water.'"[37]

Willard Richards's journal tells something of the spiritual effort that went into the conversions. September 14: "Kept this as a day fasting; felt much strengthened and refreshed"; September 18: "Kept this as a day of fasting and prayer that God . . . would make known to me his mind and will about the people of Bedford"; September 21: "Kept this as a fast day; I praise the Lord for much of his Spirit."[38]

Those who responded to the gospel were often the working poor, whose lives had been rendered nearly hopeless by England's social conditions. "It is as much as they can do to live," noted Heber. "There is not more than one or two that could lodge us overnight if they should try."[39] The missionaries who were living without purse or

scrip shared the poverty. "We have to live quite short, but the brethren are very kind to us. They are willing to divide with us the last they have."[40] Brigham Young would later say, "I have been in countries where the men, women and children had to labor—wearying their lives out of them to get the bread necessary to keep their lives in them. I have gone to bed many a time, and when I have turned down the bed I would find the sheet patched from end to end, so that I would wonder which was the original sheet. I have also known young ladies . . . come home from their work on a Saturday evening, and retiring to a room, throw a blanket over their shoulders, and wash every particle of their clothing, that they might be able to go out on Sunday to attend meeting. These are they that we have baptized. Why? Because their ears were open, and the Spirit of the Lord found a way to their hearts and they saw there was deliverance in the gospel."[41]

By September, most of Reverend James Fielding's flock had joined the Church, and Joseph Fielding was painfully divided from his brother. He wrote, "My brother James will scarcely speak to me, so I feel rather lonely."[42] What's more, all the ministers in Preston were sufficiently riled by the Church's growth that they banded together in opposition, preaching that it was "sure death" for the people to hear the Mormons preach, "for they will surely be caught in the snare."[43] Such words served only to attract curious listeners, who crammed the Cock Pit, the old temperance hall where the Church met.

If the citizens of Preston received the gospel with joy, they warned Heber not to bother traveling to the villages of Chatburn and Downham, for in these places every minister had failed to raise a church. Yet Heber received a pressing invitation to Chatburn, where he preached standing on a barrel in a large tithing barn. He later said, "These people who had been represented as being hard and obdurate were melted into tenderness and love. . . . When I concluded I felt someone pulling at my coat, exclaiming, 'Maister, Maister. . . . Please sir, will you baptize me?' 'And me?' 'And me?' exclaimed more than a dozen voices."[44] The next day at Downham the scene was repeated. In five days Fielding and Whitney would baptize one hundred and ten persons and organize branches in four towns.

Some time later, as Elders Kimball and Fielding passed through Chatburn, they said, "Having been observed approaching the village, the news ran from house to house, and immediately the noise of their looms was hushed, and the people flocked to their doors to welcome us and see us pass. More than forty young people of the place ran to meet us; some took hold of our mantles and then of each others' hands, several having hold of hands went before us singing the songs of Zion, while their parents gazed upon the scene with delight, and poured their blessings upon our heads, and praised the God of heaven for sending us to unfold the principles of truth and the plan of salvation to them. . . .

A *small amount of light streams through the windows of this Church of England chapel in the village of Old Langho, Lancashire, England.*

R I G H T *Tradition is etched deeply even in the pews of the churches of England, this one in Old Langho dating to 1688. To join The Church of Jesus Christ of Latter-day Saints and leave for Zion was to fly in the face of generations of religious philosophy.*

Breathtaking countryside near Chatburn and Downham, Lancashire, England. Heber C. Kimball recorded his feelings on departing this area: "I felt as if the place was holy ground. The Spirit of the Lord rested down upon me and I was constrained to bless that whole region of country.... I thought my head was a fountain of tears, for I wept for several miles after I bid [the people] adieu. I had to leave the road three times to go to streams of water to bathe my eyes."

"The Prophet Joseph told [Heber] in after years that the reason he felt as he did...was because the place was indeed 'holy ground,' that some of the ancient prophets had traveled in that region and dedicated the land, and that he, Heber, had reaped the benefit of their blessing."[2]

Such a scene, and such gratitude, I never witnessed before."[45] The gospel had given the people what they had never had before—a sense of themselves and a sense of dignity. They were not the forgotten backwash of the Industrial Revolution but children of a God who knew them and loved them and called their immortality and exaltation his work.

Elders Kimball, Richards, and Hyde had been away from home a year when they again set sail for America in April of 1838, leaving behind them more than fifteen hundred new Saints and Joseph Fielding as the new British mission president to continue the work.

"The standard is planted in the land and they can't root it up for it has become so powerful,"[46] Heber said.

Heber had been home only weeks when the Prophet Joseph received a revelation calling the Twelve to England, and the instructions were specific: "Let them take leave of my saints in the city of Far West on the twenty-sixth day of April next."[47] When this revelation was received, the Saints were living happily in Far West, but by April 1839, the Mormons had been driven from Missouri, children clinging to their mothers, as state militia officers pointed guns in their faces and burned their crops. Joseph Smith had spent the winter in the dank Liberty jail, and in Missouri some were boasting that if the Twelve returned they would be murdered. "It was with the greatest difficulty that many of them, especially the prominent ones, got out of Missouri," wrote Wilford Woodruff, "for at that time many people of that state acted as though they thought it no more harm to shoot a Mormon than to shoot a mad dog."[48] Indeed, with the extermination order in place, they could do so legally. The mobsters boasted that the revelation calling the Twelve to England could never be fulfilled, and thus Joseph was no prophet.

As the date approached, the Twelve met in Quincy, Illinois, to decide what to do. Brigham had no question about their course. They would go and did, traveling back through Missouri as if they were behind enemy lines, alert for sounds, wary of strangers. While it was yet dark on the morning of April 26, Brigham Young, Heber C. Kimball, Orson Pratt, John Taylor, and others met at the temple lot in Far West for a short service to begin their missions. Wilford Woodruff and George A. Smith were ordained apostles. Their enemies found out all too late that the Twelve

In this area of Downham, Lancashire, England, Heber C. Kimball recalled: "When I concluded [my sermon] I felt someone pulling at my coat....' Please sir, will you baptize me?' 'And me?' 'And me?' exclaimed more than a dozen voices."[3] Heber baptized 55 souls in one two-day period here.

A B O V E   Lucius Scovil commissioned Joseph Twigg to make these special temple plates in the fall of 1846. About 150 dozen plates were made in the Kiluhurst Old Pottery in the Staffordshire region.

F A R   L E F T   Old bottle ovens of the Gladstone Works in Longton (near Hanley), Staffordshire, England. The world-famous Staffordshire potteries were the mainstay of the economy in this region.

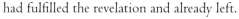

Light streams into one of the rooms of the John and Jane Benbow farmhouse where Wilford Woodruff preached beginning in March of 1840. Here in Herefordshire, England, the people opened their hearts to the preaching of the gospel.

RIGHT *The United Brethren, more than 600 strong, had been praying night and day for years that the Lord would reveal to them the Savior's ancient gospel. In response to those prayers, Wilford Woodruff was directed here by the Spirit of the Lord and preached in this barn.*

had fulfilled the revelation and already left.

Because other immediate needs pressed upon them, however, those missions would be temporarily postponed. The Saints, displaced and huddled along the Mississippi River, needed their help. Then as the steaming heat of that humid summer brought out the mosquitoes, malaria swept through their camps. Children lay in a fever, their enameled lips parched for water, their parents too weak themselves to help. Chills wracked their bodies, draining them of life. Heber, Brigham, Wilford Woodruff, and John Taylor were not excluded, lying in sickbeds trying to figure out how to walk to the front door, let alone how to leave on a mission.

Finally on August 8, Wilford Woodruff dragged himself up from his bed; blessed his sick wife, Phoebe; and "left her almost without food or the necessaries of life" to leave on his mission for England. "Although feeble," he wrote, "I walked to the banks of the Mississippi River. There President Young took me in a canoe . . . and paddled me across the river. When we landed, I lay down on a side of sole leather, by the post office, to rest. Brother Joseph, the Prophet of God, came along and looked at me. 'Well, Brother Woodruff,' said he, 'you have started upon your mission.' 'Yes,' said I, 'but I feel and look more like a subject for the dissecting room than a missionary.' Joseph replied: 'What did you say that for? Get up, and go along; all will be right with you.'"[49]

"I do not believe," Wilford later wrote, "that ever a company of men . . . attempted to perform a journey and mission of such extent and magnitude, under such unparalleled embarrassments and circumstances as did the quorum of the Twelve and others that started for England in 1839."[50] When Wilford left, Parley Pratt gave him an empty purse, and Heber Kimball gave him a dollar to put into it. Then he rode away in a lurching wagon, still suffering with

his chills and fever. John Taylor, Brigham, and Heber would themselves be weak and sick as they left on their missions. But, said Wilford, "the Spirit of God was upon me like fire shut up in my bones, urging me forward to fill my mission to England, and tarry no longer by the way."[51]

To Wilford, England appeared "like an old world sure enough, for all the fires, from the parlor to the largest public works . . . being fed alone from stone coal, that it causes the whole horizon, air, elements, earth, buildings, and everything visible to be covered with gas, soot and smoke."[52] Wilford went right to the heart of industrial England, the Staffordshire potteries, where in their gray factories, the people sweated their lives away creating bone china. There he found a branch of sixty members under the direction of a potter, Alfred Cordon, who labored six days a week and preached five evenings a week and three times on the Sabbath. Interest in the gospel took hold of the people there, and Wilford preached to crowded congregations and experienced frequent opposition from the ministers.

Wilford recounted this experience that took place on the evening of his thirty-third birthday: "I . . . met with a large assembly of the Saints and strangers, and while singing the first hymn the spirit of the Lord rested upon me and the voice of God said to me, 'This is the last meeting that you will hold with this people for many days.' I was astonished at this, as I had many appointments out in that district. . . . In the morning I went in secret before the Lord, and asked Him what was His will concerning me. The answer I received was that I should go to the south; for the Lord had a great work for me to perform there, as many souls were waiting for His word."[53]

South for Wilford was the rolling, lush farmlands of Herefordshire, where his companion, William Benbow, had a brother named John. John was a wealthy farmer and a member of the United Brethren, a group who had broken from the Wesleyan Methodists in an eager and prayerful search for light and truth. They had 600 members, including fifty preachers, who met in homes and

one or two chapels scattered over twenty to thirty miles.

Wilford spent the night with the Benbows, and the next morning, on March 5, 1840, John Benbow sent word through the neighborhood that an American missionary would preach at his home that evening. The response of the people was immediate and heartfelt; they had been prepared from long years of praying to find the ancient gospel described in the scriptures. Wilford's journal captures the electricity in the air: "On Saturday the 7th, I spent the day in preparing a pool for baptizing, for I saw there was much to be done. Sunday the 8th, I preached at Bro. Benbows before a large congregation, and baptized

seven, four were preachers. On the 9th I preached at Standly Hill and baptized seven, two were preachers. On the 10th, I preached again at Br. Benbows and baptized twelve, three were preachers."[54]

"This people universally felt willing to hear a matter before they condemned it," Wilford observed, "they opened their doors for me to preach, and searched the scriptures daily to see if the things which I taught were true." [55] Word of Wilford's astonishing work flew through the countryside and stirred the minister of Frooms Hill to action. He sent the constable out to arrest Wilford on the only count he could think of—preaching without a license—but according to Wilford, he "sent the wrong man."[56] As the constable politely waited for Wilford's sermon to conclude, he was touched by the Spirit and requested Brother Woodruff to baptize him. Exasperated, the preacher next sent two church clerks to discover what Wilford was teaching. Instead of making their report, they too were baptized.

I N FINE," SAID WILFORD, "I NEVER had seen such a work before, and the like had not been known in the last days. It was not the work of man but the work of God, the power of God was among the people, and his spirit was like a rushing mighty wind in our midst from time to time until multitudes were stirred up to inquire into these things. If any one asks why these things are so, I answer because the Lord is about to make a short work in England."[57]

Wilford could constantly see the evidence of that short work. In Ledbury, the Baptist minister "went into the pulpit with me and opened the meeting by reading the 35th chapter of Isaiah and praying mightily for me; I then arose and preached to a large and attentive audience and when I closed thirteen offered themselves for baptism, notwithstanding it was the first meeting we had held in the town."[58]

Yet even though the conversions were sometimes fast, they were not casual. John Benbow had been baptized only about a month when he and his wife, Jane, came to see Wilford. As they met in a little sitting room, they earnestly recounted that they had read in the New Testament how in the days of the Apostles, Church

members had sold all their possessions and laid them at the apostles' feet, and they felt it was their duty to fulfill that law and do the same thing. It was a moment Wilford would never forget, recounting it in a speech fifty-five years later, but for then, he said, "I gave them to understand that God had not sent me to England to take care

L ast light gently touches the pond on the Benbow farm that Wilford
had prepared and then used to baptize hundreds of the United
Brethren in Herefordshire, England. The Benbow farmhouse and out-
buildings can be seen in the background on the right. The
constable who was sent to arrest Wilford was also baptized in this pond.

of his gold, his horses, his cows and his property; He had sent me there to preach the gospel."[59] Though their offer was refused, the spirit of it continued to animate their lives. The Benbows would substantially finance the printing of the Book of Mormon in England, pay for at least forty of the United Brethren to make their journey to Zion, and later put up bail to help keep the Prophet Joseph out of jail.

Hostility to the restored gospel grew in direct proportion to its success. This American missionary with the strange new doctrine was a threat to tradition. Wilford ran headlong into animosity in some of the little villages that dotted the Herefordshire farmlands. When he arrived at Haw Cross, a vast assembly of people thronged the house, yard, and street where he was to speak, and among these were wary dissenters. When he began to preach, the mob created havoc and confusion. Then, as a number of people wished to be baptized, the mob surrounded the pool armed with stones and malicious intent. "I dismissed the meeting and went away," Wilford said, "but the congregation and mob remained on the ground till midnight; and as there was no prospect of their dispersing, and the candidates were anxious to be baptized, I went down into the water and baptized five, in the midst of a shower of stones. The water was all in a foam for a rod around me. None that I baptized were hit, and I was only hit twice, once on my hip and once on my head; the blow on my head raised a large bump, which went away while I was confirming." Then Wilford added almost as a forgotten understatement, "Subsequently I baptized many of the mob."[60]

Later he ran into similar treatment in Dymock during a prayer meeting in a home. "As the Saints began to assemble, the beat of pails, kettles, pans and sticks were heard through the streets, and soon a mob of 50 or 100 assembled and paraded rank and file before the house where we met. We closed our window shutters and doors in the room where we were, and I opened meeting by singing and prayer, and as soon as I commenced, they armed themselves with stones,

Canal and old Victorian school in Manchester, England. At the general conference held in Manchester in April 1840, 33 congregations were represented with a total of 1,517 members of the Church.

RIGHT Here, from atop the Herefordshire Beacon, on May 20, 1840, Brigham Young, Wilford Woodruff, and Willard Richards engaged in solemn prayer and made the decision to print the Book of Mormon in England. John Benbow would step forward to finance the bold undertaking.

brick bats, eggs, and every thing they could lay their hands upon, and began to throw them upon the house like a shower of hail for nearly an hour. They dashed in the windows, scattered stones, brick and glass through the rooms, broke the tile on the roof, and continued to commit such depredations until I closed the meeting."[61] Despite such opposition, all but one of the members of the United Brethren were converted to the gospel.

By April of 1840, eight of the Quorum of the Twelve were finally in England, malaria and families left behind—Brigham Young, Heber C. Kimball, Parley P. Pratt, Orson Pratt, John Taylor, Wilford Woodruff, George A. Smith, and Willard Richards. Following the

impulse and enormous talent for organization that has always marked the Church, within a week they had ready to present an ambitious program to the sixteen hundred Church members who had come for the first British conference. This included missionary labor and printing of a hymnal and a monthly publication to be called the *Millennial Star.* Soon after, Brigham Young and Willard Richards joined Wilford Woodruff in a mission back to the United Brethren, and on May 18, Brigham participated in a remarkable healing, a miracle too pointed for anyone to miss. Mary Pitt had been confined to bed for six years, unable to walk without a crutch for eleven. Brigham gave her a healing blessing, commanding her to

be made whole. She threw away her crutch and the next day walked three miles.

Work among the United Brethren spurred along one of the missionaries' major projects. "[The people] beg and plead for the Book of Mormon,"[62] wrote Brigham to the Prophet Joseph, asking for authorization to print the scripture in England since import duties were high. The urgency was such that Brigham was finally faced with the need to make a decision without Joseph's direction. On May 20, he, with Elders Richards and Woodruff, climbed the Herefordshire Beacon, which overlooked the villages where so many had responded, and asked for the will of God in the matter. After a pleading prayer, they felt they should immediately move forward on the printing. Brigham returned to Manchester, where he put a new kind of faith and himself on the line. Unschooled and unpolished, he would toil long hours editing, proofreading, and indexing the book.

Yet if publishing the Book of Mormon seemed nearly impossible, it is not farfetched to say that the Twelve in Britain trafficked in impossibilities. That same month, Brigham would tackle an even more difficult project by announcing a policy of encouraging the new Saints to immigrate to America. Here was Brigham, a craftsman by trade, called upon to organize a mass emigration of people, many of whom didn't have the means to emigrate anyway. And it wouldn't be just any emigration; its organization would be an awe-inspiring beehive of order and purpose, where each had a job and each helped the others. From the time Brigham and Heber sent the first group of forty-six emigrants, on June 1, 1840, the gathering was a remarkable feat, and a pattern was set. Priesthood leaders would be appointed to preside on the journey, and

First light touches the great city of Edinburgh, Scotland, and the edges of Arthur's Seat, the cliffs and prominence on the right. Orson Pratt hiked to the top of this hill many times. On his first climb he pleaded with the Lord for 200 converts. Orson preached the first discourse here on Sunday, May 24, 1841, and his original prayer was more than answered by the time he left the land of Scotland for America.

Scores of row houses at Merthyr Tydfil, Wales. Graded slag piles from the coal mines can be seen in the foreground. Dan Jones, shown above, made excellent use of his brother John's printing press in Wales. In all, Dan published 58 tracts and books in Welsh. By the end of 1848 he had distributed 1,850,000 pages of material.

RIGHT *Last light of day washes over old church and houses on street in Cowbridge, South Glamorgan, Wales. The mandatory 10-percent state church tax on all the produce of the farmers of Wales embittered the people. If the farmers did not pay the tax, all of their land was put up for sale at public auction. This led many to see the truthfulness of the gospel and bring them to Zion.*

those who came felt a kinship and responsibility for those who still wanted to come. This stewardship and bond would be lifelong. Thus decades later when Heber or Wilford would arise to speak to the Saints in the Salt Lake Valley, they would see in the audience their converts from Chatburn and Downham or Herefordshire and know that the gospel they had brought them had completely transformed their lives.

When the apostles left Britain in April of 1841, they left a church with a thoroughgoing organization and more than five thousand members, many of whom would follow them across the sea. They had arrived a year before, penniless, poorly dressed, and unsure of themselves in a foreign land. Thrust into a work bigger than they were, they grew to the job in a school particularly designed by the Lord. Beginning as the small and simple of the earth, they were transformed into confident, able men of God who could carry forth the work amid the many hazards that lay ahead. The firmly established work they left behind was not the only marvel of this mission; their training in leadership could hardly be duplicated in any other circumstance. The tradesmen and farmers had become kingdom builders.

Others would follow whose work would also be counted as astonishing. Short, stocky Dan Jones had left his native Wales at seventeen to go to sea, but he ended up in America plying the *Maid of Iowa*, a boat large enough to carry 300 passengers up and down the Mississippi River. His interest in the Church was piqued by a letter Emma Smith had written, and he joined in January of 1843. By 1844 he was back in his native land speaking what he admitted was rusty Welsh, but at first he found his efforts disappointing. He had traveled to Britain with Wilford Woodruff and had probably heard stories of the bountiful harvest in Herefordshire. For him, at first, it didn't happen that way. Downcast, he wrote Wilford in

February 1845, "I have neglected writing until now, expecting to have better news."[63] Later he jokingly wrote, "In the first Manchester Conference after my arrival I should have reported three [members], had I but baptized one, and included myself and wife."[64]

This state would not last long, for in a few months Elder Jones was called to preside over the entire mission and move from northern Wales to Merthyr Tydfil in the south. Now his determination and pugnacity, his raw energy, found a responsive people, and he approached missionary work as a battle for the souls of men, never timid about the personal consequences. To him Satan was his adversary, and he intended to conquer for the Lord. It has been written of him, "In spite of a lung illness that occasionally caused him great pain, he was a dynamic orator and an exceedingly fluent and colorful speaker, particularly when he spoke in his native tongue. He gloried in persecution, and he used it effectively for advertising. . . . He would often advertise in a town for several weeks that he was coming to convert the whole town. He would inform the mayor, the city council, the ministers and the police force of his intentions. He would have the local members of the church distribute thousands of tracts to all the city. When he arrived at the railroad station he was often met by all of the officials of the city and many excited citizens."[65]

As the fame of Dan Jones and his message began to spread through the hamlets and along the hedged roads of Wales, the clergy lashed out, using both their pulpits and the press, to which Dan did not have access. Seeing this as no major obstacle, he found a way to capitalize on the controversy. He said, "I delight in the trophies of war. I came here to fight for the spiritual freedom of my brethren, and I thank heaven and the God of this warfare, that He is knocking off their shackles by hundreds!"[66]

If the attacks were personal, he was still undaunted, saying, "Most of the stories that were told on poor Brother Joseph in America are here fathered on Captain Jones, and I often hear those who don't know that little man, unhesitatingly denounce him as a curse upon this nation for kicking up such a fuss."[67]

Elder Jones drew such fire that people felt compelled to find out for themselves the truth about Mormonism. As the controversy raged, Dan was shouted at and his life was threatened, but through it all he steadily baptized. The *Millennial Star* reported that Brother Jones "had lately baptized the only remaining two of an entire church of Baptists; they had now the chapel, priest, and hearers."[68]

In another place, having already baptized 150 locally, Dan Jones visited a Baptist church meeting whose purpose was to "expose" Mormonism. He wrote, "The big seat was crowded with the reverends, etc., from far and near, and although they exacted sixpence for admission, yet the chapel was crowded with anxious listeners, who, with opened mouths, eagerly anticipated to hear the funeral sermon of Mormonism. I seated myself in front, and took notes of his topics, and were you to see the fingers and eyes that evidently marked me as a gone case, you would have thought that I had seven horns."[69] At the meeting the speaker continually pounded the pulpit, crying "Down with Mormonism," and he brought out every old saw against the faith. Joseph Smith, said the lecturer was a "money-digger," "fortune-teller," "liar," and "thief."

The result of the meeting was far different from its intent. From that time, said Dan, "I have been lecturing there to audiences of eager hearers, almost without cessation, and many believing the gospel."[70]

Despite his exuberance, Dan's lungs, weakened by his early years in coal mines, bled when he was overexerted, and he knew the pang of loneliness. He wrote to Orson Spencer, "Would that I were near you—near somebody! But here I am alone, like a beacon at sea, or a reed in the gale."[71]

WHEN DAN JONES LEFT Wales in February 1849, largely due to his influence seventy-two branches were in operation with Church members numbered at 4,645. One out of every 278 Welsh people was a Mormon—and like so many before them, most of the Welsh Saints would have Zion planted in their hearts and, while family protested, pack their bundles to head for Liverpool.

Dan took 249 converts with him bound for New Orleans aboard the ship *Buena Vista.* They were those who had found a way to earn the forty-five dollars per person it cost in the Church's disciplined pipeline to bring them to Zion and who had probably followed the advice he would later pen in a pamphlet called *Guide to Zion:* "First, pay your rightful debts to everyone, or obtain the kindness of those you owe either to freely forgive or to allow you time to pay at the end of your journey; without doing one or the other we do not advise anyone to emigrate towards Zion."[72]

With or without a guide, they would have come. Dan Jones paced back and forth on his ship bound for Zion, comforting and administering to the sick, forcing gruel down the weary, and urging everybody out of the stale air below to come up on deck. One said, "Many would hide from him by covering up in bed while he passed," and he joked in return that he would get them up into healthier circumstances if it took a rope and a pulley.

The homesick flock, like those who had been leaving steadily since 1840, wouldn't see home again. They had turned their faces to Zion.

*The fields of Wales would become a bountiful harvest
for Dan Jones and his missionary companions.
For generations to come, many Church members would trace
their spiritual roots to ancestors who had heard
and accepted the gospel in villages that dotted this countryside.*

Two

My people must be tried in all things

Western light touches panes of glass in the
Nauvoo home of Lucy Mack Smith, mother of the Prophet
Joseph. By the time Lucy passed away in 1856,
she had buried her husband, seven sons, three daughters-
in-law, one son-in-law, and eight grandchildren.

PAGES 42–43 *Sun sets over the fro-
zen Mississippi River at the end of Parley Street where the
Saints crossed over from Nauvoo to Iowa. The
shore-to-shore distance today is a foreboding 6,565 feet.*

NGLISH CONVERTS GEORGE Q. AND MARY ALICE CANNON, brother and sister, were hardly more than children when they traveled up the Mississippi River and arrived at the landing of Nauvoo, but that first impression would linger forever. It wasn't of the city, set like a jewel on the bend of the river, with its cultivated gardens and orderly streets laid out on the square. No, what indelibly impressed them in the crowd of people thronging the dock was the Prophet Joseph Smith. Young George said he would have known him among ten thousand: "There was that about him that distinguished him from all the men he had ever seen."[1] Mary Alice said, "I knew him the instant my eyes rested upon him, and at that moment I received my testimony that he was a Prophet of God, for I never had such a feeling for mortal man as thrilled my being when my eyes first rested upon Joseph Smith."[2]

For the converts who streamed in from England and various parts of the eastern United States, Nauvoo was their city on a hill, a religious refuge, an expression of the beauty of the Spirit they felt in the restored gospel. In only seven years, its citizens would transform a stinking, malaria-infested swamp into the fairest and largest city in Illinois, a place where a substantial number of homes were made of brick, made to endure and grow old in. Here cultural events and university classes expanded the mind, and the Nauvoo Legion with their strutting horses and colorful uniforms marched in parades and gave the citizens, many who had been driven from their homes in Missouri by mobs, a sense of safety.

Eliza R. Snow called Nauvoo "our beloved city,"[3] and it was, but not because building it was easy. The Saints' journals are filled with descriptions of roofs that leaked and meals of hard Johnny-cake, of husbands leaving for missions and children dying of chills and fever while they were gone. Somehow, for the gospel they loved, it was worth it. "I did not put my hand to the plough to look backward,"[4] Electa Williams said when her husband's parents offered them a home and

security in Michigan. A newspaper reporter who visited the city wrote, "No sect of religious enthusiasts were ever more firmly convinced of the entire truth of their creed than these people."[5]

Their faith was centered in the gospel restored through the Prophet Joseph Smith, and his presence animated their city. He was a window to the heavens, a source of authority, and they loved him. They listened to him with rapt attention when he addressed them in the grove. They were refreshed by the doctrine he preached and buoyed up in the midst of turmoil by his "native cheery" temperament. "Never be discouraged," he said. "If I were sunk in the lowest pit of Nova Scotia, with the Rocky Mountains piled on me, I would hang on, exercise faith, and keep up good courage, and I would come out on top."[6] Even while hiding from his enemies in William Hunter's attic, where he could not stand up to his full height, he wrote, "Shall we not go on in so great a cause?"[7]

He pulled sticks with his friends, played with the children of Nauvoo, and inspired deep loyalty in the hearts of the people who joined him in the work. When Margaret Judd Clawson's mother went shopping one day, she passed the Prophet's home. He was standing on the lawn conversing with some elegant gentlemen. Though he had never met her, he turned from that circle and reached over the fence, grasped her hand, and gave it a hearty shake. It was simply a kind gesture of the moment, but for her it was worth recording and remembering for generations. "In the midst of difficulties he was always the first in motion; in critical positions his counsel was always sought," said John Taylor. "As our Prophet he approached our God, and obtained for us his will."[8]

But faith is not something well understood by the outside observer. It seems extreme, its power of motivation unexplainable, and the people of Illinois who had no trouble believing in a Moses or an Abraham found the idea of a modern prophet and the devotion that followed his teachings dangerous. The old citizens of Illinois looked at the converts swelling the roads and the river that led to Nauvoo and felt they were being overtaken.

The industry and order that built Nauvoo were at odds with the rambling individualism of frontier America. The unity of the Saints; the concentration of economic, religious, and political power in one group; the very dedication with which they approached the building of their city—all were threats to the older settlers.

Thomas Sharp, the spiteful editor of the *Warsaw Signal*, came to Nauvoo and immediately hated the Prophet and his expansive ideas about building the kingdom of God. Fueled also by disappointment in a real-estate venture when the Saints settled in Commerce instead of Warsaw, Sharp began a relentless attack upon the Saints in his newspaper. When the Mormons began to vote consistently Democratic, two pro-Whig newspapers joined in. Soon, these newspapers had fuel for their fire; John C. Bennett, Nauvoo's first mayor, was excommunicated for

immorality and began widely publishing a series of flamboyant stories about the Church and Joseph Smith. Included in his charges was a sensational and distorted description of polygamy, a practice Joseph had received by revelation and had quietly introduced among select leaders of the Church.

Anti-Mormon sentiment was whipped into a frenzy by the half-truths, lies, and exaggeration in the media. Then, motivated by apostates, the anti-Mormon media came home to Nauvoo with the publication, on June 7, 1844, of the libelous *Nauvoo Expositor*. The city council met and decided that to allow its continued publication would lead to rising mob action and open violence on the Saints. Following earlier precedents in Illinois and acting under the Nauvoo Charter, they had the press destroyed.

It was just the chance Joseph's enemies had been waiting for, their opportunity to nip rising Mormonism in the bud by destroying its founder. The *Signal* trumpeted, "War and extermination is inevitable. Citizens ARISE ONE and ALL!!!—Can you stand by, and suffer such INFERNAL DEVILS! To ROB men of their property and RIGHTS, without avenging them. We have no time for comment, every man will make his own. LET IT BE MADE WITH POWDER AND BALL."[9]

For some time, Joseph had been telling his closest confidants that he sensed the end was near for him. Charged with treason, he was taken to "the safest place in Hancock County" under Governor Thomas Ford's promise of protection—the Carthage jail. Joseph knew it was a scam, knew he was traveling to his death. He took a last look at Nauvoo and said, "This is the loveliest place and the best people under the heavens; little do they know the trials that await them."[10] On the afternoon of June 27, a mob of from one to two hundred, with faces blackened to hide their identity, stormed the prison with the guard's cooperation and murdered Joseph and Hyrum Smith. "Oh Lord, my God," Joseph cried as he was shot four times and fell or leaped from the window of the jail.

That night the sultriness of the afternoon turned to rain, and Carthage was deserted as people fled for their lives, not taking time to shut their doors after them, because they believed the Mormons would come seeking revenge. Lewis Barney noted, "Stores were left open and

*J*oseph and Hyrum, Willard Richards, and John Taylor were in
this jailer's bedroom when the mob stormed the jail.
Hyrum lay dead on this floor, and John Taylor rolled under the
bed after being hit five times. Joseph received four balls
and leaped from the window on the left. Willard was unharmed.

L E F T *Original door in the Carthage jail still has*
marks of the martyrdom. The latch was broken, so the brethren braced
the door with their bodies. The upper-right hole in the
panel was the place through which the ball blasted that killed Hyrum.

there was gloom cast over the country, so much that strangers passing through the country spoke of it."[11]

THE PEOPLE'S FLIGHT ON THE sodden roads shows how little they knew of the Mormons. Though the Saints had the largest militia in Illinois and though an enormous crime had been committed against them with warnings of more to come, much to their credit the people of Nauvoo held themselves in restraint. Willard Richards, who had been in the jail but had been the only one not wounded, nursed the stricken John Taylor and sent a note to Nauvoo, saying, "The citizens here are afraid of the Mormons attacking them: I promise them no!"[12] A few hours later he wrote more details, adding, "I say to all the citizens of Nauvoo, . . . be still, and know that God reigns." That the Mormons were not just grief-stricken but also terrified for their lives is evident in another comment of Willard's: "Stay at home, and be prepared for an attack from Missouri mobbers."[13]

The next day the bodies of Joseph and Hyrum were brought to Nauvoo, where thousands of the Saints thronged Mulholland Street about a mile east of the temple, and "the most solemn lamentations and wailings that ever ascended into the ears of the Lord of Hosts were heard."[14] Zina Huntington was among the crowd who pressed to the Mansion House to see Joseph and Hyrum lying in state. She wrote, "Little did my heart ever think that mine eyes should witness this awful scene."[15] For the Saints, the loss was personal, a stinging, searing vacancy in their hearts. "I don't think Mother could have felt worse if it had been a member of her own family,"[16] said Bathsheba Smith.

Distress prevailed the night after the funeral in Nauvoo. Jane Richards said, "Word was brought to us from the prairies that the mob was coming in to exterminate the whole fraternity. All night men were on guard and women and children prepared for flight.

"Even the dogs howled and manifested great uneasiness and hourly we thought we heard the noise of horsemen. At midnight a terrific thunder storm broke on us. So unusual in its violence that as we were afterwards told it drove the mob back. A thousand men we were told were on their way bent on our destruction. But the rain wet their ammunition, and so rendered them powerless to destroy us."[17]

Mourning overcame all other emotions: "What dreariness and sorrow pervades every being," Vilate Kimball wrote her husband, Heber. "The very streets of Nauvoo seem to mourn."[18] Heber did not need to be told that Joseph and Hyrum had been murdered. On the day of the martyrdom, ten of the twelve apostles were away on missions, but a heavy melancholia overtook them and brought them home to a city that was lost without its prophet. Traveling between Philadelphia and New York City, Heber felt as mournful as if he had just lost a friend. In Boston, Orson Hyde was combing over maps in a hall rented by the Church when he was borne down with such heaviness that tears ran down his cheeks and he turned from his studies to pacing. Parley P. Pratt learned of the martyrdom as passengers on a steamboat on the Great Lakes buzzed with excitement about the news. In grief, Parley plodded 105 miles across the Illinois plains, hardly able to eat or sleep, wondering, "O Lord, . . . what shall I say to thy people?"[19]

Most of the apostles had arrived home in Nauvoo by August 6, 1844, finding a people who felt like "sheep without a shepherd, as being without a father, as their head had been taken away."[20] The Church was at a turning point.

Sidney Rigdon arrived in Nauvoo claiming to have had a vision that he was to be guardian of the Church, though Wilford Woodruff wryly commented in his journal that it was a "long story. It was a kind of second class

Winter sun of evening warms the home of Sarah Melissa Granger Kimball in Nauvoo. Here the women gathered to make clothing for the brethren who were working on the temple. Later this group would form the Female Relief Society of Nauvoo. Sarah would make the exodus west at age 27.

February scene of Nauvoo, looking southwest across to the Seventies Hall. Chancey Webb's old home can be seen on the left. The Saints had laid out this great city and had built it as if to stay for a lifetime, yet the main body of thousands would leave just seven years after the first furrow was turned.

vision."[21] Nevertheless on August 8, a gathering of the Church was held to decide on succession of leadership. First, Sidney presented his claims in a long-winded speech that awakened no response. Next, Brigham Young stood and gave a brief but stirring statement: "If any man thinks he has influence among this people to

lead away a party, let him try it. . . . The Twelve were appointed by the finger of God. Here is Brigham, have his knees ever faltered? Have his lips ever quivered? Here is Heber and the rest of the Twelve, an independent body who have the keys of the priesthood—the keys of the kingdom of God to deliver to all the world: this is true, so help me God. They stand next to Joseph, and are as the First Presidency of the Church."[22]

As Brigham Young spoke, in an event attested in numerous journals, he was transfigured before the people to look and sound like Joseph Smith. George Q. Cannon wrote, "If Joseph had arisen from the dead and again spoken in their hearing, the effect could not have been more startling than it was to many present at that meeting; it was the voice of Joseph himself; and not only was it the voice of Joseph which was heard, but it seemed to the eyes of the people as if it were the very person of Joseph which stood before them."[23] The detractors who thought the gospel was held together by the charismatic personality of a single leader—Joseph Smith—simply did not understand the careful organization of God's kingdom. They had murdered Joseph, but they could not murder the stirrings of the Spirit in the hearts of those who had a testimony, nor could they take away the priesthood keys. Though some groups would splinter away, the majority of the Saints followed the Twelve, led by Brigham Young. With enemies on every side, new converts still pouring in to Nauvoo, and a temple to build, he was the man for the hour. Tough, pragmatic, insightful, able to cut through any difficulty and stir a beleaguered people to action, he was as necessary for his time as Joseph had been for his. Though, like Joseph, he was born in humble circumstances, he had a natural genius for administration. In the harrowing months to come, he would simultaneously build a temple, negotiate with a citizenry who wanted him and his people gone, comfort and uplift those whose homes would be burned out from under them, write countless letters to government officials, and create and execute a plan to move a city of twenty thousand people to build their Zion somewhere else.

It wasn't enough at this meeting to determine succession. Brigham, showing the solidity of character that would hold the Church together through all the assaults to follow, energized the people for the future. Though reeling from the recent murder of their prophet, they still voted for themselves a program of action—to tithe themselves to complete the temple and expand the missionary work. Now their zeal was fueled by testimony and the blood of martyrs.

By unanimous decision of her citizens, Nauvoo was renamed the City of Joseph, and in the next few months the Saints enjoyed a brief respite from the thunderings of the mobs. In September, two of those charged with the murder of the Prophet Joseph, Colonel Levi Williams and Major Aldrich, both of independent militias, extended invitations to the captains of the military of neighboring counties to "attend a great wolf hunt in Hancock County." It was privately announced that the wolves to be hunted were the Mormons and Jack Mormons (those who sympathized with the Mormons).

To aid the movement, the anti-Mormon newspapers began again their description of thefts, robberies, and other alleged Mormon "outrages." When Governor Ford raised five hundred volunteers to march into Hancock County, the malcontents were thwarted, though their emotions continued to seethe. The interlude of peace would be fragile and brief.

Meanwhile, missionaries still went forth. Wilford Woodruff was sent to England, and Dan Jones to Wales. Eastern Canada and the states of the Union were divided into missions. George A. Smith wrote Wilford Woodruff in England, "An immense immigration is expected this spring, and notwithstanding the departure of apostates and their followers from our city, it is almost impossible to find an empty house or a room to rent. The tithing is coming in from nearly all the branches, and business moves as busily around the temple as it does around a beehive in May."[24] One of those immigrants, Irene Pascall Pomeroy, who arrived in May of 1845, expected Nauvoo to "look like poordunk or something," but she found it "the prettiest place [she] ever saw for a large place."[25]

Building continued to thrive in Nauvoo. Brigham wrote Wilford in England, "[The city] looks like a paradise. All the lots and land, which have heretofore been vacant and unoccupied, were enclosed in the spring, and planted with grain and vegetables, which makes it look more like a garden of gardens than a city. . . . Many strangers are pouring in to view the Temple and the city. They express their astonishment and surprise to see the rapid progress."[26] For his part, Brigham added two rooms to his home, and in 1845 Heber completed the brick home he would occupy only five months. Even as they built, the leaders sensed they would not be able to stay in their beautiful city.

A week before his death, Joseph had warned the people, "It is thought by some that our enemies would be satisfied with my destruction; but I tell you that as soon as they have shed my blood, they will thirst for the blood of every man in whose heart dwells a single spark of the spirit of the fulness of the gospel."[26] In the spring of 1844, Joseph had told the apostles to send a party to look for possible sites in Oregon or California for a haven for the Saints. They should find a place, he said, "where we can remove after the temple is completed and where we can build a city in a day, and have a government of our own, get up into the mountains where the devil cannot dig us out."[28]

Brigham, too, knew the solution to their problems lay to the west.

But the temple had to be completed first, a poignant effort that would eventually find them building as they packed, cutting stone as they cured hickory for wagon wheels. Only a believer who knows the temple's significance would understand the million dollars of expenditure and one out of every ten days of labor to complete a place that would be abandoned. Here they could take upon themselves sacred covenants that might allow them to live again with God, a reality that put all their suffering into perspective.

It was a project built out of their devotion and poverty. Louisa Decker said the women "sold things they could scarcely spare"[29] to get money toward its construction, and some gave more than that. Elizabeth Kirby, a widow, donated the only keepsake with which she would grieve to part—her husband's watch. She said, "I gave it to help build the Nauvoo Temple and everything else I could possibly spare and the last few dollars that I had in the world, which altogether amounted to nearly $50."[30]

Men like Charles Lambert worked on the temple by day and guarded the city by night, half-asleep with exhaustion. He had covenanted, "I would stick to the temple pay or no pay until finished." One day he came home to find his wife crying at the door, saying she could stand anything but hearing her children crying for bread and having none to give them. The two parents went to

their bedroom and pled for help. In about an hour, Lucius Scovil came and asked Charles to make a gravestone to mark the spot where his son was buried. He had no money but instead would pay with wheat—in advance. That very evening, Lambert picked up about four bushels of wheat, went to the mill, and came home with grist. "Thus," he said, "was our prayers answered."[31]

In this time of need, the hounded people saw many answered prayers. With the undaunted faith that marked him, Brigham Young said, "A few months after the martyrdom of Joseph the Prophet, in the autumn and winter of 1844, we did much hard labor on the Nauvoo Temple, during which time it was difficult to get bread and other provisions for the workmen to eat. I counseled the committee who had charge of the temple funds to deal out all the flour they had, and God would give them more; and they did so; and it was but a short time before

Brother Toronto came and brought me twenty-five hundred dollars in gold. The bishop and the committee met, and I met with them; and they said that the law was to lay the gold at the Apostle's feet. Yes, I said, and I will lay it at the bishop's feet; so I opened the mouth of the bag and took hold at the bottom end, and gave it a jerk toward the bishop, and strewed gold across the room and said, now go, and buy flour for the workmen on the temple and do not distrust the Lord any more; for we will have what we need."[32]

Nancy Tracy, whose home was near the temple, remembered, "Out of my bedroom window I could see the masons at work and could hear the click of their hammers and hear their sailor songs as they pulled the rock in place with pulleys. It was grand to see."[33]

Far from thinking it grand, Illinois' "old citizens" were infuriated by the energy of the Saints. This majestic white

limestone temple rising on a prominence overlooking the Mississippi was a sign to them that the Saints were digging in to stay, an unthinkable idea. As the temple rose, the designs of the enemies of the Church grew as well.

The anti-Mormons first concentrated their efforts on the state legislature, motivating the repeal of the Nauvoo Charter in January 1845. The charter had been a thorn in the side of the old citizens, as they believed it gave the Mormons too much power. Under the charter, the mayor and aldermen were also judges in the municipal court, and since Church leaders were inevitably elected to these positions, such mingling of powers brought criticism. The Nauvoo Legion was also empowered under the Nauvoo Charter. Of this repeal, state legislator Josiah Lamborn wrote to Brigham Young, "I have always considered that your enemies have been prompted by political and religious prejudices and by a desire for plunder and blood, more than the common good."[34]

With the charter gone, Nauvoo was without a city government, and, much worse, without police protection. As a riverside city, it became a breeding ground for the thieves, counterfeiters, and gamblers who trafficked the river—and now they could run loose. What's more, their activities were blamed on the Church. Some renegades claimed their activities were, in fact, sanctioned by the Church, which further fed the hostility of the surrounding countryside.

To protect themselves, the Saints turned to a home-grown remedy. The older boys in the town were formed into a "whistling and whittling brigade." Lolling about the streets, they watched for dubious-looking strangers and followed them en masse, whittling with their jackknives and whistling tunelessly. The message was clear—get out of town.

Ironically, while the river riffraff had their way in Nauvoo, the leaders of the Church were constantly barraged by vexatious lawsuits, so much so that one of the

*O*riginal Nauvoo Temple sunstone. Thirty of these stones topped the pilasters of the temple. Moonstones and starstones also respectively matched that number. Only three sunstones and two moonstones exist today.

L E F T *Actual photograph of the Nauvoo Temple (circa 1846).[2] This magnificent structure, overlooking the rolling waters of the Mississippi River, was 128 feet long, 88 feet wide, and 60 feet high at the overhang. The belfry and clock-tower dome was 158½ feet above the ground. The cost of the temple is estimated at $1 million.*

Wooden bin of spices that dates to the Nauvoo period. These were found behind a loose rock
in one of the foundations of the homes in Nauvoo in
recent years. Spices were very expensive in
the 1840s, and apparently the sister who hid them in
the cellar expected to come back and get them.
Each small container had ample spices still intact.

city's landmark ceremonies had to be held in secret. When Joseph died, the temple was only one story high. Only eleven months later, in May of 1845, a people eager for their temple ordinances and bound to show themselves that truth would prevail were ready to place the capstone. John Taylor said of the event, "On the morning of Saturday, May 24th, 1845, we repaired to the temple with great secrecy. . . . There were but few that knew about it, [but] the band playing on the walls and the people hearing it, hurried up. About six o'clock A.M. . . . we proceeded to lay the stone. Although there were several officers watching for us to take us, yet we escaped without their knowledge when the singing commenced."[35]

By September, a scattered group of anti-Mormons of Lima and Green Plains met to devise a means of expelling Mormons from their neighborhood. As they met in one of their homes, one of their own number fired upon it. Then they announced through the neighborhood that the Mormons had fired on them—just the excuse they needed to begin a work of death and massacre. They began by burning the homes of the most vulnerable—those who lived in the outlying areas beyond the protection of Nauvoo.

The burnings were almost a ritual. The mob would arrive at a house and pull the family out, women and little children being dragged sometimes from beds of sickness. Then the family watched helplessly as their cattle were scattered, their crops destroyed, and their homes, barns, and haystacks burned to piles of smoking ashes. The roads to Nauvoo were strewn with the homeless whose living had been off the land and now had no choice but to seek shelter from the compassionate. Bathsheba Smith said, "Our house was filled with refugees."[36]

One night James Porter told Mary Bigelow and her family, who lived at Camp Creek near Nauvoo, that the mob was coming to burn down their house and kill every family member. Terrified, they scurried to hide everything valuable, then took their bedding and camped out in their corn, near the bean patch. "We took all of the children in bed with us, never undressing them, and having everything dark about the bed so that the mob wouldn't see us," she said. They prayed and then lay sleeplessly on the ground, waiting. Soon they heard firing and whooping at the house. Mary later wrote, "My husband said, 'lay still and pray, children.' We all prayed silently.

"They yelled and set the bloodhounds on our track but the Lord preserved us from them. We could see them loping around and heard the mob racing through the corn field in search of us." The mob stayed from 10:00 P.M. until 3:00 A.M., hours that stretched out endlessly for the Bigelows. When daylight came, Mary's husband got up, gesturing for the family to lie quietly while he went to see if the mob was completely gone. "He found the house still standing but the windows were broken," Mary wrote. "The tracks of horses' feet were all around the house."

MARY SENT HER SON ASA to the beautiful, large spring under the porch of the milk house to get water for breakfast. Mary wrote, "He brought the water to the house, but said he believed the spring was poisoned as there was a glistening green scum on the water. He poked it away and got another pail full and it was the same. I felt that the child was inspired by God, and as the water stood the scum rose again."[37] They got their water from another source that morning and took a sample of the scum water to Dr. Willard Richards for analysis. He said it contained four ounces of arsenic and would have killed ten men.

drive the Mormons into the river.'"[38]

The Twelve advised the people not to resist these attacks nor to defend themselves but, according to John Taylor, "to keep all things as quiet as possible and not resent anything."[39] Sheriff J. B. Backenstos of Hancock County told the people, "The Mormon community had acted with more than ordinary forbearance, remaining perfectly quiet and offering no resistance when their dwellings, their buildings, stacks of grain, etc., were set on fire in their presence. They had forborne until forbearance was no longer a virtue."[40]

About that same time Lewis Barney was approached by a committee of three men asking him to give up Mormonism. Of the event he wrote, "They said, 'We know you are an honest man and we feel sorry for you and if you will give up Mormonism and the Book of Mormon, you are welcome to stay with us and we will protect you. The determination is to drive all the Mormons into Nauvoo then surround it and then burn the city and

Forbearance wasn't enough. While the smoke rose from charred homes, the citizens of Quincy, the same town who had greeted the driven Saints from Missouri with open arms just six years before, met on September 22, 1845, and demanded the removal of the Saints from Illinois. "It is a settled thing," reported the Quincy *Whig,* "that the public sentiment of the state is against the Mormons, and it will be in vain for them to contend against it."[41]

Governor Ford confessed to the Saints that "while the state has no power to insist upon their removal . . . [and] it is a great hardship on them to remove from their comfortable homes and the property which they have accumulated by years of toil," yet the state of Illinois could and would do nothing to protect them. If they decided to stay, they would be living in a state of "continual war."[42] Two days after the Quincy convention, the Twelve issued a proclamation they hoped would bring a truce. They would move out of their homes, they said, "for some point so remote that there [would] need to be no difficulty with the people and ourselves,"[43] but they wanted an agreement in return—an end to lawsuits and persecution so they would have time to prepare. They would go the following spring, when the grass grew and the water ran.

The Twelve had already begun gathering information on possible sites for relocation. In that October 1845 conference, they also unanimously covenanted, "We [will] take all the saints with us, to the extent of our ability, that is, our influence and property."[44] The poor would not be left behind at the mercy of their persecutors.

Two thrusts busied the Saints that fall in Nauvoo— finish the temple and become prepared to leave according to an orderly plan designed by Brigham and the Twelve. The plan called for twenty-five companies, each comprised of one hundred families and headed by a company captain. Parley P. Pratt estimated that a family of five would need one wagon, three yoke of oxen, two cows, two beef cattle, three sheep, a thousand pounds of flour, twenty pounds of sugar, one rifle with ammunition, and one tent with poles—a total weight of 2,700 pounds. Immediately Nauvoo became a hive of activity as men wore themselves out cutting and drying oak and

Fire of the blacksmith is kept at a steady temperature to work the raw iron into various products such as horseshoes, chains, tools, cooking utensils, and various parts of wagons. If metal is heated too hot for too long, it can lose its temper.

RIGHT *Tools of the blacksmith trade were critical to the exodus of 1846. The blacksmiths in Nauvoo were the hub of the community and the centerplace of activity (with the exception of the temple) for the last months of 1845 and all of 1846.*

FAR RIGHT *Yoke leaning on a fence in Nauvoo. One of the great challenges of the exodus was inexperienced converts dealing with unruly oxen and other draft animals for drawing their wagons.*

hickory for wagons and sweating over hot forges to pound out chains and wheels. The women dried fruit and stitched bags for flour and salt, then wore callouses sewing wagon covers.

A reporter from the *Daily Missouri Republican* gave this account of a city in preparation: "Nearly every work-shop in the city has been converted into a wagon maker's shop. Even an unfinished portion of the Temple is thus used, and every mechanic appears to be employed in making, repairing or finishing wagons, or other articles necessary for the trip. Generally, they are providing themselves with light wagons, with strong, wide bodies, covered with cotton cloth—in some instances painted, but mostly white. These are to be met with in every direction, and contribute greatly to the singular and mournful appearance of the country."

Though Brigham intended the exodus to be well-provisioned and orderly, not everyone was adequately prepared, which the reporter noted: "Many of them are going with poor teams, and an amount of provisions insufficient for their subsistence for two months, if so long. . . . If they should fail to make a good crop this year, at the stopping place, it cannot be otherwise than that many of them, especially the women and children, and the aged and decrepit, must be sorely pressed by starvation, if many of them do not literally perish from

famine on the plains. . . . Of those whose condition is calculated to arouse sympathy are a number of women, many of whom have large families of children, inadequately provided with provisions, and without the assistance of protection of any male person. How they expect to get through the journey, we cannot conceive."[45]

The problem for many, of course, was gathering the means to go. Speculators knew that property was in abundance in Nauvoo and that buyers were few. The Saints, forced to sell, were selling cheap, and since little money was in circulation, they took most of their pay in trade. "As a stranger passes through," the reporter observed, "he will find himself frequently beset mostly by women and children, with inquiries, 'Do you wish to purchase a house and lot? Do you wish to buy a farm?'" Then the stranger would "be pressed and entreated to go and examine, and all the advantages [and] cheapness" of the property would "be fully explained."[46]

"We have sold our place for a trifle to a *Baptist minister*," Martha Haven wrote to her mother. "All we got was a cow and two pairs of steers, worth about sixty dollars in trade."[47] The problem was that such a trifle was not enough to secure an outfit and provisions. Heber C. Kimball was one of the fortunate whose lovely brick home brought six hundred dollars, mostly in goods, but as time wore on buyers were rare. "The frequency and earnestness manifested everywhere, in the city and country, indicate the great anxiety which they entertain to get off," observed the newspaper reporter. "In the city, houses and lots are selling at from two to five and ten hundred dollars, which must have cost the owners double that sum. They are willing to sell for cash, or oxen or cattle, or to exchange for such articles of merchandise as they can barter or carry away with them."[48]

Money for an outfit wasn't the only problem. Margaret Judd Clawson watched her father struggling to prepare. She said, "How well I remember what a hard time he had breaking in the animals to draw the wagon. There were six cows and two oxen. The oxen were well broken and quite sedate. But the cows were wild and unruly. He would get help to yoke them up, and then would start to drive them. All at once, they would run off in an opposite direction to where he wanted them to go. Or would run around to the back of the wagon, and get all tangled up. Well, this went on for days and days, and while Father was breaking the cattle, Mother was praying. She told me afterwards that many nights when we were in bed asleep that she would go out into the orchard at the back of our house, and there pour out her soul in prayer, asking the Lord to open the way for us to go with the Saints."[49]

They were a mistreated but happy people; their accounts show little sign of resentment or self-pity. "The spectator cannot fail to be struck with the lightness of heart, apparent cheerfulness, and sanguine hopes with which families . . . set out on their journey," noted the reporter.[50] They were sustained by faith that they would build their Zion in a place beyond the torment of angry mobs, that in leaving their city, they would be sustained in the wilderness by the God they loved.

Like Priddy Meeks, many abandoned their possessions: "I had a small flock of sheep which I had not time to sell. These I left, together with my house and lot, the former containing my furniture and books."[51] They packed and

The east room of Brigham Young's Nauvoo home, where the great exodus of the Saints was discussed. Brigham declared that the planned exodus was part of the "merciful design in our Heavenly Father towards all such as patiently endure these afflictions until He advises them that the day of their deliverance has come."[52]

RIGHT Flowers by a picket fence at Wilford Woodruff's home in Nauvoo. Brigham Young, though burdened with the leadership of the exodus, was positive and powerful: "Wake up, wake up, dear brethren . . . to the present glorious emergency in which the God of heaven has placed you to prove your faith by your works."[53]

repacked wagons, trying to make room for keepsakes that would give them some sense of civilization in a new land. Some, in an optimistic gesture, hid their china in the bottom of privies, hoping they might someday come back to reclaim it. They never did. The white and gold temple, with its inscription "Holiness to the Lord," was the symbol of their faith and their sacrifice, the sorrow of their abandonings. When the rooms were opened on December 10, 1845, they flocked to the temple for the sacred ordinances that would sanctify their loss. In January Brigham Young wrote, "Such has been the anxiety manifested by the saints to receive the ordinances, and such the anxiety on our part to administer to them, that I have given myself up entirely to the work of the Lord in the Temple night and day, not taking more than four hours sleep, upon an average, per day, and going home but once a week."[52]

THEIR ENEMIES CONTINUED their relentless pressure, and the thought of leaving in the spring became a pipe dream. Governor Ford warned that federal troops in St. Louis planned to intercept the Saints and destroy them. An indictment was filed against Brigham and eight others of the Twelve, charging them with counterfeiting, and in February they knew it was time to go. Brigham had planned to stop the ordinance work on February 3 to make final preparations for the trip west, but so many still clamored for their endowments, he delayed his trip two more weeks. In all, 5,615 would receive their endowments before they shut the temple doors behind them and turned their faces west.

They left their beautiful Nauvoo with feelings like those of Bathsheba Smith, who said, "My last act in that precious spot was to tidy the rooms, sweep up the floor, and set the broom in its accustomed place behind the door. Then with emotions in my heart which I could not now pen and which I then strove with success to conceal, I gently closed the door and faced an unknown future, faced a new life, a greater destiny as I well knew, but I faced it with faith in God and with no less assurance of the ultimate establishment of the Gospel in the West and of its true, enduring principles, than I had felt in those trying scenes in Missouri."[53]

It was a miserable day, February 4, 1846, when Charles Shumway led the first group of refugees with their sagging wagon loads down to the Mississippi River. Soon, in a miracle the Saints would always remember and recount, the river would freeze to let a wave of refugees across, but most, like Charles, would stand at the river and watch dangerous ice floes drift by, waiting for that moment when they would clump together and leave a momentary opening so the immigrants could get to the other side. Between February 8 and February 16, nearly five hundred families would leave, their rickety wagons waiting in line down Parley Street for their turn at the ferry. Among these was eight-year-old John Young, a nephew of Brigham Young. When his father's wagon stood before the door of the home and his father was packing their household goods into the wagon, he looked up to see the ashen face of his mother. "Mother," he asked, "what is the matter?" "We are going to leave our home," she answered, "and we will never see it again."[54]

It was a cold, wet, muscle-straining job to load the Saints' reduced possessions onto flatboats to make the treacherous crossing. Ferrymen worked tirelessly, night and day, to transport the refugees, halting only for weather. As the wagons crossed the river one by one, wind buffeted them, frightened oxen lurched, and unexpected

Morning light touches the last 300 yards of Parley Street leading to the launching point on the Mississippi River where the wagons lined up for the exodus west. This street would come to be known as the "Trail of Tears" for the Saints. The photograph was taken the first week of February to depict how it was when the Saints departed Nauvoo.

ice chunks threatened to cut through the frail boats.
More than one boat and its cargo swamped and sank to
the bottom. Brigham Young noted, "A filthy wicked man
squirted some tobacco juice into the eyes of one of the
startled oxen attached to Thomas Grover's wagon,"[55] and
the oxen kicked a hole in the boat, which sank as it
neared the Iowa side. The people were rescued; the oxen
and all their possessions sank to the bottom of the river.

Because members of the Twelve were endangered by the
law, they were among the first to leave, and once they had
gone, the people followed quickly, sometimes abandoning
their thorough preparations. Still, it would become the
most remarkable exodus of an entire people in American
history. They were the camp of Israel, the Lord's people
making a wilderness trek, led by their own Moses and
watched over by God, whose miracles would carry them.

They were resolute and hopeful but only partly suc-
cessful in hiding their sadness. Parley's Street, where
the wagons lined up that February waiting for their turn
to cross the river, became known as the Trail of Tears.
The pangs continued on the western shore where, at the
last prominence where Nauvoo could still be seen, the
Saints turned for a wistful, parting glance. "The top of
this hill, I was aware," wrote Priddy Meeks, "was the last
point from which I could see the Nauvoo temple. I have
no words with which to convey a proper conception of
my feelings when taking a last look at this sacred monument. . . . After the lapse of thirty-six years, I can
scarcely restrain my feelings when I write of it."[56] After
their final departure, most of them, including Brigham
Young, who lived thirty-one more years, would never see
Nauvoo again. "By the rivers of Babylon, there we sat
down, yea, we wept, when we remembered Zion."[57]

Three

URING FEBRUARY OF 1846, THREE THOUSAND WEARY Saints crossed the Mississippi River and plodded the seven miles to Sugar Creek. They thought they were on their way to a permanent home that year, but permanence would elude them. The main Camp of Israel would take 131 days to wade through the three hundred miles of Iowa in the worst spring weather the residents could ever recall. By contrast, the next year the 1,050 miles from Winter Quarters to the Great Salt Lake Valley would take only 111

days. Most of the refugees would come to regard that first trek to Winter Quarters as the worst trial of their lives, harder even than abandoning their homes in Nauvoo.

In those first days of February, the weather was spring-like, but then the temperature at Sugar Creek plunged to a flesh-numbing twelve degrees below zero, and the snow raged. Gilbert Belnap described the scene at Sugar Creek: "Some had covers drawn over their wagons while others had only a sheet drawn over a few poles to make a tent. Sometimes these rude tents were the only covering for the invalid forms of the unfortunate. Many was the time, while keeping the watchman post in the darkness of the night . . . I wept over the distressed condition of the Saints. Toward the dim light of many a flickering lamp have my eyes been directed because of the crying of children, the restless movements of the aged, infirm and mournful groan of many suffering from fever. These have made an impression on my mind which can never be forgotten."[1]

Patty Sessions, a midwife, was one of those not entirely prepared for the journey. "The wind blows," she wrote on February 14. "We can hardly get to the fire for smoke, and we have no tent but our wagon."[2]

Shivering, the sisters visited each other and nursed the sick; some gave birth.

Large, dry burs like these at the camp of Sugar Creek, Iowa, would be a prickly irritation for man and animal alike.

PAGES 68–69
First instant of light is captured as it begins to warm twisted trees and icy grasses on a bitterly cold February morning at Winter Quarters, Nebraska.

RIGHT Steep, soft banks and deep, uneven channels made Sugar Creek and other creeks in Iowa difficult to cross. Sometimes it took a large portion of the day to dig down the banks for the wagons to pass through.

Eliza R. Snow, the cultured and dynamic poet of Zion, reported that on the first night at Sugar Creek nine children were born, and she would continue to note that in their journey mothers would deliver children in every variety of circumstance: "I heard of one birth which occurred under the rude shelter of a hut, with a bark roof, the sides of which were formed of blankets fastened to poles, stuck in the ground, through which the rain was dripping. Kind sisters stood holding dishes to catch the water as it fell, thus protecting the new-comer and its mother, from a shower-bath, as the little innocent first entered on the stage of human life."[3]

Eliza R. Snow spent many of her days at Sugar Creek confined by the snow and cold to a buggy: "Saturday, February 14. After breakfast I went into the buggy and did not leave it till the next day. Sister Markham and I did some needle work, though the melting snow dripped in through our cover. . . . Thursday, February 19th.

Snowstorm commenced in the night and continued through the day. It was so disagreeable that I did not leave the buggy. Suffered considerably from a severe cold. Amused myself by writing the following." In her journal she penned the mood of most of the refugees:

"Altho in woods and tents we dwell,
Shout, Shout, O camp of Israel!
No Christian mobs on earth can bind
Our thoughts, or steal our peace of mind.
We better live in tents and smoke
Than wear the cursed Gentile yoke.
Far better from our country fly,
Than by mobocracy to die . . . "[4]

The camp was cheered on February 15 when Brigham Young's party finally arrived. Brother Brigham spent the next day organizing the group into companies "and acting the part of a father to everybody,"[5] a job that would eventually exhaust him. Still, on the morning of the 17th,

Evening glow touches the Des Moines River where
the Saints crossed at Bonaparte Mills,
Iowa, on March 5, 1846. The channel of this river is
slow and deep and difficult to ford. Scouts
would look for rapids and then go to their head to test
for a safe ford. The place of the pioneer
crossing here is evident: where the still waters break.

he stood in a wagon and called, "Attention, the whole Camp of Israel." This was not just a call to come to a meeting but to rally their spirits. The Saints' misery at Sugar Creek had not been from the weather alone; now they were face to face with their own lack of preparation and disorder. In the next hour, the prophet's presence and extraordinary leadership would brace and encourage everyone. He explained they were delayed in the cold to wait for Heber C. Kimball, William Clayton, and Bishop Newell K. Whitney to secure Church property and put things in order for the trustees who would be left behind. He said if he could have, he would have been there sooner, even, as he said, "If I had come without a shirt to my back." Then in his practical, no-nonsense manner

he told the brethren to stop wasting their time and "fix nose baskets for their horses and comfortable places for their wives and children to ride." He ordered that dogs be tied up and that horses with distemper be taken from camp at once. He advised, "Never borrow without asking leave, and be sure to return what was borrowed," and finally he thundered, "We will have no laws we cannot keep, but we will have order in the camp."[6]

Brigham Young stood for order and community. If the Saints were going to survive, it would be by bearing one another's burdens in an inspired, systematic scheme. He told the captains of hundreds to raise money in their respective companies to send for cloth for tents and wagon covers. He told the pioneer company under the direction of Stephen Markham to move ahead and prepare roads, seek out campgrounds, dig wells, and find where hay and corn could be purchased for the camp. He said, "If the brethren [cannot] bring their minds to perfect order, they had better leave the camp and I [will] have no feelings against them." He stressed that God was the source of their strength: "Every man must call upon the Lord night and morning at every tent or wagon, and we shall have no confidence in the man who does not." [7]

As the people stamped through the freezing weather to thaw their feet, Brigham spent the last days at Sugar Creek working on details of route and organization to ready the Saints for departure. He went back to Nauvoo to hurry along the elders doing Church business; he wrote the governor of Iowa, asking if he would shield and protect the Saints as they were passing through; and he shepherded a people not sure what they were going to eat. Even for a prophet of such immense ability, it all was taxing.

Brigham confided to his journal, "Unless the people are more united in spirit and cease to pray against counsel, it will bring me down to my grave. I am reduced in flesh so that my coat that would scarcely meet around me last winter now laps over twelve inches. It is with much ado that I can keep from lying down and sleeping to wait the resurrection." [8]

LITTLE CHILDREN HAD THEIR own set of woes leaving home. One small lad cried night and day; no one could comfort him or determine why he was so forlorn. Finally his father, John Taylor, coaxed from him the reason for his tears. In loading their wagon with only the absolute necessities, the Taylor family had been unable to bring his rocking horse, his prized possession. Though Elder Taylor was a member of the Twelve, pressed with other responsibilites and in some danger if he returned to Nauvoo, he got on his horse, rode back toward Nauvoo, crossed the river, found the rocking horse, and brought it back to his son. Even the anxieties of their situation could not thwart the tenderness of this father's heart toward his child. The rocking horse, tied to the side of the wagon, would make the journey to the Saints' new home.

At last, after nearly a month of camping at Sugar Creek, on March 1 the Camp of Israel was ready to roll forward to an undecided location in the West. The uncertainty of their destination would surely have devastated fainter hearts. Orson Pratt, noting that the Saints sang each evening, wrote, "All were cheerful and happy in the anticipation of finding a resting place from persecution in some of the lonely, solitary valleys of the greater interior Basin of Upper California." [9] Though the Twelve had begun researching possible destinations much earlier, even Brigham was as yet uncertain where they were going, but he firmly believed that "the Lord had in reserve for us a good place in the mountains, and that he would lead us directly to it." [10]

The route they would follow from Sugar Creek took them northwest along the Des Moines River, through the village of Farmington and then across the river at Bonaparte. From there they went essentially west until they dipped south to stop at Locust Creek near the Missouri border. Across sparsely settled Iowa, the only excuse for a trail was an occasional trace of mud and ruts. As the Saints crossed, they would create a permanent road.

Just before they left Sugar Creek, having spent a month just a day's journey from their homes in a cold so severe it froze the Mississippi, Brigham recorded these thoughts: "We could have remained sheltered in our homes, had it not been for the threats and hostile demonstrations of our enemies, who, notwithstanding their solemn agreements, had thrown every obstacle in our way. . . . Our homes, gardens, orchards, farms, streets, bridges, mills, public halls, magnificent Temple and other public improvements, we leave as a monument of our patriotism, industry, economy, uprightness of purpose and integrity of heart; and as a living testimony of the falsehood and the wickedness of those who charge us with disloyalty to the Constitution of our country, idleness, and dishonesty." [11]

On the morning of March 1, they took down their tents from the frozen ground, rolled up bedding, and placed camp utensils in their wagons. Then they started a routine they would continue to follow in the weeks to come. They moved out at the blare of a trumpet, were led by the gonging of the temple bell in one of the lead wagons—a symbol that they would build a temple

Small wooden rocking horse that belonged
to the young son of Elder John
Taylor, now on display in the Taylors' home
in Nauvoo. This extravagant possession was strapped onto the side of the wagon
and made the nearly 1,400-mile journey to the Great Salt Lake Valley in the West.

again—and stopped early enough to make dinner and eat. That first day they lumbered only a few miles before making camp, and that night Orson Pratt took a sighting on Polaris, the North Star, to determine the latitude of the camp for future pioneers. He wrote, "After scraping away the snow, we pitched our tents upon the hard, frozen ground and after building up large fires in front, we found ourselves as comfortable as circumstances would permit. Our beds were placed upon the frozen earth, and after bowing before our great Creator, and offering up praise and thanksgiving to him, and imploring his protection, we resigned ourselves to the slumbers of the night."[12]

As the pioneers made their way along eastern Iowa, the men helped replenish dwindling supplies by hiring out to split rails, shuck corn, or clear land, taking their pay in corn or fodder. William Pitt's Brass Band, one of the Saint's best assets for propping sagging spirits, hired out to do concerts for the settlers, whose ears were aching

for music. On March 4 Pitt accepted an invitation for his band to play in Farmington. They started at the main hotel, moved on to a school, and continued until darkness, when they accepted an invitation to dinner. William Clayton said the Farmington folks gave the band three cheers as they left, but as the band neared camp they were met by a guard of thirty Mormons who had started for Farmington to see if the band members were safe. From years of persecution, Brigham Young had learned

caution and was taking no chances.

For Eliza R. Snow, the first few days of travel were a marvel of community spirit. She recorded in her journal, "Tuesday, March 3. Our encampment this night may truly be recorded by this generation as a miracle. A city reared in a few hours and everything in operation that living required and many additional things which, if not extravagancies, were in fact conveniences. Wednesday, March 4. This morning was ushered in with the music of the band which was delightfully sublime. Thursday, March 5. Sister Miller and I are nicely seated in an ox-wagon, on a chest with a brass kettle and the soap box for our foot stools, thankful that we are so well off. The day was fine."

After one week of travel, the group arrived at Richardson's Point, fifty-six miles from Nauvoo, a place they would stay until March 19 waiting for drier, more moderate weather. Eliza wrote, "Monday, March 9. Our town of yesterday morning has grown to a city, laid out in the form of a half hollow square, fronting east and south on a beautiful level, with an almost perpendicular hill on one side, and on the other side a gradual descent to a deep ravine. On the west and north at nine this morning I noticed, but a few rods from our tent, a blacksmith's shop in operation and everything indicated real life. Not a cooking utensil was idle. Sister M. baked a batch of 11 loaves, but the washing business was necessarily omitted for the want of water an inconvenience which the present location suffers more from than any previous one."[13]

While they tarried at Richardson's Point, Brigham wrote his brother Joseph, who had been left to preside in Nauvoo and urge on the emigration. The letter shows how seriously Brigham had taken the covenant the Saints

Last light paints an orange tint on overhanging limbs of a tree along the banks of the Des Moines River. Iowa rains caused small creeks and streams to swell from a shallow 6 inches to a raging 16 or 20 feet in a matter of hours. The Saints sometimes waited for days to cross once-small creeks.

had made at the October 1845 conference to bring out the poor. He said, "I shall write to Brother Babbitt to sell my house and the two lots there by yours. They will bring enough to bring all my friends. If you sell your house and lot you will be able to help brother John and others that we want to help."[14]

While the Saints camped at Richardson's Point and then slogged on through eastern Iowa, it rained, poured relentlessly more than half the days in March, turning the ground into a sticky gumbo that stuck to their feet

in heavy clumps and gummed up the wheels of their wagons. At night in the gusts of wind, their tents blew down, the rain pounding them and soaking their bedding. In the morning they slipped their chilled and aching feet into soggy shoes and began tramping again. Brigham's brother Lorenzo, chronically ill, noted in his March 23 journal entry, "We camped on the hill. It began to rain about noon, and rained the rest of the day. About nine o'clock P.M. it began to blow. I stepped to the door of my tent and took hold to hold it, but in a moment there came a gust of wind and blew the tent flat to the ground. My next care was to hold my carriage, which was

under the tent, from blowing away. The rain came down in torrents so fast that it put out the fire. In a few minutes, it was all darkness, and it was so cold that it seemed as though I must perish. I stood and held the . . . end of the carriage about one hour. The rain wet me through and through, and I never felt in my life as though I must perish with the cold more than I did then."[15]

Wet clothing, sodden shoes, March rain that chilled them to the sinews, bedding that was spread out each evening still soaked from the day before—all these took their toll on the health of the Saints. They sickened with colds, flu, and pneumonia; their joints ached; they had toothaches and migraines, croup and dysentery. They suffered from the plagues of the day, diptheria and typhoid. All this was not only miserable physically, but it also plagued the hearts of parents whose children shivered, then sniffled, weakened, and died. Eliza, who rode through the mud, noticed her friends who were less fortunate. "Many of our sisters walked all day, rain or shine," she wrote, "and at night prepared suppers for their families with no sheltering tents; and then made their beds in and under wagons that contained their earthly all. . . . How frequently, with intense sympathy and admiration, I watched the mother, when forgetful of her own fatigue and destitution, she took unwearied pains to fix up, in the most palatable form, the allotted portion of food, and as she dealt it out, was cheering the hearts of her homeless children, while, as I truly believed, her own was lifted to God in fervent prayer, that their lives might be preserved and, above all, that they might honor him, in the religion in which she was an exile."[16]

The rain made traveling laborious, sometimes impossible, as the teams slithered down embankments and slipped in boggy stream bottoms, heaving the wagons up the endless rolling hills of Iowa, double-teaming when

Music played a critical role in rallying
the Saints as they crossed the plains and
mountains. A few of the towns along the
trail across Iowa invited William Pitt's
band to play concerts for some remuneration.

LEFT *Close-up of English brother William
Clayton's fife and drum set now located
in the Heber C. Kimball home in Nauvoo.*

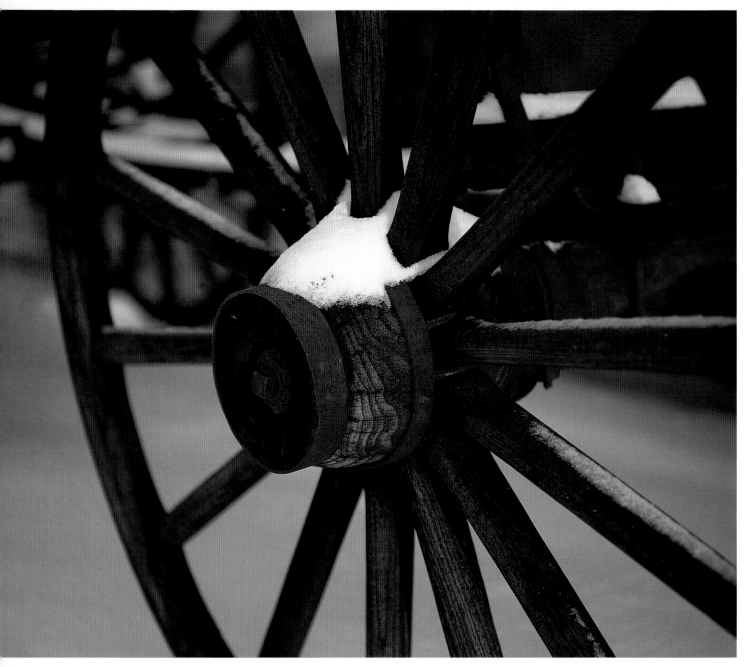

the pull became too hard. Brigham commented one day in late March that they had passed through one mud hole that day "which was about six miles in length."[17] Broken axles, broken wagon wheels, wallowing in mud, and finally camping out only four miles from where they had started that day, horses sinking up to their bellies in goo—this was the Iowa crossing that spring. It was as much as flesh could endure.

They were traveling in the season "between hay and grass," and the teams that were called upon to do so much were wasted in flesh, weakened by hunger as they fed on browse or the twigs and bark of felled trees. Eliza wrote, "It was painful at times, to see the poor creatures straining every joint and ligament, doing their utmost, and looking the very picture of discouragement. . . . From the effect of chills and fever, I had not strength to walk much or I should not have been guilty of riding after those half famished animals."[18]

Progress was slow as the Saints waded through the mud and the wagons became spread out one from another. One broke down, another held sickness, a third was stopped to bury a child. Already Brigham could see that the Saints would have difficulty making the journey all the way to the West that year. Not only the animals were hungry in those dark days. The fathers and mothers, who often had to look through a sheet of rain to see the wagon ahead, wondered what they would feed their children at night. George Q. Cannon wrote that even at Sugar Creek, "eight hundred men reported themselves in camp without a fortnight's provisions."[19] By March 24, even Brigham Young, who had shared with everyone, found his supplies gone.

As the Saints traveled westward across Iowa into a country less and less populated, opportunities for work dried up even as food supplies dwindled. They hunted for deer, turkey, duck, and elk. They sipped gruel, chewed parched corn, and traded off their most precious keepsakes, even venturing down into border towns in Missouri, where they feared for their lives. "They not only sold their feather beds, but they sold their crockery, cooking utensils and such things as they could possibly spare. They thought they were destitute enough when they started from Nauvoo, but they were becoming accustomed to hardships and they were willing to deprive themselves of articles which, under other circumstances, they would have thought they could not have lived without."[20]

The naturally robust had the advantage. On a cold, blustery March day on the banks of the Chariton River, Zina Huntington

(Young) called out for her group to stop their march. She was in labor, and the incessant pains told her she was ready to deliver immediately.

There on the banks of the river she had a fine son, whom she named Chariton, and her health she attributed to a heavenly promise. She said, "I had been told in the Temple that I should acknowledge God, even in a miracle in my deliverance in woman's hour of trouble, which hour had now come. . . . I did not mind the hardship, or my situation, for my life had been preserved and my babe seemed so beautiful."[21]

For the frail, the conditions seemed impossible. Orson Spencer had studied for the ministry in an eastern college and become a popular Baptist preacher, a career that had suited him well enough until he and his cultured wife, Catherine, had met the missionaries. Despite the stern disapproval of their families, and after giving up their livelihood, they had come to Nauvoo. After their winter departure from the city, delicate Catherine began to sink under the mounting hardships until her husband wrote her parents, imploring them to receive her until the Saints should find their home. They answered, "Let her renounce her degrading faith and she can come back, but never until she does."[22] When her husband read this letter

Icy-gray winter waters of the Des Moines River. With each river ferried, each wide prairie and forest crossed, the Saints were putting distance between themselves and their persecutors.

LEFT *Typical early morning view during the early days of Iowa. Keeping wagon wheels true, servicing the wagon, and working with draft animals were some of the journey's challenges.*

M*orning sun bursts through thick forest at the*
Chariton River Crossing in Iowa. The main
body of the Saints arrived here on March 22, 1846,
marking 100 miles from Nauvoo. They were de-
tained here for 10 days because of the inclement weather.

to her, she called for the Bible, turned to the story of Ruth, and read, "Entreat me not to leave thee or to return from following after thee; for whither thou goest I will go, and where thou lodgest I will lodge. Thy people shall be my people and thy God my God."[23]

In the severe cold, she continued to waste away, still singing the songs of Zion to her six children, all under the age of thirteen. From time to time she would call them to the wagon box and say, "I think you will have to give me up and let me go." Then one night she told her husband, "A heavenly messenger has appeared to me tonight and told me that I had done and suffered enough, and that he had now come to convey me to a mansion of gold." Finally, unable to get comfortable in her rain-soaked bedding, she made a request to be in a house. A man named Barnes, living not far from the camp, let her come to his home, where she quietly passed away.

Rain came almost continually between mid-March and mid-April. One journalist said, "We were strung along clear across Iowa and such roads, from one rod to a mile in width on those bottomless prairies. When the turf would hold the wagons up, it was ok, but there might be a dozen or more all sunk in the mud at once, a short distance apart."[24] Benjamin Johnson said, "Our mules feet like pegs, could find no bottom, and could go no further. So in the open treeless prairies we were compelled to stay."[25]

Maintaining the organization of so many people under such trying circumstances was frustrating for Brigham Young. Instead of rolling out in single file, the wagons were scattered, fan-like, for miles across the Iowa prairie. Wagons were spread so far afield that they did not reassemble for Sunday worship for eight weeks. The disastrous weather slowed the coming of grass just as the cost of provisions skyrocketed. Corn that had sold for twelve to fifteen cents a bushel doubled in cost beyond the Chariton. Instead of driving their wagons, moving their families along, men were off desperately trying to find work. Consequently, on March 27, on the banks of the swollen Locust Creek, Brigham called a meeting to thoroughly reorganize the camp, with new captains and leaders chosen where necessary and much stricter laws adopted requiring the companies to stay together.

Brigham had been agonized by the delays, worried

Morning light paints across the deep greens of Iowa at the beautiful Locust Creek Camp of the Saints in Iowa. Hundreds gathered here in April 1846 and reorganized the Camp of Israel.

RIGHT *Ancient oak tree at the Saints' camp by Locust Creek. It was near this spot that William Clayton would pen what would become the most sung of all pioneer hymns: "Come, Come, Ye Saints!"*

over the decaying condition of the hungry draft animals, and exasperated by wagons in constant need of repair. He knew how depleted their food supplies were, how much the people suffered, and the dream of reaching the Rockies that year was fading yet further away. Thus, he prayerfully devised a new plan that would meet several needs. The people and animals needed rest. Since food had become so expensive, crops must be planted and money raised to continue the journey. An express company must be sent ahead across the mountains to plant crops, and others should go back to bring the rear companies along a better, more direct route that avoided the creeks.

Though Brigham had originally planned to build villages that would be relief stations through the Nebraska Territory, the plan was revised because help was needed now for the pioneers strung out in the mud across Iowa. The first station with its growing crops to feed the the hungry refugees would be located somewhere on the Grand River, not far from where they were.

Meanwhile, on April 15 at Locust Creek, British convert and secretary to the Twelve William Clayton suffered

from rheumatism that was exacerbated by the wet and cold. Still, when he received word that his plural wife, Diantha, who had remained in Nauvoo, had given birth to a fine son, he rejoiced and gave a party that night in his tent to celebrate. William Adriel Benoni Clayton had been born! The times were not auspicious for a little Mormon to come howling into the world, but the pleasure at his entry was real.

That night Clayton wrote a song there in the mud, a song that would have as great an impact on the Saints as Brigham Young's decision to build a way station. Despite his aches and his worries about Diantha (who was suffering from the ague and the mumps), despite the problems that plagued the Saints on every side, he wrote with a spirit that would animate every pioneer to follow a hymn called "All Is Well."

> Come, come, ye Saints, no toil nor labor fear,
> But with joy wend your way:
> Tho' hard to you this journey may appear,
> Grace shall be as your day.
> Tis better far for us to strive
> Our useless cares from us to drive;
> Do this and joy your hearts will swell
> All is well! All is well![26]

The mudholes of Iowa were extremely challenging. Often the rain would come down so hard that the wagons in front were completely obscured from those trying to follow.

R I G H T *Because the Saints had left Nauvoo earlier than planned, provisions were in short supply. The meals were simple, and hunger was pervasive during those early Iowa days.*

The words, put to a haunting English melody, would be sung around campfires and graves, sometimes with tears streaming down the faces of those whose loss for their faith was great. "And should we die before our journey's through, Happy day! All is well!" Those who sang had a firm belief that God would compensate them for their suffering. In another crossing, a few years beyond that night at Locust Creek, a man came into camp late, delayed by sickness. "Some of us," wrote Oscar Winters "unyoked his oxen and attended to his part of the camp duties. After supper, he sat down before the camp-fire on a large rock and sang in a very faint but plaintive and sweet voice, the hymn, 'Come, Come Ye Saints.' It was a

rule of the camp that whenever any-body started this hymn all in the camp should join, but for some reason this evening nobody joined him. He sang the hymn alone. . . . The next morning we noticed that he was not yoking up his cattle. We went to his wagon and found that he had died during the night. We dug a shallow grave and after we had covered the body with the earth we rolled the large stone to the head of the grave to mark it—the stone on which he had been sitting the night before when he sang."[27]

With their cooperative energy, the Saints could build a settlement nearly overnight, and at Garden Grove, their first way station on the Grand River, they did. A hundred men raised axes against the trees; forty-eight more cut them into logs for cabins; some started making wooden plows; others dug wells.

The wilderness was miraculously transformed under their touch. In three weeks they had built several log cabins, cultivated the fields, and were ready to aid the weary travelers who would follow them. For Helen Mar Whitney, Garden Grove was a much needed respite: "I shall never forget how I feasted at Garden Grove on my mother's first white bread and fresh churned butter. I had been famishing for a fortnight or more for the want of nourishment, or the lack of appetite to eat such as was set before us."[28]

For others, Garden Grove was a grimmer experience, the hunger and exposure having been too much to take. Hosea Stout had been the captain of the Nauvoo police; in travel, policing and guarding the camp was still his responsibility. As the Saints passed through potentially hostile territory, Hosea's job was weighty—watching for dangers from without and shirkers from within. He was to learn firsthand that hunger and illness are no respecter of persons, no matter how great their duty. Early on his

family ran out of food, and his pregnant wife, Louisa, stricken with pleurisy, ached as the wagon lurched over the muddy ground. On April 21, she gave birth to a little namesake, Louisa, but three days later the two older children, William and Hirum, came down with whooping cough. Hungry and hacking with coughs, the fevered children and their parents traveled to Garden Grove. Hosea wrote in his journal on April 28 that he and his family were completely out of provisions, that it had rained without stopping for several days, that he was not well. On May 2 he was hardly able to herd his cattle. "I came in before night almost fainting with a sick headache," he wrote. "I felt that my constitution was giving away." Two days later, Hosea got some flour and meat, but by the next day the family were entirely without provisions again. Finally, on the ninth, heavy with misery, he went to the woods with a friend to talk over his feelings. Then someone came with word that his little son Hirum was dying. "I returned immediately home,"

Thousands of acres were cleared by the Saints here at Mt. Pisgah, Iowa. Cabins were erected, land was cultivated, and a cemetery on the hill would mark the resting place for as many as 800 of the pioneers.

wrote Hosea, "and found the poor little afflicted child in the last agonies of death. He died in my arms about 4 o'clock. . . . I shall not attempt to say anything about my feelings at this time. . . . My wife is yet unable to go about, and little Hosea my only son now is wearing down with the same complaint, and what will be the end thereof? We are truly desolate and afflicted, and entirely destitute of anything even to eat, much less to nourish the sick, and just able to go about myself. Arrangements made

the poor, who were helpless before the unwavering hostilities of their neighbors. He reached into the resources of his spirit to face each day and improvise solutions to the countless problems that presented themselves. One of the most pressing was the need for money to supply an express company to the mountains far ahead of them. But where does one find money in a wilderness? Since the property in Nauvoo was not selling well, it was decided to put the Nauvoo Temple, only recently completed, up for sale for a meager $200,000. As the weeks waned and no sale was forthcoming, even that hope was dashed.

MEANWHILE, GARDEN GROVE had been found too small to accommodate the needs of the oncoming companies, so Parley P. Pratt and a small group were dispatched some miles ahead to find another place for a way station. Parley said, "I steered through the vast and fertile prairies and groves—without a track or anything but a compass to guide me—the country being entirely wild and without inhabitants. . . . We crossed small streams daily, which, on account of deep beds and mirey banks, we had to bridge." Finally, after several days of travel, he "came suddenly to some round or sloping hills, grassy and crowned with beautiful groves of timber [that] . . . seemed blended in all the beauty and harmony of an English park." Parley, who, like his fellow pioneers, had a keen sense of their journey as a type of the children of Israel's, exclaimed, "This is Mount Pisgah."[30] It was a reference to the ancient mountain in Palestine from which Moses viewed the Promised Land.

But even with two villages for way stations, the promised land was still a long way off for the Saints in 1846. As the spring sun dried up the land, the Saints began to pick strawberries by the quart, but the rattlesnakes came out as well, biting and sickening their animals and becoming unwelcome guests in the tents at night.

It is difficult to know how many Saints were strung out across Iowa that May. John Taylor, who had traveled back to Nauvoo on a short business trip, wrote in a letter that he had passed twelve hundred teams. George A. Smith said the original company that left Sugar Creek on

to bury him this evening."[29] Hosea would lose his wife and all his children on this pioneer journey.

It is hard to imagine the emotions of Brigham Young, who bore the responsibility of leading a people across a trackless prairie to an unknown destination as he watched them suffer and starve. Several times in these weeks, he huddled with the leaders to reassess the route they traveled, unknown as it was by any of them. He pondered how to feed the people, how to bring out from Nauvoo

March 1 had numbered "between four and five hundred wagons."[31] Most estimates suggest that by May about five thousand people had left Nauvoo in about two thousand wagons and were journeying west.

One that May who was barely getting started on his journey was Lucius Scovil, who had run one of Nauvoo's bakeries and sent wonderful smells into the neighborhood on winter mornings. He had lost everything when he was driven from Missouri; he arrived in Illinois penniless just in time for his family to be stricken with the bilious fever and malaria and his daughter Sarah to be afflicted with the black canker, which ate a hole through her lip, two teeth, and chin. He had worshiped and suffered with the Saints in Nauvoo, and then, when it was time to go, even as his friends were packing out, his wife had died while giving birth to twins, Mary and Martha. Ten days later, as some of the earliest wagons were making their way down the road to the river, the twins died too.

The grief would delay his trip, but it would take him longer than he might ever have imagined to join the main body of the Saints. By May he was ready to travel, but while making final preparations, on the 6th, he received a mission call to England. It is hard to conceive that in this hour of desperation, with the Church members scattered and homeless, missionaries were still being called, but Lucius was called. He had not gone this far to ignore what the Lord required of him. Thus, he traveled with his remaining family members a few days into the prairie "to get their property regulated." Having made arrangements for someone to care for them, he blessed them.

Tombstone at Pioneer Cemetery, just east of Nauvoo, marking the graves of Lucy Scovil (died January 27,
1846—just eight days before the Saints would begin to leave
Nauvoo) and infant twins Martha and Mary.

LEFT Morning light warms homey Scovil Bakery interior in
Nauvoo, Illinois. Lucius Scovil lost nearly everything,
yet never his testimony of the restored gospel of Jesus Christ.

Then, leaving them collapsed in tears, he turned back east to go on a mission six thousand miles away without purse or scrip. "This seemed like a painful duty for me to perform," said Lucius," to leave my family to go into the wilderness and I to turn and go the other way. It cost all that I had on this earth, . . . [but] I thought it was best to round up my shoulders like a bold soldier of the crop . . . and assist in rolling forth the Kingdom of God."[32]

Lucius was not the only missionary called that spring. In the four years that Franklin D. and Jane Richards had been married, they had already been separated several times while Franklin had served on missions. Sacrifice for their faith was nothing new to them. Jane had been baptized in midwinter through a foot of ice, and Franklin's brother had been shot to death at Haun's Mill. By denying themselves in every way, they had economized to build a house in Nauvoo, which they had lived in only two months before they were driven from it. Jane and her daughter, Wealthly Lovisa, lived downstairs; Elizabeth McFate, Franklin's new, plural wife, moved in upstairs. Polygamy seemed strange to Jane, but since she was satisfied that the doctrine had come as revelation, she opened her arms and home to Elizabeth. "Never in our association together was there an unkind word between us," Jane wrote, a comment that became all the more remarkable in light of what they would face together.

IN MAY 1846, SO THREATENED BY the mob that they dared not stay longer, Franklin and his family sold their house and everything in it for two yoke of half-broken cattle and an old wagon. They would head west without the means to travel, taking only one trunk of clothing and a few provisions, mostly breadstuffs and no sugar or luxuries of any kind. As they left, a neighbor gave them a pound of tea, a gift that would see Jane through the suffering that lay ahead.

They got as far as Sugar Creek and stayed there six weeks trying to break their cattle and prepare for the trip ahead. Then Brigham Young sent word to Franklin that he had been called on a mission to England. Ever devoted, Franklin blessed his family and went, leaving Jane eight months pregnant, Elizabeth tubercular and

pregnant, and fewer provisions than when they had first crossed the Mississippi. "I felt as though it was doubtful if I was living on his return," Jane said. So now, with the woman with whom she had to share her husband and Philo Farnsworth to drive her teams, Jane started out.

Spring had turned to the muggy, insufferable heat of summer with the innumerable sicknesses of the season. Little Wealthy Lovisa became dangerously ill the day after her father left, and exposure and anxiety brought on early labor for Jane.

In a ceaseless rain that seeped into the wagon and onto her bedding, Jane gave birth, just three weeks after Franklin had left, to a son he would never see. Isaac Phineas died just an hour after his birth, and not only did Jane not have the comfort of her husband in this wet hour but the fuel was too damp for cooking. They had not eaten much anyway on this journey, and Jane's little girl hung on, feverish and miserable on the brink of death.

For three weeks, Jane kept tiny Isaac's corpse with her, waiting to arrive at Mt. Pisgah for a proper burial. By the time she reached Mt. Pisgah, Jane and Wealthy were so pale and sick that the elders gathered around the wagon, rolled back the curtains, and administered to the sick family. They "anointed Wealthly and myself and prayed earnestly for us," Jane wrote. "Everything was done for us that kindness could suggest." Then, because she had no alternative, Jane traveled on.

By this time, the Camp of Israel had arrived on the eastern shore of the Missouri River and had begun building another settlement—Council Bluffs. Along the way, hearing of Jane's wretched condition, Brother Brigham came back to find her. Seeing her misery, he told her that if anyone had passed through tribulation she had, and if he had known of her circumstances, he would have never sent Franklin on a mission. He also promised that her team would not have to wait in line with the other wagons to cross the ferry at the Missouri River but move to the front of the line.

Somewhere on her way to Cutler Park, not far from Council Bluffs, Jane passed the last remnant of civilized life, a house with a small farm. Her little girl, gaunt and weak and having eaten little since Franklin had left eight to ten weeks earlier, asked for some potato soup. It was

Open ground near Richardson's Point, Iowa. In the
midst of incessant rain, sleet, and hunger,
Patty Sessions noticed the prophet coming with his team
in mud up to his knees and exclaimed,
"Here comes Brother Brigham as happy as a king."[1]

her dying request. Jane's mother, having joined the group, went to the house, stated the circumstances, and asked for some potatoes. The farmer's wife listened impatiently, then put her arms on this grandmother's shoulders and marched her out of the house, saying, "I won't give or sell a thing to one of you damned Mormons." Jane, still sick, said, "I turned on my bed and wept as I heard the Grandmother trying to comfort my little one in her disappointment."

This was not the end of her tears. Sickness was rampant at Cutler Park. One night while Jane lay in the wagon too sick to move, her child beside her let go of her feeble hold on life. Jane called it her "crowning affliction." But grief and anxiety are not polite. They give no recovery time between disasters, as Jane had come to know. Outside in the tent, she could hear Elizabeth, who was steadily wasting away with tuberculosis, screaming in delirium that she wanted Jane. A few hours after Wealthy's death, some friends carried Jane to see Elizabeth, whom she had come to love. Elizabeth, her friend with whom she had shared so much, would last only until that next March. In the irregular mail between Jane and Franklin, he would learn of the birth and death of his son, the death of his daughter, the death of Elizabeth. Jane would not hear from him until April 1847, and then only to hear that he was taking care of his brother who had smallpox. "What could I expect but to hear next that he himself was dead from that disease?" This fear would stalk the halls of her mind along with hunger and loss. Speaking of that period, she said, "I only lived because I could not die."[33]

The June that found Lucius Scovil's and Jane Richard's family just starting across Iowa found Brigham Young

camping at Council Bluffs on the Missouri River, en-
tangled in problems. Iowa had spent the people and
supplies beyond all expectation.

Malnutrition and sickness were rampant in the camps.
Moreover, the Saints had reached the Missouri too late to
plan on taking the Camp of Israel over the mountains
that season. Brigham reiterated his plan to send a pioneer
company of the ablest and strongest, unhindered by families, to locate a place, but even getting them to the
mountains in time to plant crops and prepare shelter
seemed difficult. Yet staying brought its own set of challenges as the Saints were on Pottawattami Indian land,
and they had no permission from the government to stay.

In their camps on the bluffs that sprawled over the
Indian villages below, Brigham adopted a policy of good
relations with the Indians and the Indian agents, a policy
that served the Mormons well. The Pottawattami had
sympathy for the Mormons, seeing them as fellow victims
who had also been treated badly by the government.
However, in that time of rumors on the wind, the Indian
agents were watching anxiously to make sure the
Mormons weren't allying with the Indians in a conspir-
acy against the government. Some believed they were
having powwows with the Indians to incite a holy war.
The agents were friendly but wary about letting the
Mormons stay and build winter camps. Brigham found

his people on the eastern shores of
the Missouri without permission to
stay or time or money to move ahead.

But the dilemmas were about to
be solved. Earlier, Brigham had sent Jesse Little back to
Washington to see what help the government could give
in moving the Mormons west. Brigham had volunteered
them to build roads or bridges, establish ferries, con-
struct way stations, transport troops—anything that
would infuse some capital into their journey and give
them official sanction to cross the plains. On his way to
Washington, Little had preached at a Church conference
in Philadelphia. In the audience was twenty-four-year-old
Thomas L. Kane, an attorney from a prominent family who had been following the news reports of the
Mormons with genuine sympathy and would write
eloquently of their plight to a public that had heard
mostly negative rumors. Kane gave Little some letters of
introduction to highly placed government officials,
including the vice-president. Little's May arrival in
Washington couldn't have been better timed. The United
States had just declared war on Mexico and needed western detachments. President James K. Polk decided to
enlist the Mormons to help.

When Captain James Allen arrived in Mt. Pisgah on
June 26, the people were immediately alarmed at the
sight of uniforms. Mothers hid their children, and the
men walked warily out to greet him. When they were
told why he had come—to enlist 500 of them to become
a battalion of the United States army—anxiety was

On July 1, when Captain Allen arrived at Council Bluffs with the government's request, Brigham saw it as a godsend. If the enlistees would forego uniforms and turn the $42 clothing allowance into camp to be used for the needs of all, it would be $21,000 of badly needed money for food and supplies. Beyond that, wages would be paid throughout the year. Brigham saw too that the government's need for a battalion from the Mormons gave him just the bargaining chip he needed. With the men gone, the Saints could not move on that season. Would the government give them permission to stay on the Indian lands on both sides of the Missouri River? Captain Allen agreed, and with that agreement came Brigham's final decision to stay put until the next spring.

Recruiting for the battalion was not easy. With the feelings many of the Saints had toward the government and the desperation of their circumstances, men did not want to volunteer. It was not easy to leave a sick wife or a family with only a tent for shelter. Brigham told the people at Council Bluffs, "I am as well acquainted with the situation of every man in the Camp as they are themselves. At this time, surrounding circumstances must recede from our minds; let them go. . . . If we want the privilege of going where we can worship God according to the dictates of our conscience, we must raise the Battalion. I say it is right and who cares for sacrificing our comfort for a few years? . . . After we get through talking we will call out the companies, and if there are not young men enough, we will take the old men, and if there are not enough we will take the women."[36] It took three weeks of such hard recruiting at the camps across western Iowa to gather the 500.

The Saints hid their tears and bid the battalion farewell by holding a ball at Council Bluffs. Thomas Kane, who with Little had come to be with these people he liked, noted that the folks who danced in the primitive

transformed to indignation. The Saints remembered only too well an official extermination order against them in Missouri, President Martin Van Buren's remark that their cause was just but he could do nothing for them, the murder of their prophet by men who were quickly acquitted in unjust courts, and the mobs who had driven them from their homes under the indifference of the Illinois governor. Now, driven and sick, they were supposed to give up 500 of their strongest men to help the government?

Not surprisingly, though they revered the Constitution, some of the Saints had hard feelings against the government. Lucius Scovil, for instance, said he longed to get his family "out of this boasted Republic, where they will suffer men to be butchered in cold blood and the guilty go unpunished."[34] Hosea Stout was downright suspicious. "In the event that we did not comply with the requisition," he wrote, "we supposed they would now make a protest to denounce us as enemies to our country and if we did comply that they would then have 500 of our men in their power to be destroyed as they had done our leaders at Carthage. I confess that my feeling was uncommonly wrought up against them."[35]

*Council Bluffs, Iowa (also
called Kanesville), on the eastern shore of the
Missouri River, was named for
the sharp rise of hills seen here in the background.*

L E F T *Saw leaning against a wall in Nauvoo. The 500 men and 80
women and children of the Mormon Battalion
marched more than 2,000 miles
to San Diego, arriving January 30, 1847.*

shelter had been bred to a better life. The women had sold their trinkets and brooches to raise money—their ears were pierced but had no earrings; the men wore vests cut with empty watchpockets. The white stockings were darned, the lawn and gingham gowns faded and patched, but on this night the Saints kicked up their heels with merriment. Kane noted, "With the rest, attended the Elders of the Church within call, including nearly all the chiefs of the High Council, with their wives and children. They, the gravest and most troubleworn, seemed the most anxious of any to be the first to throw off the burden of heavy thoughts. Their leading off the dancing in a great double cotillion was the signal which bade the festivity to commence. . . . They did dance . . . French fours, Copenhagen jigs, Virginia Reels. . . . Light hearts, lithe figures and light feet had it their own way from an early hour till after the sun had hid behind the sharp skyline of the Omaha hills."[37]

THE THOUGHTS OF LEAVING MY family at this critical time are indescribable,"[38] said William Hyde, a sergeant in the expedition. William Draper, who may have watched the battalion until they disappeared beyond the horizon, wrote, "We could look in every direction and see the prairies dotted with wagons and tents and speckled with cattle, whose owners had gone. Now it was that something must be done for the women and children that was left unprovided for and without protection and in an Indian country, so a meeting was immediately called and the country divided up into districts or wards, and bishops appointed and a bishop to each ward. It fell to my lot to be one of them and when I went to look up those that were in my district there was 33 families and each bishop was to take charge and provide for all that was left in the ward that fell to him."[39]

He would have a challenge on his hands immediately, for with the heat of August came malaria. Few escaped it. Unmilked cows bellowed in misery while their owners lay sick in their tents. Few voices joined in the songs at Sunday services. Thomas Kane noted that the burials were so far behind that "you might see women sit in the open tents keeping the flies off their dead children,

some time after decomposition had set in."[40]

Kane, who had come to understand the suffering of the Mormons, even shared it with them as he, too, lay sick with chills and fever. He later wrote of this nightmare of sickness, "I still kept my tent in the camp line, but, for as much as a month, had very small notion of what went on among my neighbors. I recollect overhearing a lamentation over some dear baby, that its mother no doubt thought the destroying angel should have been specially instructed to spare." The howls of another sufferer interfered so much with Kane's fitful slumbers that he wrote, "I was glad when death did relieve him."[41]

While the vulnerable in Council Bluffs writhed in fever, the even more vulnerable were still in Nauvoo. These were the destitute, the sick, those who for many reasons had not been able to gather the resources or the strength to leave their homes. When the gentiles saw that some of these planted crops, their hostility erupted. Thirsting for violence and made bold by having gotten away with it before, a wolfpack of from fifteen hundred to two thousand men descended on Nauvoo in mid-September, armed and ready for war. Though the city still held about a thousand people, only 150 or so were capable of defending themselves by throwing up barricades in the road or creating makeshift land mines. Through the next days, shots rang in the air and cannonballs exploded, while the sickly cowered in their homes. Badly outnumbered, their defenses were hopeless, and by September 17, the last of them had given up, thrown whatever they could into bundles, and been driven across the Mississippi.

In a letter to Franklin Richards, Thomas Bullock described the Nauvoo War:

"Beloved Franklin:

"In the month of August, 1846, I was taken very sick with the ague and fever, and soon after my wife and four little children were taken with the same disease. In this condition we continued until the 16th of September. On that day a friend, George Wardell, packed up my goods on two wagons and removed them to his house to be out of danger from the cannon balls, which were flying about too thick for anyone to feel anyway comfortable. He located us behind his house out of danger. As I did not see this battle, I don't write much about it. But I know for a whole week the roar of cannon and the sharp cracking of rifles kept us in awful suspense and anxiety.

"Our devoted city was defended by about one hundred and fifty poor, sickly, persecuted Saints, while it was cannonaded by from fifteen hundred to two thousand demoniacs in the shape of men, who had sworn to raze our temple to the ground, to burn the city, ravish our wives and daughters and drive the remainder of the people into the river. With what desperation our little band fought against such an overwhelming horde of desperadoes, I leave you to judge. My flesh seems to crawl on my bones at the remembrance of those scenes. On the 17th of September, two thousand men with five hundred wagons marched into the city. Such yelling and hooting I never heard before from civilized men, nor even from the wild savages. . . .

"The next morning at nine o'clock saw me, my wife, my four children, my sister-in-law Fanny, my blind mother-in-law, all shaking with the ague in one house, only George Wardell to do anything for us, when a band of about thirty men, armed with guns, with fixed bayonets, pistols in belt, the captain with sword in his hand, and the stars and stripes flying about, marched opposite my sheltering roof. The captain called and demanded that the owner of the two wagons be brought out. I was raised from my bed, led out of doors, supported by my sister-in-law and the rail fence. I was then asked if those goods were mine. I replied, 'They are.' The captain then stepped out to within four feet of me, pointed his sword at my throat, while four others presented their guns with bayonets within three feet of my body, and said, 'If you are not off from here in twenty minutes my orders are to shoot you.' I replied, 'Shoot away, for you will only send me to heaven a few hours quicker, for you may see I am not for this world many hours longer.' The captain then told me, 'If you will renounce Mormonism you may stay here and we will protect you.' I replied, 'This is not my house; yonder is my house,' pointing to it, which I built and paid for with the gold I earned in England. I never committed the least crime in Illinois, but I am a Mormon, and if I live I shall follow the Twelve.' Then said the captain, 'I am sorry to see you and your sick family, but if you are not gone when I return in half an hour, my orders are to kill you and every Mormon in the place.'

"But, Oh, the awful cursing and swearing these men did pour out! I tremble when I think of it. George and Edwin drove my wagons down to the ferry and were searched five times for firearms. The mob took a pistol, and though they promised to return it when I got across the river, I have not seen it to this day. While on the bank of the river I crawled to the margin to bid a sister who was going down to St. Louis goodbye. While there a mobber shouted out, 'Look! Look! There is a skeleton bidding death goodbye.' So you can imagine the poor, sickly condition of both of us.

"On Wednesday, the 23rd of September, while in my wagon on the slough opposite Nauvoo, a tremendous thunder shower passed over which drenched everything we had; not a dry thread left to us; the bed a pool of water, my wife and sister-in-law lading it out by basins full, and I in a burning fever and insensible, with all my hair shorn off to cure me of my disease. Many had not a wagon or tent to shelter them from the pitiless blast. One case I will mention. A poor woman stood among the bushes wrapping her cloak around her three little orphan children, to shield from the storm as well as she could through the terrible night, during which there was one continued roar of thunder and blaze of lightning while the rain descended in torrents.

"The mob seized every person in Nauvoo they could find, led them to the river and threw them in. I will mention one individual case. They seized Charles Lambert, led him to the river and in the midst of cursing and swearing one man said, 'By the holy saints, I baptize you by the order of the commanders of the temple,' plunged

him in backwards and then said, 'The commandments must be fulfilled, G—d—you, you must have another dip.' They threw him in on his face, then sent him on the flat boat across the river, with the promise that if he returned to Nauvoo they would shoot him."[42]

Six hundred and forty people shoved out of their homes with pitiful possessions camped on the western bank of the Mississippi in the most miserable conditions the Mormons had yet seen. Known as Poor Camp, the people were gaunt, scarecrows, shaking with malarial chills and unsheltered from the elements. Thomas L. Kane, now recovered from his malaria and returning from Council Bluffs, came back and left this lasting description, first of the empty city, then of the homeless at

new dwellings, set in cool green gardens ranging up around a stately dome-shaped hill which was crowned by a noble marble edifice, whose high tapering spire was radiant with white and gold." Everywhere Kane turned, he saw the hallmarks of industry and educated wealth, yet the city "lay as in a dream under some deadening spell," a ghost town. He said, "I went into empty work-shops, ropewalks and smithies. The spinner's wheel was idle, the carpenter had gone from his work-bench and shavings, his unfinished sash and casing. . . . I could have supposed the people hidden in the houses, but the doors were unfastened, and when at last I timidly entered them, I found dead ashes white upon the hearths," unpicked apples on trees heavy with fruit. "On the outskirts of the town was the city grave-yard; but there was no record of plague there." Instead he found freshly sodded mounds and stones newly set at the graves of loved ones that would never be visited.

IN THE STILLNESS OF HIS SOLI-tary walk, Kane finally came to the temple, now surrounded by armed men and their stacks of musketry. Drunken and rowdy, they boasted of their prowess in battle, of the father and his fifteen-year-old son they had murdered. They took him into the temple, which, like ancient pagans, they had diligently defaced, spreading their bottles, bodily filth, and rubbish everywhere, particularly desecrating the baptismal font on its twelve marble oxen because here, they explained, these "deluded persons, most of whom were emigrants from a great distance," believed their Deity countenanced proxy baptisms. They stained it with their vomit and

Poor Camp. As he traveled, he said, "My eye wearied to see everywhere sordid vagabond and idle settlers; and a country marred without being improved by their careless hands. I was descending the last hillside upon my journey when a landscape in delightful contrast broke upon my view. Half encircled by a bend of the river, a beautiful city lay glittering in the fresh morning sun, its bright

urine because it was sacred to the Mormons.

It was after nightfall when Kane left this disgusting scene and arrived across the river to find the homeless and desperate of Poor Camp. Seeing a light, he observed, "I found it came from a tallow candle in a paper funnel shade . . . which . . . shone flickeringly on the emaciated features of a man in the last stages of a bilious remittent fever. They had done their best for him. Over his head was something like a tent, made of a sheet or two, and he rested on a but partially ripped open, old straw mattress, with a hair sofa cushion under his head for a pillow. His gaping jaw and glazing eye told how short a time he would monopolize these luxuries, though a seemingly bewildered and excited person, who might have been his wife, seemed to find hope in occasionally forcing him to swallow awkwardly measured sips of the tepid river water from a burned and battered, bitter smelling tin coffee pot." An apothecary, a man "familiar with death scenes," Kane wrote, "mumbled in his patient's ear a monotonous and melancholy prayer, between the pauses of which I heard the hiccough and sobbing of two little girls who were sitting upon a piece of driftwood outside."

*K*ANE LATER DESCRIBED WHAT he saw as he wandered through the heaps of human misery: "They were there because they had no homes, nor hospital, nor poor house, nor friends to offer them any. They could not satisfy the feeble cravings of their sick, and they had not bread to quiet the fractious hunger cries of their children. Mothers and babes, daughters and grandparents, all of them alike were bivouacked in tatters, wanting even covering to comfort those whom the sick shiver of fever was searching to the marrow."[43]

To this sorry scene Brigham had already sent rescue, the wagons beginning to arrive at Poor Camp in early October. The faithful here would always remember that God sent another kind of rescue, too. On October 9 as the wagons were getting ready to pull out, there came a miracle. Flocks of quail flew into camp. Abundant and tame, they were easy to catch. To the people they meant food and much more—they meant that God remembered

them in their anguish. Thomas Bullock wrote, "But hark! What noise is that? See! The quails descend. They alight close by our little camp of twelve wagons, run past each wagon tongue, when they arise, fly around the camp three times, descend and again run the gauntlet past each wagon. See! The sick knock them down with sticks and the little children catch them alive with their hands! Some are cooked for breakfast.

"While my family were seated on the wagon tongue and ground, having a washtub for a table, behold, they come again! One descends upon our tea-board in the midst of our cups, while we were actually around the table eating our breakfast, which a little boy eight years old catches alive with his hands. They rise again, the flocks increase in number, seldom going seven rods from our camp, continually flying around the camp, sometimes under the wagons, sometimes over, and even into the wagons where the poor, sick Saints are lying in bed; thus having a direct manifestation from the Most High that although we are driven by men He has not forsaken us, but that His eyes are continually over us for good. At noon, having caught alive about fifty and killed abouty fifty more, the captain gave orders not to kill any more, as it was a direct manifestation and visitation from the Lord. In the afternoon hundreds were flying at a time. When our camp started at three P.M. There could not have been less than five hundred, some said there were fifteen hundred, flying around the camp."[44]

Along the Missouri, the leaves died and drifted off the trees in the river bottoms, and the Saints began to hole up for the winter in Council Bluffs on the east side of the river and Winter Quarters on the west. With the cooling weather, the malarial season was past and the starvation season was again upon them. The fortunate threw up their crude cabins made of logs with dirt or sod roofs; others lived in dugouts carved into the hillsides. Their homes, their church, their workshops in this temporary settlement were surrounded by a stockade to protect them from the Omaha Indians.

The winter would be a trying one, yet these Saints were not a jumble of sorry souls, forced to survive by looking out for themselves. They were a community, their settlement divided into forty-one five-acre blocks,

each with twenty lots per block. All houses were to be laid out on the outside of the lot to promote community camaraderie. Blocks were to have five wells, and each outhouse was to be at the back of the dwelling, dug at least eight feet deep. Misery had not made the Saints sloppy.

Eliza R. Snow, who would spend the dark winter huddled in her cabin writing poems of tribute to friends who had died, said, "The log house we moved into was partly

Morning light begins to add warmth to a wagon at Winter Quarters, Nebraska. Just as the rescue wagons were ready to bring the more than 640 Saints from their miserable circumstances in the poor camp, quail came by the hundreds.

B OTH PHOTOGRAPHS
Full-scale reconstruction, with detail, of
cabin at Winter Quarters, Nebraska. Ursulia
Hascall described her cabin here: "We
have a brick chimney and hearth (two thirds of
the people have them made of sod and they
do very well).... The furniture consists of sacks,
barrels, chests, trunks and ... my chest
for a table.... I think we shall get along first rate."[2]

chinked and mudded, leaving large crevices for the wind—then cold and blustering. This hastily erected hut was roofed on one side, with a tent cloth thrown over the other, and withal was minus a chimney. A fire, which was built on one side, filled the house with smoke until it became unendurable. . . . Our cooking done out of doors until after the middle of November, when a chimney was made."[45]

*L*IKE GARDEN GROVE AND MT. Pisgah before it, Winter Quarters was another instant city. Brigham noted with some satisfaction, "I went through the city—where, nine weeks ago there was not a foot path, or a cow track, now may be seen hundreds of houses, and hundreds in different stages of completion—impossible to distinguish the rich from the poor. The streets are wide and regular and every prospect of a large city being raised up here."[46]

With husbands and brothers gone in the battalion or off in Missouri on trading or working trips, there would be a glaring absence. A census taken at the end of 1846 revealed a population of 3,483, only 500 of them men. Many thousands more were spread from Council Bluffs eastward across Iowa. Those men who were left carried a heavy burden to help feed the people. Brigham called to his followers, "Unite with us in the principles of self-preservation,"[47] and the people did, sacrificing personally for the welfare of the community.

Benjamin Brown, called to be a bishop of one of the thirteen wards in Winter Quarters, looked at his new stewardship with some trembling. He wrote, "We could not put in any grain until the next spring. We began, then, more than ever, to feel the destitution of our position, for want of vegetables had brought on the scurvy, the provisions of many become exhausted, and our prospects of a fresh supply seemed rather distant. . . . One of the wards was committed to me, and this, of course, entailed upon me the care of the poor—no trifling matter under such circumstances. It would take no small space to describe all the expedients to which I was driven in fulfillment of this duty, for the little stock I had of my own was soon gone, and still the poor had not done eating. What was to be done? I went to President Young,

and very pathetically told him that all my grain was gone, and I had not the first shilling in my possession with which to get any more grain. All the consolation I got from him was some instruction to feed them well and take care they have enough to eat, and it would not do for a Saint to say he could not. So I had to scheme. I borrowed ten dollars from a sister who possessed a small store. I then crossed the Missouri River, and laid the money out in meal and some meat. But when this was gone I had to borrow of someone else to pay her, and then of someone else to pay him. I borrowed until I made my debt up to fifty dollars, and no more chance of payment appeared than at the first. Who would not have been a bishop then? Fortunately, just at this juncture, the lost cattle of one who had died in my ward came into my hands, and I sold them for fifty dollars. I paid my debt, and I was just right, and ready to commence borrowing again with a clear conscience."[48]

Borrowing, working, trading, or back-breaking industry couldn't stave off the hunger of that season. Once the wild grapes, plums, and berries that the pioneers had feasted on had withered away, the Saints turned to the scant diet of coarse flour and corn meal, a diet which, without vegetables, brought on Winter Quarter's worst disease—what the pioneers called black canker or scurvy. John D. Lee described it as a disease "that falls into the feet and legs and commences on the toes first with a pain, then they die away without feeling and so on continuing until the person expires."[49] The canker swelled

with empty, aching arms for lost children. Best estimates suggest that six hundred died there. Another twelve hundred died at Council Bluffs. One out of every three babies passed away in infancy. So great was the concern for survival in that long, dark season that there was little time for mourning the dead. Archibald Gardner recorded that "when little Janet died [there was] so much sickness that care of living left no time for mourning the dead—the baby [was] laid away hurriedly and unceremoniously."[51]

Skeletally thin, Jane Richards, her own babies dead, spent her winter nursing dying Elizabeth and her child in a twelve-by-fourteen-foot cabin just big enough for two little beds and a fireplace. She had wood for a fire only when she begged for it. Then, when the sister wives ran out of food, she traded her last possession of any worth, Franklin's violin, to Brigham Young's nephew for a gallon of wine. She was grateful to trade it for anything. During the dark winter, by sipping it sparingly, like two stranded birds, the women managed to stay alive. When Jane hurried along the snowy paths to visit her sisters in the sociability that made life bearable, ice clung to her tattered skirts. She wrote, "Often my clothes would be frozen stiff about my ankles remaining so day after day that you could hear them rattle as they struck against anything. What was there to thaw them out?"[52]

Still, in what must have seemed like a living nightmare, they praised God, looked for his grace, and hung on. Lorenzo Snow, living in a fifteen-by-thirty-foot cabin

their gums, turned their flesh black, and ate it. Their heads hurt, their joints ached, their fevers raged. One woman, spent from delivering a stillborn child, said, "The scurvy laid hold of me, commencing at the tips of the fingers of my left hand, with black streaks runnng up the nails with inflammation and the most intense pain, and which increased till it had reached my shoulder." "The flesh would rot and drop off, some to the bones,"[50] another recalled.

The chills and fever, tuberculosis, and exposure all took their toll on the driven people, and the cemetery at the place they came to call "Misery Bottoms" began to fill, leaving families without fathers and mothers, parents

with a dirt floor and turf chimney, even managed to throw a party. He covered the floor with straw, hung the walls with the sheet casings from the long-ago discarded feather beds, and lit the room with tallow dips stuck in hollowed-out turnips. Lacking a band, the guests entertained themselves with songs, riddles, and recitations. Refreshments were a bowl of succotash. It was not much of a party by today's standards, but in that bleak midwinter, it was a moment of warmth the guests would always remember.

That January in a room of Heber C. Kimball's log house, Brigham Young received a revelation that would become section 136 of the Doctrine and Covenants. In that revelation, the Lord gave the pattern for the exodus. The companies were to be organized with captains of hundreds, captains of fifties, and captains of tens. They were to select an advance pioneer company to leave for the West in the spring with teams, seeds, and farming utensils; this company would put in spring crops in their new place of refuge. Each company was to bear in equal proportion, according to the dividend of their property, the poor, the widows, the fatherless, and the families of those who had gone into the army. The Saints were also to prepare houses and fields for those who would be left behind. All these things were to be done with a covenant to walk in all the ordinances of the Lord. The promise for those who would obey was clear: "Go thy way and do as I have told you, and fear not thine enemies; for they shall not have power to stop my work. Zion shall be redeemed in mine own due time."[53] As winter melted into spring, the citizens of Winter Quarters, Council Bluffs, and a string of temporary settlements across Iowa began casting their eyes west toward the setting sun. None of these towns was meant to be a permanent resting place. Brigham Young wanted a mountain range between the Mormons and their old enemies. Those who had endured the winter with their faith intact were as tested and tough as any pioneers who would ever head west. The limits of their faith had been tried and not been found wanting.

At the north end of the pioneer cemetery at Winter Quarters is this sculpture by Avard Fairbanks depicting a father and a mother standing beside the shallow, open grave of their child. Accounts of the deaths at Winter Quarters are humbling and heart-wrenching.

Four

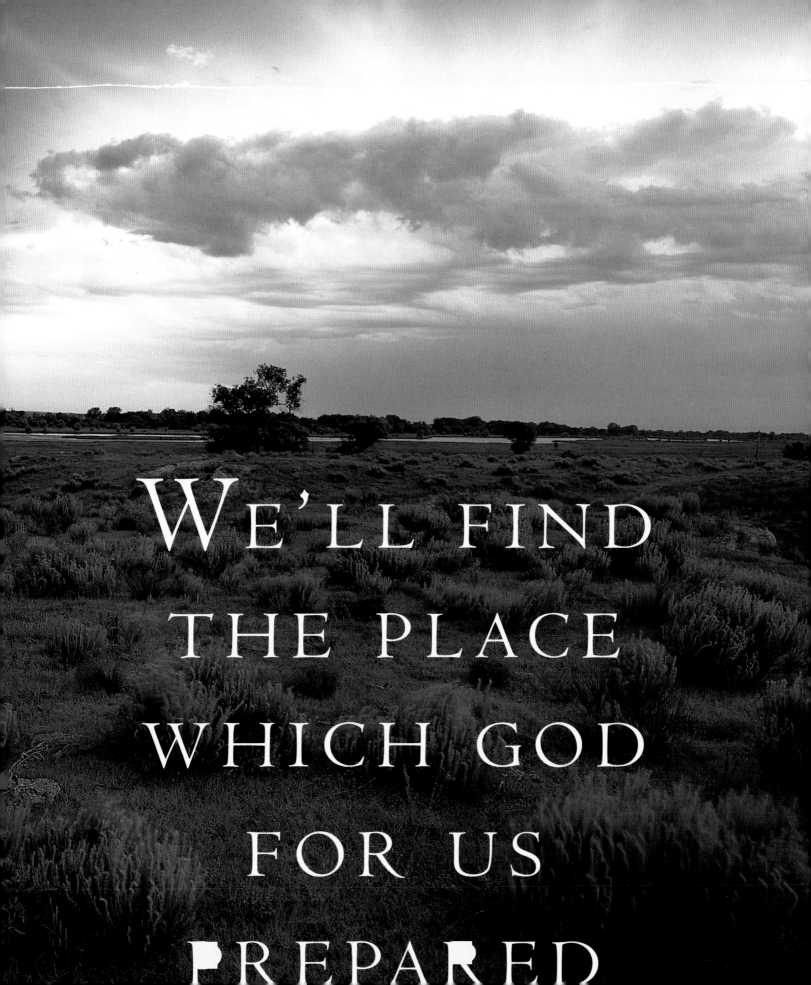

WE'LL FIND
THE PLACE
WHICH GOD
FOR US
PREPARED

WINTER QUARTERS WAS A
TURNING POINT FOR THE
Saints. The winter of misery would
evolve into a spring of hope, and burying the dead would be replaced by patching
wagon covers to prepare to travel to Zion. The
uncertainty of the trek across Iowa with its vague destination and route was replaced by the certitude of revelation, a sure knowledge of where they were going and
how to organize for the trip. Brigham Young assigned
Orson Pratt to hurry back to Mt. Pisgah and Garden
Grove to organize the stragglers into companies according to the new instructions in the January revelation.
From the depleted ranks of the men, 144 were called to
make up the advance pioneer company. They were able-
bodied, well-organized, and highly skilled, 144 men
based on the 12 times 12 spoken of in the book of
Revelation. In contrast to the dreary, hardship-ridden
hike across Iowa, this would be a truly glorious journey,
and in the journals of the fifteen in the company who
kept vivid day-by-day accounts is a sense of awe, the
mouth-gaping excitement of the sightseer thrilled by the
scenery and new experiences.

In the group would be nine of the Twelve apostles and
a variety of others chosen for their varying abilities.
Orson Pratt, the philosopher and scientist, would spend
his journey taking note of barometric readings and lon-
gitudes and latitudes. His journal tells less about people
than it does about fluctuations in temperature. He would
travel "with his eye glued to an artificial horizon and his
wet finger up to test the wind."[1] Wilford Woodruff
would enjoy fly fishing and, true to his remarkable spiritual abilities, see an open vision of the temple that
would be built. William Clayton, who was invited along

at the last minute and had only three hours to throw his
clothes together, would take copious notes and invent an
odometer for measuring mileage. Their impressions were
as different as their personalities, but we are not left to
wonder what happened day by day on the journey.

As it turned out, the number was less and more than
the scriptural 144. One man dropped out, and Lorenzo
Young's wife Harriet, spent by her winter at the "Misery
Bottoms," begged to come along with her two children.
At the last moment Clara Decker Young, Brigham's wife,
and Ellen Sanders Kimball, Heber's wife, came too,
bringing the total to 148, along with seventy-three wagons, ninety-three horses, fifty-two mules, sixty-six oxen,
nineteen cows, seventeen dogs, and a few chickens.

Those left behind would follow the vanguard group
a few weeks later—if they were prepared. Willard
Richards gave a friend this advice on what that would
entail: "A few families may follow us this spring, after
grass starts, such as have teams and provisions plenty to
last them one year and a half, or from 300 to 500 pounds
of bread-stuff per soul; but few can do this, and none
can depend upon the labors of the pioneers. If you can
thus fit yourself, you are at liberty to go on this spring,"
but if not, "I would recommend you to come here as
early as you can and join my sons to plant at least twenty-
five acres of corn, and as many beans, pumpkins,
squashes, onions, cabbages, turnips, parsnips, carrots,
spring rye, wheat, buckwheat, barley, [and] oats."[2]

Those 148, who would be fondly remembered for generations, were probably conscious enough that they were
making history, but they did not leave town in a parade
with cheering crowds. Though they had been watching carefully to take off as soon as the prairie had
dried, when at last the time came, they arrived at their

Foxtails dancing in the winds of the prairies were a com-
mon sight along the Iowa and Nebraska trails.
The vanguard company, under the direction of Brigham
Young, would make the journey from Winter
Quarters, Nebraska, to the Great Salt Lake Valley in 111 days.

PAGES 112–13 Beam of light shoots
from behind the clouds as if marking the trail with hope
for the pioneers here along the Platte River. The
Saints would follow the river's course for more than 600 miles.

rendezvous point at the Elkhorn ten miles from town in a piecemeal fashion and were further held up by a series of last-minute errands. Heber C. Kimball moved six teams out of Winter Quarters on April 5, counted by many historians as the official day the trek began, but the next day was the annual spring conference of the Church, at which the members would covenant to pray continually for the pioneer camp. Even the day after that, April 7, when Brigham left Winter Quarters to join the twenty-five wagons already gathered at the Elkhorn, the journey would not begin, for news came that Parley P. Pratt had arrived from England, and Brigham returned to Winter Quarters to hear a full report on the missionary work there. On April 9, the Twelve started again, only to be delayed by word that John Taylor had returned from England, bringing with him a much-needed $2,000 in gold gathered from the British Saints. He was also bringing scientific instruments that would be precious to Orson Pratt in keeping meticulous records of the trail for those who would follow—two sextants, one circle of reflection, two artificial horizons, two barometers, thermometers, and a telescope.

Despite the delays, on April 16 when the pioneer company finally left the Elkhorn, they knew where they were going. They had a fixed purpose to head to the valley of the Great Salt Lake, and they were certain of their route. Before them lay the endless Platte River Valley, which stretched out as a fifteen-mile-wide highway for hundreds of miles clear to the mountains, presenting none of the problems they had seen when they had lurched through Iowa the year before. No inclines to heave a load up. No steep banks to shimmy a wagon down. Instead, edged by cottonwoods, the Platte was in most places wide and shallow with a soupy bottom, a gray, braided ribbon as far as the men could see. Still, it had its unique dangers.

Wilford Woodruff wrote of it, "It is from three quarters to a mile wide and its shores and bed one body of quicksand. It is a rapid stream, yet in many places a person can wade across. Frequently the whole bed of the river is covered with but a few inches of water and at other places it is deep and rapid. . . . Horses and cattle can walk down to the edge of the river and drink, like

walking on the edge of a smooth sea beach, and sometimes while walking on the apparent hard beach or bed of the river a man or horse will suddenly sink into the quicksand. . . . Many men and horses have been lost in this way on the Platte."[3]

As the company moved into this new world, a land not yet tamed at the very brink of the West, camp order was immediately established. Other wagon trains inspired by gold or the promise of quick wealth might travel this road with rowdiness and brawling, the rough-and-ready lawlessness that came to mark the West. True to form, however, the Saints were a disciplined

community who would ever bear in mind those who would follow, marking and improving the trail as they went. They were a village on the march, transplanting a vision a thousand miles from its beginnings.

The pioneer company had an elaborate and overlapping series of jurisdictions. In addition to their captains, they had a complete military organization to schedule guard duty, and as they traveled, every man was to walk beside his wagon within reach of a loaded gun. Their precautions were born of years of persecution and justifiable fear of the Indians. Wagons were to travel in double file, and no one was to stray more than twenty rods from

One historian recorded about the Platte River, "It furnished fish, turtles, fowl, protection from prairie fire, and, above all, water." A lazy stream "a mile wide, six inches deep, too thick to drink, too thin to plow, and maybe a pretty good river if it hadn't flowed upside down." [1]

camp, rules that would gradually be relaxed on the trail. At five o'clock in the morning, a bugle sounded a signal for every man to arise and see to his prayers. Cooking, eating, and feeding teams occupied them until seven o'clock. As they rolled out, the wagons rotated, so all got a turn to travel without the taste of dust in their mouths. At night, the bugle sounded at 8:30, and after prayers and for Orson Pratt a searching look at the skies through the new telescope, the men were in bed at 9:00 p.m., their wagons pulled into a circle with the stock tied inside for security.

William Clayton started out the trip with a toothache, which plagued him for several days until Luke Johnson, the unofficial dentist of the camp, yanked the tooth out. But the pain didn't squelch his ideas. As an official recorder for the camp, he kept a daily log estimating the distance they had traveled. Yet he was bothered by the discrepancy in the men's estimates of their travel for the day, especially as those who followed would count on the information. Pondering the problem, he had an idea that he shared with Orson Pratt only three days into the trip. Cogs could be rigged to a wagon hub so as to measure distances accurately. As with most groundbreaking ideas, it was a notion he would have to repeatedly champion before it was adopted. In the meantime, he measured the wheel of Heber C. Kimball's wagon and found it to be fourteen feet eight inches in circumference, which, much to his delight, was exactly 360 revolutions to the mile. He tied a red flannel rag to the wheel and then spent his days walking beside it, doggedly counting the revolutions, a dizzying job that did not allow for a moment's distraction.

The first four days of the trip, the pioneers made twenty miles a day, which carried them into the heart of Pawnee country. The Pawnee were considered less dangerous than the Sioux but were noted for petty thievery. Early in the morning, a lone Indian rode out of a clump of trees on the side of the road, and soon six or eight others came running up on foot. The only English they could speak was "How de do?" By that afternoon the pioneers passed a Pawnee village, and the Indians came wading across the river demanding gifts. Brigham gave them powder, lead, salt, and flour, but the chief thought the booty insufficient. He warned them that he did not like them going west through their country as he was afraid they would drive off the buffalo, and he refused to shake hands at their parting. Braced for trouble, that night the camp had a hundred men acting as guards, fifty shivering until midnight in a hard wind and rain and fifty more who planned to stand until morning. At one o'clock, however, no Indians had appeared and the guard was released, after firing off a few warning rounds from the cannon.

The next day the pioneers came upon an abandoned Pawnee mission and, not far away, an equally deserted government station. James Case, a member of the pioneer party, had been dismissed from government service a year earlier when the raiding Sioux had swooped down, burned most of the buildings, and stolen the equipment. What was left were a few wagon boxes, some iron plows, and other odd but useful equipment. Some of the pioneers naturally wanted to take it, but Brigham sized up the circumstance with an eye to the thousands of his people who would follow on that trail, and he forbade that anything be taken away. It would not do to have any embarrassing incidents or participate in anything that could be construed as dishonest. Better to let the iron plows rust into the earth than to unwittingly create trouble. Later, learning that James Case was owed back pay from the

Wagon hubs were generally made of dried lumber so they wouldn't contract, crack, and cease to turn on the axles. Most wagon trains along the trail were hampered by Indians, adverse weather, poison water, and lack of feed, yet this first company would lose more time to Sabbath Day observance than any other challenge.

ABOVE *Spyglass and leather case used daily by Heber C. Kimball on the trail to Zion.*

government, he allowed the animals to eat some of the station's hay, which was deducted from Case's back pay.

To this point the pioneers had been angling northwest along the Loup Fork of the Platte, hunting for a ford or ferry across the swift, sandy river, a diversion that had left them twenty miles north of the main Platte. They had to cross the Loup Fork to get back to the main valley, but this was not easy on the boggy river floor, so thick with quicksand that in some places it would quickly sink both men and horses. They had two channels to cross with a sandbar in the middle, a total of three hundred precarious yards, an untried river with dangerous goo at its base.

But it couldn't be avoided, and Wilford Woodruff had the job of leading the initial ten to try fording the river. Luke Johnson went first with no load and no difficulty, but Orson Pratt had not gotten far across with his load before his horses began to sink in the deceptive quicksand.

A NUMBER OF MEN LEAPED INTO the water, lifted his wheels, and got him to the sandbar in the middle, but meanwhile Wilford was behind him, his cattle hopelessly sinking in the mire. "I jumped out of my carriage into the water up to my waist," he said. "About ten men came to my assistance with a rope and hitched it to the oxen and helped me in getting across the first stream, though with great difficulty. We stopped on a sandbar out in the water, but my horses and wagon began to sink. By treading the ground a little, it would become a perfect quagmire, and though we were sinking in it, the men had to leave the wagon where it was and go to the assistance of Orson Pratt,"[4] who was struggling in the sand in the second half of the river.

The Revenue Cutter, a leather boat that was carried on a wagon bed, rescued the sinking men and their goods, but no one else would cross the river there that day. Orson, Wilford, and their companions would be stuck alone on the Pawnee side of the river through the long night. The rest of the party would find a different crossing point the next day and learn that quicksand became less muddy as wagons crossed over it and packed it down.

The crossing of the Loup Fork at the 98th meridian

brought the pioneers into the West, a reality they sensed immediately. It was a change of climate, of vegetation, of animal life. The grasses became shorter and less verdant. The men's skin, used to higher humidity, became dry and rough; their lips cracked, and their hair became like straw. William Clayton noted, "The wagons and everything else is shrinking up, for the wind is perfectly dry and parching; there is no moisture in it. Even my writing desk is splitting with the drought."[5] It was about this time, too, they had a Sunday service at Brigham Young's wagon where a choir hastily formed from the group sang "This Earth Was Once a Garden Place." Erastus Snow said he had never been happier in his life, and George A. Smith recommended that the brethren be careful not to destroy animal life unnecessarily. At this point, as if on cue, a wolf approached the camp, and all unanimously agreed to let him live and continue their meeting.

The next morning brought more Indian trouble as two crept upon their hands and knees toward camp, apparently to steal horses. They made it to within three yards of the camp guard before they were discovered. Then they rose and ran, amid gunfire, and four more leaped out of the grasses and joined them. That evening, after a day of hunting, the pioneers returned to camp to find that the Indians had finally succeeded in stealing two horses. The next morning four men, including Porter Rockwell, who would become known as an accurate and deadly shot, started back over the trail on horseback in search of the lost animals. They found the trail of the horses and followed it to a clump of willows and trees. Suddenly fifteen Indians sprang out of the grass, armed with bows, arrows, and guns, and came toward the men

The Saints crossed the Loup River at this point just 100 miles from Winter Quarters. On the whole journey to the Great Salt Lake the vanguard company would come upon only three white habitations, one of them abandoned; namely, the Pawnee Mission (evacuated because of Sioux raids the year before), Fort Laramie, and Fort Bridger. They would meet Pawnees, Otoes, Omahas, Sioux, Crows, Shoshones, and finally the Utah Indians.

Hundreds of miles of the trail along the north bank of the Platte
River in Nebraska looked similar to this. Since large cottonwood
trees grew along the fertile banks, firewood in this area was plentiful.

RIGHT *The Saints carried as many of their necessities
as they could on their journey to the West. Scraps of cloth were used
for patching clothing, bedding, wagon covers, and even quilts.*

FAR RIGHT *Small butterfly collects nectar from a thistle
along the Mormon Trail. One time, while leading the camp
in prayer, Heber C. Kimball's hat blew off from a swirling, quick
wind. He refused to interrupt his conversation with the
Lord and ended up chasing his hat nearly three-quarters of a mile.*

on their horses, grabbing at bridles, hoping to steal these horses too. Porter Rockwell was convinced he had found the thieves, but he did not feel like provoking a fight with them. He knew it would lead to bloodshed and endanger the lives of the companies to follow. The Indians kept the horses.

Past the Loup Fork and on into the Platte River Valley, the eyes of the pioneers were trained on the prairie, straining for that first glimpse of buffalo. These shaggy creatures, the sight of which exhilarated the early pioneers, roamed the Platte River grassland in the tens of millions during the nineteenth century. Later travelers would decimate the buffalo with wanton killing, leaving decaying carcasses strewn across the plains, but the Saints were conservationists, true to the message they had shared the Sabbath before. In an era when Mark Twain would set fire to the forests around Lake Tahoe just for the sport of watching them burn, Brigham Young would tolerate no such waste. He told the men that only enough buffalo could be taken to feed the company. The word was:

"If we do slay when we do not need,

we will need when we cannot slay."[6]

This advice would turn out to be easier to say than to follow.

The first day of May was a cold 30 degrees, but a sense of skin-tingling electricity filled the pioneer company as they caught sight of their first buffalo—three of them, quietly grazing on the bluffs off to the right. Four miles farther a large herd was discovered, and through their telescopes William Clayton counted seventy-two and

Orson Pratt seventy-four. Those of the company designated as hunters—eight on horseback and eleven on foot, as well as members of the Twelve—were anxious to go after them. The wagons halted while the hunters began a spirited chase, resulting in the killing of ten buffalo by that afternoon. The meat was distributed equally among the companies, a quarter of a buffalo for each ten people. They feasted that night and spent the next morning cutting their meat into strips and drying it over a fire to preserve it for future use. The hides were cut into strips to be used for ropes and thongs. "The meat is very sweet," wrote William Clayton, "and as tender as veal."[7]

The savory buffalo was probably a welcome treat from the usual pioneer diet—corn-meal mush, white or navy beans, salt-rising bread, and, for the fortunate, a few potatoes or dried apples and peaches—but at first it was a little rich for their systems. George A. Smith wrote, "I ate heartily of buffalo meat, and was routed out very early by its effect."[8]

In the treeless wilderness through which they passed, the pioneer company found another use for buffalo. Just when cold suppers were becoming tedious, they discovered that buffalo dung, which dried quickly and dotted the landscape in great plenty, was an adequate substitute for wood. They learned to scoop out a hole in the ground, fill it with what they called buffalo chips "to save a hard word," and make a fire in the most desolate regions.

In the days that followed, herds of buffalo, hundreds of thousands of them, crowded the trail and cropped the grasses, making it difficult for the pioneers to feed their own cattle. The sight of a country literally black with buffalo as far as the eye could see astonished the men. Wilford Woodruff said, "It looked as though the whole face of the earth was alive and moving like waves of the sea."[9] Heber C. Kimball noted that he had heard many buffalo tales told, but he had never expected "to behold what his eyes now saw."[10]

Herds in such immense numbers posed their own danger to the men. One earlier traveler of the trail said, "We saw them in frightful droves, as far as the eye could reach, appearing at a distance as if the ground itself was moving like the sea. Such large armies of them have no fear of man. They will travel over him and make nothing of him."[11] Brigham Young thought a much greater danger was spiritual—that many of the men continued eager to kill more buffalo for sport after the company's needs were satisfied. He issued an ultimatum that he would remind the men of again and again: "There would be no more game killed until such time as it should be needed, for it was a sin to waste life and flesh."[12]

In his private moments, Brigham wrote a yearning letter home to his wife, Mary Ann. "I want to write a long letter," he said, "but have not time. We are all pretty well at present though my labour has been very hard for me on the journey. I pray for you continually. . . . I am glad you are not going to come on this summer for I want to be with my family when they come this journey."[13]

THE INDIANS CONTINUED TO be an ominous presence, burning the prairies in the Saints' path as far as they could see. Whether this was to drive the buffalo or to destroy the grasses necessary to feed the pioneer's cattle, Brigham did not know, but the air smelled charred. "The wind blew the ashes of the burnt grass in all directions," wrote Thomas Bullock, "which caused us to look like [chimney] sweeps. However by washing, after our halt we were enabled to discern each other again." But the burnt grass and the hungry buffalo made it nearly impossible to feed their own stock. "The feed is so short and teams so weak that we are unable to travel but a short portion of the day,"[14] complained Wilford.

To this point, though the better-traveled Oregon Trail was on the south side of the Platte River, the Saints had been traveling on the north. Now they faced a dilemma. They saw wagons on the opposite of the river heading east, and one of the traders, Charles Beaumont, eager to see a fresh face, forded the river to talk. He advised the Saints to cross the Platte here and take the south side trail, as it was good and hard and the grass had not been burned off by disgruntled Indians. It was tempting. Ahead of them the prairie was burning for miles, and feed for their already hungry animals was bound to be scarce. They voted and determined to continue on the more challenging north side because of their sacred responsibility to forge a trail for thousands of others. Even if they could cross the Platte here, they might be putting at risk future companies whose wagons would be laden with women and children. Besides, they wondered at the wisdom of taking a trail hard-driven by gentiles who might be hostile to them. No, they would stick to the north side.

They didn't get far before second-guessing their decision. The next day a strong south wind fed the fire, and they had traveled only fourteen miles before meeting a wall of fire that stopped them short. Their animals were starving and things looked grim until a rain came that night—blessed, lifesaving rain, a gift from God to douse the prairie flames. The next day, in a hard push, they were able to get beyond the charred stubble into the good grass again.

About this time William Clayton put up the first marker on the Mormon trail, a marker that thousands would see over the years, a kind of encouragement that said others had gone this way, that others knew the hardships and pitfalls. Come along to Zion, it said. This marker, a cedar post written in pencil, said, "From Winter

On the arid land at the western end of
Nebraska, the pioneers saw new vegetation. Robert Sweeten, who came as a six-year-
old, said, "One time... driving two yoke
of oxen... I stepped on a prickly pear, and
being bare-footed the needles ran into
my feet, and mother had to pull them out."[2]

Quarters, two hundred ninety-five miles, May 8, 47. Camp all well. Wm. Clayton." It was a hard-earned calculation, born of Clayton's tenacity in counting the revolutions of the wagon wheel. That day alone he had measured eleven and a quarter miles plus twenty revolutions. The next day when they moved on again to find better grass, even though it was Sunday, a day they usually rested, he put up a second sign: "From Winter Quarters three hundred miles, May 9, 1847, Pioneer Camp All Well." Soon William Clayton would be relieved of the tedium of counting because Brigham had asked Orson Pratt to help create the roadometer Clayton had suggested. Appleton Harmon was set to work whittling the cogs for the wheel. The roadometer was designed as an endless screw; six revolutions of the wheel turned the screw once, which then acted upon a wheel of sixty cogs. One full turn of the wheel equaled a mile. Clayton must have felt great relief when the roadometer was installed and he got to enjoy long scenic views as he walked along.

In addition to these mileage markers, Brigham and other leaders decided to leave periodic messages along the trail—advice and instructions for those who would come later. Thomas Bullock, the camp historian, wrote down a list of the laws that governed the camp. When Brigham saw these he said, "That's scripture," and, adding it to a digest of their journey thus far, he put it in what he called the Platte mailbox atop a twelve-foot

pole. Other letters would be left about every ten miles for the rest of the trek, messages that would restore vitality and urge on the sometimes drooping pioneers who would find them.

As the company continued to push west along the Platte, filling their shoes with sand, the weather was often cloudy and cool. The buffalo began to decrease in numbers, and the landscape became more variegated as the long valley began to pinch down in a broken series of hills and ravines. Orson Pratt, who thought of the company as "adventurers in . . . savage and inhospitable wilds," saw in the new contours of the land "a tumultuous confusion of ocean waves, when rolling and tumbling in all directions by violent and contrary winds."[15] Farther on, when the land was broken by bluffs, their ideas became even more romantic. Wilford wrote, "[The bluffs] presented the most singular natural scenery that I ever beheld in my travels on the earth. It has the greatest appearance of the old walls and ruins of the castles of Europe."[16] One of these they called Ancient Bluff Ruins. Wilford hiked to its top carrying a bleached buffalo skull on which he wrote the names of the Twelve and the distances from several places for the benefit of the next camp. It would become for the generations that followed the very symbol of the trail and the community of spirit that was felt by pioneers in companies widely scattered from each other. Like the gospel, the trail bound them to each other.

Of all the landmarks along the Platte, none caused more stir than Chimney Rock, an ancient cylindrical rock tower that could be seen for at least forty-two miles and stood like a beacon before them for several days' travel. "Chimney rock still grows plainer to our view," Wilford wrote while miles out, and Orson Pratt, using a trigonometric measurement with his sextant, guessed the height to be 260 feet. Joseph Fish, who came as a child in a later company, captured the sheer fun of it for a child: "I remember that when we came in sight of it that it was thought by us boys that it was not far off and some of us boys started out to go to it thinking that we could go there and then take across and meet the train on ahead. We traveled some little distance when we gave it up and we did not get even with it until the next day."[17]

*The greatest natural landmark along the trail, Chimney
Rock, could be seen for 45 miles. Though it was only
425 miles from Winter Quarters, the Brethren later liked to consider this the halfway mark. Many pioneers noted this
country as the most romantic and sublime they had ever seen.*

L E F T *Big game, like this pronghorn, was abundant along the trail, but the brethren were taught to kill only
those animals that were essential for food. The
lessons of Zion's Camp 13 years before had taken well.*

It was a time of new sensations. The pioneers captured a baby eagle and brought it into camp; they found the petrified leg bone of a prehistoric mammoth; they laughed at the prairie dogs, which popped into their holes so quickly it was hard to get a good view of them; and they stripped the needles from a prickly pear and tasted its fruit, which was pronounced delicious. The air was perfumed by "southern wood," an herb that flourished in the dry, barren soil. Even without their wives, the men danced one evening for sheer exuberance.

Like Arabs who travel the deserts and name the geography to suit themselves, the pioneers gave this western wilderness names. Rattlesnake Creek was named for a snake that rattled in warning and then made a lunge at Thomas Woolsey's foot. The snake lost its head in the encounter. Heber C. Kimball had an even more compelling reason to name Wolf Creek. One day, traveling ahead to search out the way, he went down a deep hollow surrounded by high bluffs. As he was riding along, he turned his head to see two large wolves gazing fiercely at him. When he looked to the other side, to his surprise he saw several more. Having no gun and growing more anxious by the moment, he made a loud noise, hoping to frighten them away. They didn't move, but he did—riding away without further incident.

Indians continued to be a threat. Even when the pioneers didn't see Indians, they noted their fresh tracks. Orson Pratt said, "It is their custom frequently to follow emigrants hundreds of miles, keeping themselves secreted during the day, and watching the best opportunities for stealing during the night."[18] Near Chimney Rock, one day in late May, during the noon halt two Indians appeared, and later that day there came thirty-five more of their tribe. They were not the thieving Pawnee of the plains but the noble appearing Sioux, and the pioneers were impressed with their bearing, their clothing, and their friendliness. They wore broadcloth, blankets, and fur caps ornamented with brightly colored beads, and the Saints gladly fed them and invited the chief and his wife to stay for the night, a memorable one since Orson enthralled the chief by showing him the moon through the telescope.

It wasn't Indians that troubled Brigham at the end of May as the party made their way through the western end of what would become Nebraska. On Saturday, May 29, he had the Revenue Cutter dragged to the center of camp, the bugle blown, and the roll called, and he blasted the brethren with a call to repentance that turned out to be the longest entry in William Clayton's trail diary. It was a shakedown that left some of the men in tears. They had left their persecutors behind: "We are beyond their reach, we are beyond their power, we are beyond their grasp. What has the devil now to work upon?" He didn't wait for their answer; he was about to give it. For days he had been quietly seething about the frivolity of the camp. They were on the Lord's errand with a sober responsibility, and what did they do? "When I wake up in the morning, the first thing I hear is some of the brethren jawing each other and quarreling because a horse had got loose in the night. I have let the brethren dance and fiddle . . . night after night to see what they will do. . . . Well, they will play cards, they will play checkers, they will play dominoes, and if they had the privilege and were where they could get whiskey, they would be drunk half their time, and in one week they would quarrel, get to high words and draw their knives and kill each other. . . . Do you suppose that we are going to look out a home for the Saints, a resting place, a place of peace where they can build up the kingdom and bid the nations welcome, with a low, mean, dirty, trifling, covetous,

View from the top of Scott's Bluff, Nebraska, looking southwest to the valley far below. The geography was so different from anything the pioneers had seen before that many noted in their journals the magnificence of the landscape, thinking it romantic and sublime.

wicked spirit dwelling in our bosoms?" Brigham declared, "I had rather risk myself among savages with ten men that are men of faith, men of mighty prayer, men of God, than to be with this whole camp when they forget God and turn their hearts to folly and wickedness."[19] The men stared at the ground as he spoke and gave each other long guilty looks, chagrined at the biting truth of his words. How could they build Zion and raise a standard to all the earth if they embraced evil at the same time? Brigham asked every member of camp who was willing to turn from his sins to the Lord to raise his hand. All hands went to the sky.

*I*T WAS A CLEANSING MOMENT, A reminder that the Saints were not merely finding a place to settle. They were about a far larger and heavenly work—and they had to act like it. The next day was the Sabbath, and William Clayton noted that the spirit of repentance swept the camp: "I have never seen the brethren so still and sober on a Sunday since we started."[20] "It truly seemed as though the cloud had burst and we had emerged into a new element, a new atmosphere, and a new society"[21] Wilford Woodruff knew why Brigham had been so worked up: "A burned child dreads the fire. He had not forgotten his

journey in the Camp of Zion in 1834; and should he live to the age of Methuselah, he should not forget the hour when the Prophet and Seer, Joseph Smith, stood upon the wagon wheel and addressed that Camp and said that because they had not hearkened unto his counsel, but disobeyed and transgressed from time to time, judgment would come and that we should be visited by the destroying angel. And so we were, and more than twenty of our members fell by the stroke"[22] when cholera had swept through that camp.

The same thing would not happen to this camp. That Sabbath was appointed as a day of fasting and prayer, and in the afternoon, the Twelve climbed a nearby bluff and, once out of sight of the camp, changed into their temple clothes and had a prayer circle, pleading with the Lord to bless the camp, the brethren in the army, their families, and all the Saints. The timing was perfect, as renewed contact with the rabble-rousing gentile camps lay just ahead at Fort Laramie.

For the westward traveler in 1847, Fort Laramie was an oasis in the wilderness, the only outpost of civilization along the trail. Here traders came to barter, travelers picked up supplies at sometimes inflated prices, and information and trail gossip were willingly and happily shared. The Saints were anxious to get news of their Pueblo contingent—sick members of the Mormon Battalion and a group of Missippippi Saints that John Brown had taken there in the fall of 1846, and in this they were about to be satisfied. On June 2, Brigham Young, who had turned forty-six the day before, took a small group and crossed the Platte to visit the fort. True to form, Orson Pratt made careful measurements. The river was 108 yards wide and, Orson wrote, "the water is deep in the channel and the current runs about four miles

an hour." It was important information, because the company needed to cross the river soon. The Mormon trail on the north of the Platte was fast becoming impassable.

James Bordeaux, who ran the fort, had the friendliness and wealth of information typical of the old-time innkeeper who ran the "last chance" store before his customers hit the mountains. He greeted them cordially and confirmed that the company needed to cross there. Clayton recorded, "We learned that we cannot travel over four miles further . . . before we come to bluffs which cannot be crossed with loaded wagons."[23] His advice came with an offer—he would ferry them over for twenty-five cents a wagon or rent them his flatboat for fifteen dollars. He offered them a forge for wagon repair, which the Mormons didn't need, and gave them a piece of information on which they hung with interest. Their old enemy, former Missouri governor Lilburn W. Boggs, who had signed an extermination order against the Saints and had personally overseen driving them from the state, had just passed in a wagon train heading west and had warned Bordeaux against the Mormons, telling him to take care of his "horses and cattle or the Mormons would steal them."[24] It was a hard accusation, borne of meanheartedness, but even harder for Bordeaux to take seriously because Boggs was having so much trouble with his own company. Fighting and contention among them had risen to such a pitch that many had deserted, and Bordeaux had told the ex-governor that no matter how bad the Mormons were, they could not be any worse than he and his men.

For the pioneer company, ferrying the Platte began before sunrise the next morning, June 3, and they made a

contest between the first and second hundreds to see who could move the fastest. The winners averaged a wagon crossing every eleven minutes, undoubtedly spurred on not so much by the thrill of victory but by reports that two thousand wagons from Missouri were on the road just behind them. To this point in the journey, they had chosen an unbeaten path and had the trail to themselves. With this crossing they would be in the mainstream of traffic on the Oregon trail and would be competing for campsites and feed for their animals. More worrisome, like the scalawags of Boggs's wagon train, many of the travelers were rough Missourians at whose hands the Mormons had been beaten or burned out. It would be hard to flee from their enemies along the very trail their enemies were traveling, and time had not dimmed the memory of a state militia, armed to kill, surrounding their community at Far West. In the next few days, Missourians would camp near them, pass by them—and at last overcome their mutual suspicion and talk. Some of the Missourians dropped by to see the roadometer, whose fame was spreading along the road, and the Mormons, in turn, set up their forges and did a little repair work on the gentiles' wagons.

Laundry tents at Fort Laramie, Wyoming. The fort was the last taste of civilization before pioneers headed into the rugged Wyoming mountains. Though the trail information, gossip, and trade were attractive, after 1850 the Saints would generally avoid the fort because of their fear of contamination by gentile companies.

LEFT *The post commander's office was located in this room at Fort Laramie, Wyoming. This rugged wilderness outpost was established in 1835, and whether travelers were headed to California, Oregon, or the valleys of the mountains, all would pass this way, replenish supplies, and gather news.*

Western eye of a storm opens and the sun's
last rays burst upon Register Cliff
just beyond Fort Laramie, Wyoming. Though none
of the fifteen diarists of the 1847
vanguard company recorded stopping at Register
Cliff, hundreds of westward-bound
wayfarers later carved their names and the date of
their passage into this rock, making
it one of the most famous "frontier post-offices"
of the Oregon/Mormon Trail.
Brigham Young's Company would pass by this
dramatic location on June 4, 1847.

*L*ight touches dramatic shoulder-deep trail ruts
at Guernsey, Wyoming. Shown above are Ellen Saunders
Kimball (wife of Heber), Harriet Young (wife of
Lorenzo), and Clarissa Decker Young (wife of Brigham),
the only three women in the 1847 vanguard company.

Though their meeting was not one of hostility, neither was it one of camaraderie. A Mormon trail scout, John S. Higbee, was disgusted at the mess one Missouri camp had left. "In cleaning up breakfast," he wrote, "they strewed meal, salt, bacon, shortcake, beans and other things on the ground,"[25] and the Mormons were dismayed by the cursing and brawling they could hear in the gentile camps. Brigham Young even made the contrast between the Saints and the Missourians part of the subject of a Sunday discourse. "They curse and swear, rip and tear, and are trying to swallow up the earth," he said, "but they do not wish us to have a place on the earth." He drew a contrast between the Missourians and the Saints, explaining that the most acceptable way to worship God "is to do each day the very things that will bring the most good to the human family."[26]

Beyond Fort Laramie, as the Saints left the long river valley, the country began to be rougher, and they entered higher country where it was colder at night and timber grew. It was a land of wolves and grizzlies and meals of sweet antelope meat. The men tried their hand at fishing. One day William Clayton caught "two dozen good fish," but Wilford Woodruff, out with his fly rod, heard something rustling in the bushes and, remembering he was in bear country, "thought it wisdom to return to camp" empty-handed. Orson Pratt's journal is filled with descriptions of a countryside that excited his senses, of springs and timber, mountain cherry and wild currants, "pine, and cedar thinly scattered upon the bluffs." He wrote, "The wild rose flourishes in great abundance. The principal herbs and plants of this elevated region are highly odoriferous, perfuming the atmosphere with their fragrance."[27]

Part of the men became a road crew, tossing rocks off the trail and digging down the steepest banks. William Clayton put up his trail markers every ten miles. Late on June 8, a group of eastbound traders told the Saints they had left a boat made of buffalo hides hanging in a tree ahead on the trail, and the Saints could have it. It was a welcome gift, since the Mormons knew they had one last, dangerous crossing of the Platte ahead. The problem was that a camp of Missourians was traveling ahead of them and would probably find it first. Brigham wanted to beat them to the boat.

The next day, June 9, he dispatched nineteen teams and forty-nine pioneers to march ahead to find the traders' boat. They were also to build a raft of their own for a ferry. The advance party rolled out that morning a half-hour before the rest and made nineteen miles that day, hiking through one long valley of unusually red sand. The next day they saw the Platte again as well as the Missourians probing various places along the river to find a good spot for the next day's crossing. They had traveled nearly ninety miles since leaving Fort Laramie and were now at the location of present-day Casper, Wyoming. By June 12, they had not found the buffalo boat (nor would they ever), but they were already at work building a raft to ferry the river. Meanwhile, the Missourians had arrived at the spot and were impressed with the Revenue Cutter and its capacity to carry fifteen hundred pounds of cargo at a time. They struck a bargain with the Saints to ferry their own supplies across at $1.50 a load, payable in flour valued at $2.50 per hundred pounds, corn meal at fifty cents a bushel, or bacon at six cents a pound. Wilford Woodruff saw it plainly for what it was—not luck, and not a just reward for having become handy at fording rivers. "It looked as much of a miracle to me to see our flour and meal bags replenished in the midst of the Black Hills as it did to have the Children of Israel fed with manna in the wilderness," he said. "But the Lord has truly been with us on this journey. We have had peace and union in our midst, our horses and cattle have been wonderfully preserved from death and accident on the way and our wagons from breaking down."[28]

Though most of the Missourians were from Jackson, Clay, Lafayette, and Daviess counties, the very places the Saints had been scalded by persecution, the Mormons were treated to a hearty meal that night and, during the conversation, learned of the sad fate of one of their old benefactors. The father of Bill Bowman sat with the Saints around the fire that night and told a dark tale. Eight years earlier his son had been a sheriff in Daviess County and had provided horses for Joseph and Hyrum to escape when they were being transferred from Liberty Jail. For his son's kindness, a mob headed by Obadiah Jennings, the same ruffian who had spearheaded the massacre at Haun's Mill, rode Bill "on an iron bar until they killed him."[29]

A SPARK OF FRIENDSHIP, KINship born of shared pain, passed between the Mormons and the Missouri travelers, and it was further fanned by the gratitude of one Missourian who had been saved from drowning that day when he had tried to swim the river at a point one hundred yards wide. Partway out, he had become frightened and had been saved by some Mormons in the Revenue Cutter.

After the Mormons got their clients across the river, it was their turn to ferry themselves across the place that came to be called Last Crossing. Late in the season, the river would be shallow enough to wade, but with the swell of early June, it was a hundred yards wide and fifteen feet deep. Their goods crossed handily enough in the Revenue Cutter, but the wagons were a different story. A wagon floated across singly would get caught in the current and roll as if it were nothing but a log, wheels and bows appearing alternately above the water. Two wagons lashed together were no better, and four wagons provided more stability but too much weight. The pioneers finally had to climb the mountains, bring

Next to Chimney Rock, Independence Rock (shown here) was the most famous natural landmark along the trail. Here the pioneers passed the 700-mile mark from Winter Quarters on June 20, 1847.

RIGHT Hundreds of 19th-century travelers left their names on Independence Rock in Wyoming as if it was a toll required for passage. John Brown and Wilford Woodruff, scouts for the lead company, hiked to the top, noting that they were "the first Latter-day Saints that ever went onto that rock."[1]

down lumber, and begin work on a more elaborate raft. Then, soaked to the skin in the icy water, they ferried one wagon across at a time, a tedium that took an entire day to transport only twenty-three wagons. To make matters worse, the wind came up, the rain and hail pelted them, and the river rose. It took four back-breaking days, starting June 14, to get across the river, but by the last day the raft, now steadied with two long dugout canoes, was in full operation, and Brigham saw an opportunity.

One hundred and eight Oregon wagons were on the other side of the river eager to cross, and more would be coming. Why not set up a ferry business whose profit would help the Saints' companies that would soon follow? Brigham, whose natural business sense was sharpened by his prophetic calling, liked the idea, and even in their exhaustion, the men waded back into the water and spent the night ferrying the gentiles. When all was finished, the Saints were $400 richer in provisions, and a detachment was chosen to stay behind to operate the ferry on a more permanent basis.

Now, a few men shorter, the pioneer company left the Platte, the river that had given them water and timber and sometimes frustrated them, and moved into the worst stretch of the trail. The fifty miles from here to the Sweetwater River was a depressing trek that, through the years, was strewn with animal carcasses and abandoned equipment, the telltale leavings of exhaustion and despair.

A pioneer in a later train described the scatterings left by others: "Innumerable articles of all kinds were left by the wayside. I even noticed an old broken fiddle. . . . We found many wagons and parts of wagons were found, the owners having made carts or put their effects on pack animals. . . . My father's team was failing fast so to help them some he left his wagon and took another that was

A fternoon clouds gather and light dances
along the peaks of the Rattlesnake
Range of mountains that approximate the course
of the Sweetwater River in the highlands of Wyoming. The trail fords the meander-
ing Sweetwater so many times that the
pioneers' clothing did not completely dry out
between the crossings for five days.

lighter that he found by the wayside."[30]

The Saints' campsites offered more opportunity for endurance than rest. Wilford Woodruff called the campsite on the evening of June 19 "the most wretched of any ground we have found on the way,"[31] and Brigham thought it should be called Hell Gate. Two creeks fed the spot, one poisonous and stinking of sulphur. Mosquitoes rose from the bog created by the smelly creek, and the stock were in constant danger of miring in the mud. It was, according to Heber C. Kimball, "a gloomy, cheerless, filthy place, most dangerous for cattle and unhealthy for families."[32]

They pushed on, up over Prospect Hill, where they got a view of the Sweetwater Mountains, and then across the rough road that led to Independence Rock. The road had its own stink from the alkali lake it crossed, and the water, standing in shallow ponds, tasted "sickly." Later travelers would be warned to avoid it as poisonous; the cattle that didn't would bloat and die. Here, too, they found "saleratus," the white bicarbonate of soda that was said "to raise bread equal to the best bought in eastern markets."[33] Lorenzo Snow gathered up a pailful of the stuff to try it, but the bread it made was a strange cast of green and not appetizing.

BEFORE THEM AND behind them were Missourians, and when John Brown and Wilford Woodruff went ahead to scout for campsites, they saw what they believed to be six Indians, wrapped in blankets, who blocked the trail and motioned for the horsemen to go back. When the two men ignored them, the "Indians" spurred their horses and were soon out of sight behind a rise. When the scouts mounted the ridge, they came upon a camp of Missourians, and the six were just entering camp. Brigham later called it "an old Missouri trick" and was convinced that the hucksters were just trying to keep the Saints from a good campground. Though he advised his men to "press on a little faster and crowd them up a little,"[34] the Missourians and Mormons would leapfrog along the trail for several miles.

The night of June 20, the camp felt some anxiety for Wilford Woodruff and John Brown, who had left camp and not returned. They built a bonfire as a beacon and fired the cannon, but unbeknownst to their friends, the two were happily settled. They had accepted a Missouri company's invitation to spend the night, and they shared bacon, buffalo meat, cornbread, coffee, and milk with them and appreciated their hospitality. Still, Wilford noted, "I found that there was a great difference between these Missouri companies and our own, where there was no thing as cursing, swearing, quarreling, contending with other companies, etc., allowed or practiced."[35]

The next morning Wilford and John Brown climbed Independence Rock, which sits like an enormous, gray, beached whale in the Wyoming highlands and is one of the trail's most famous natural landmarks. Painted with the names and dates of travelers who had passed before, the granite hump gave Wilford a wide view of the surrounding country. Beyond six miles was Devil's Gate, another noted landmark of the trail, through which the Sweetwater River gushed with the unrelenting power of water, cutting pillars of the rock. Even farther away stood the Sweetwater Mountains, a spill of rugged contours painted in muted grays and browns, and the place that travelers who followed would freeze and die. The old, green world they had grown up in was behind the pioneers now, and the two men, as the first of the Mormon pioneers on the rock, did what those who know God are apt to do at such a moment. They offered up prayers "according to the order of the priesthood," and Wilford said, "While offering up our prayers the spirit of the Lord descended upon us."[36]

Soon the rest of the pioneers caught up with them and, like thousands after them, had their own turn to scramble to the top of the rock. Farther on at Devil's Gate, they stopped long enough to put up another sign. Devil's Gate was 50 ¼ miles from Last Crossing and 175 ¼ from Fort Laramie. In the next few days they crossed and recrossed the Sweetwater, marveled at the sheer wildness of the mountain views and wide spaces, and found that in the ups and downs of the landscape the going was hard even for the best of teams. The Sweetwater was swift and cold, and at night, even in June, the men were chilled in the gaping vastness of the high country.

The pioneer company never did get ahead of the Missourians, and as common challenges will often create unusual bedfellows, so the trail continued to make almost friends of those who had once been sworn enemies. Lorenzo Young broke his axle in the worst possible place, without a foot of timber to be found, and William Henrie dropped back from the main company, found a piece of wood, and began helping him make the repair. Just then a Missouri company came upon them, and its members, seeing that Young's heavy load might damage his hobbled-together wagon, took the cargo into their own wagons. The exchange of information and goodwill marked the mountain crossing. An advance scout from the Missouri company returned to tell about South Pass. William Clayton noted, "He says it is not over twenty-eight miles to the pass from here."[37] In turn, Burr Frost, one of the Saints, set up his forge and repaired one of the wheels of the Missouri wagons.

*S*OMETIMES IN THEIR JOURNALS the pioneers sound like tourists, agog with excitement at each discovery. Norton Jacob found what he called a "great curiousity."[38] In one hole about a foot deep under the prairie was an ice spring that yielded as clear an ice as William Clayton said he ever saw. "Some of the brethren had broken some pieces off which floated," he said, "and I ate some of it which tasted sweet and pleasant."[39] Yet under the awe of fresh scenes was a sober reality. These were the vanguard group of a displaced people who would not find the happiness and stability of a home again until they had faced the most challenging rigors of this very trail. Each difficulty this first company met would be multiplied geometrically when women, children, and elderly were added. Some would falter by the wayside; thousands would die. This was brought home poignantly when, on June 23, the company came upon the grave of a young woman who had perished the previous year. "Matilda

Crowley," the marker read. She was born in July 1830 and died the same month sixteen years later in a place her loved ones would never see again. William Clayton wrote, "On reflecting afterward that some of the numerous emigrants who had probably started with a view to spend the remainder of their days in the wild Oregon had fallen by the way and their remains had to be left by their friends far from the place of destination, I felt a renewed anxiety that the Lord will kindly preserve the lives of all my family."[40]

They pushed on, climbing higher, finding snow in the shady ravines and having to breathe more deeply to catch their breath in the thin mountain air. Up they mounted, over the rock-ribbed back of Rocky Ridge, a long, high climb that would challenge every fiber of those who followed in bad weather. In the mornings they found ice on their water buckets and their milk a chunky slush. At the ridge, Wilford measured snow that was still ten feet deep, unmelted by the summer sun. Still he liked what he saw on the trail, writing, "I should almost have thought myself traveling over the beautiful prairies of Illinois and Missouri except that the country was covered with more sage than prairie grass."[41]

The Saints heaved their loads through the famous South Pass and then met the type of character they had

been longing to see—a genuine mountain man. His name was Moses "Black" Harris, and he had tramped these mountains and valleys and had firsthand information about the Great Basin. They hung on his every word, a report that must have made their hearts sink.

"From his description . . . ," Clayton wrote, "we have little chance to hope for even a moderately good country anywhere in those regions. He speaks of the whole region as being sandy and destitute of timber and vegetation except wild sage."[42] In their secret thoughts they

must have wondered, "To what new heartache are we leading the almost two thousand people who are following only weeks behind us?"

Then, in a symbolism that didn't escape them, on June 27 they arrived at the Continental Divide. It had been three years to the day since Joseph and Hyrum had been reading scriptures and listening to John Taylor sing in the Carthage Jail, three years since multiple balls had entered their bodies and killed them, three years since the Saints had waited in their homes for the mobs to come. Now those who had taken up the Lord's cause with Joseph were at a great divide. Wilford noted, "For the first time in my life [I have] tasted water running into the Pacific."[43] They had escaped the grasp of their enemies. It was a Sunday, and many would have liked to stop for fasting and prayer, but competition with the gentiles for grass and water kept them moving— moving toward a place they hoped they could finally stop. In what must have seemed like a further message to them, the next day, just six miles farther, the trail divided. Most of the gentiles took the righthand fork; the Saints went left toward Fort Bridger and a fresh start.

On that day, too, they met the most famous mountain man of all, Jim Bridger, of whom it was said that at age twenty in 1824 he had discovered the Great Salt Lake. Weathered, profane, and no stranger to alcohol, which kept him warm on Rocky Mountain nights, Bridger spun tales of the region and his own vast experience, which Wilford, at least, was not certain about. "We found him to have been a great traveler, and possessed a great knowledge of nearly all of Oregon and California . . . if what he told us was true."[44] His conversation was rambling rather than helpful, but at least his report of the region was more cheering than "Black" Harris's had been. He did, however, suggest that the nights in the Salt Lake Valley might be too cold for the maturing of corn. Brigham noted

that Bridger "considered it important not to bring a large population into the Great Basin until it was ascertained that grain could be raised; he said he would give one thousand dollars for a bushel of corn raised in the Basin."[45] If Bridger had known the Mormons a little better, he would have seen it wasn't a good wager. Legend claims that Brigham replied, "Wait a little and we will show you." And, of course, they did.

The next two days were excruciating, including a hard push of twenty-four miles across a hot, barren desert "with scarcely any green thing."[46] Many in the company began to complain of blinding headaches and severe pains

Afternoon light touches tenacious flowers in the highlands of Wyoming. This ground was made sacred by the trodding of 70,000 Saints on their way to Zion.

LEFT *Remnants of the old trail can still be seen in remote areas of Wyoming. Near the Continental Divide in the highlands of Wyoming, the trail passes over the 7,500 foot elevation, through the South Pass, and into the final 200 miles of the journey. Even in the summer crossing, here the pioneers found chilly nights and ice on their milk in the morning.*

the Mississippi fleeing Nauvoo. He had come by way of the Horn, arrived in San Francisco the end of July that year, and established the coast's first newspaper. Now he came extolling the virtues of California, hoping to convince Brigham Young to bring the emigrants on to the coast. The rivers ran with salmon, clover grew there as high as a horse's belly, and wild geese and horses moved in great abundance, he said. Sutter, who seven months later would discover the gold fields, would welcome a colony of Mormons, and besides (this must have been a jab since they had just passed through such barren country), there were more trees here along the Green River than he had seen on the entire trip from California. Brigham was unmoved. Despite all the dour descriptions of the Salt Lake Valley, and despite the glow that surrounded California, Brigham went for the drabber choice. His people had been pushed around enough by people who had found their land desirable. God had a place for them in the tops of the mountains, and that's where they were going.

Independence Day was not celebrated by the pioneers. It was a hot, dusty, mosquito-ridden day like many others to come. Wilford Woodruff stopped writing in the middle of his journal because, as he wrote, "the mosquitoes have filled my carriage like a cloud and have fallen upon me as though they intend to devour me. I never saw that insect more troublesome than in certain places in this country."[48] That day, the company sent a contingent back to help bring up the large group of Saints behind them, which was just then crossing the Loup Fork, and then, because it was the Sabbath, they had a prayer and also a rare treat. George Smith rode into the mountains and returned with a heap of snow. They mixed it with sugar and made ice cream.

in the back and joints. Some came down with high fevers that led to delirium. Clayton noted that John Fowler "was seized this afternoon and this evening is raving."[47] They called it mountain fever, brought on, they supposed, from the severe alterations in hot and cold and the breathing in of alkali dust. Later scholars suppose it was, instead, Rocky Mountain spotted fever, transmitted from tick bites. No matter what it was called, jolting along in the wagons with the dust rising around them was a torture for the sick, and it was a relief to arrive at the more pleasant Green River, which was lined on either side by a narrow strip of land that was suitable for farming and held patches of wild apple trees.

The Green, named for an earlier explorer and not for its color, was too swollen with winter runoff to ford, and the Missouri companies that had come before them had turned loose their rafts to prevent the Mormons' using them. The men rolled up their sleeves and started building rafts again, a job they were about when they looked up to see Samuel Brannan arriving on horseback from the west. Brannan was a Mormon who had sailed from New York with a shipful of Saints on February 4, 1846, the same day Charles Shumway had been the first across

Treats were few and far between in those days as they passed over soil as hard as cast iron, barren of anything

but sage. Just before they arrived at Fort Bridger, which one journalist admits wasn't very impressive, the grass improved. Wilford, who loved to angle, found a trout stream and got a chance to try out the artificial flies he had purchased on his last mission in England. It was, he said, "the first time I ever tried the artificial fly in America or ever saw it tried. I watched it as it floated upon the water with as much intent as Franklin did his kite."[49] He caught twelve trout and returned to camp with a fishing creel stuffed to the brim.

At Fort Bridger, the terrain was the most mountainous they had yet seen, and the most challenging part of the journey lay ahead. The route they proposed to follow over the rugged mountains was practically virgin, having been taken by only fifty-seven wagons the year before, and their faint traces were almost grown over. It had been proposed and promoted by Lansford Hastings in his *Emigrant's Guide to Oregon and California* as a way to save hundreds of extra miles over the well-worn Oregon Trail,

but following it had taken the Donner-Reed party an entire month to travel from Fort Bridger to the Salt Lake Valley, a delay that led to one of the West's most grisly tragedies. They were marooned in an early snowstorm in the high Sierras, and more than half of the party's eighty-seven members died, while the others survived only by eating the flesh of their dead companions.

Now the trail became rugged, a trudge made possible only by the sheer strength of the oxen and the sheerer will of the pioneers. They struggled up high ridges that seemed impossible to climb, only to arrive at the top and find there was no way down without making a new path. Thomas Bullock recorded that one afternoon the party "descended by two steep pitches, almost perpendicular, which on looking back from the bottom looks like jumping off the roof of a house to a middle story, then from the middle story to the ground and thank God there was

On August 3, 1855, the Church purchased Fort Bridger for $18,000, enlarged it, and built this cobblestone wall around it (a small remnant remains). On September 27, 1857, at the approach of Johnston's Army, the Saints evacuated and burned the fort to the ground.

FAR LEFT *Light warms the fence and buildings of Fort Bridger, Wyoming. According to William Clayton's roadometer, the vanguard company had now come 919 miles from Winter Quarters. Remaining were 113 ½ of the hardest miles of the entire journey.*

ABOVE *The vanguard company of 1847 dragged a cannon, similar to this one at Fort Laramie, across the plains and mountains, sometimes firing it in the evenings to give a clear message to the Indians of their presence. It was a warning to hostile natives to keep their distance.*

no accident happened. Priests Young and Kimball cautioned all to be very careful and locked the wheels of some wagons themselves."[50] William Clayton observed, "There are some in camp who are getting discouraged about the looks of the country, but thinking minds are not much disappointed, and we have no doubt of finding a place where the Saints can live which is all we ought to ask or expect."[51]

Some men were disabled with mountain fever, which made the trail more difficult as others had to do double-

duty. Then, on July 12, Brigham "was attacked with fever." By noon he could not travel, and by evening he was "very sick . . . raving and insensible." He described himself as "almost mad with pain."[52] Debilitated with illness, Brigham could not travel, and so a division was made that eventually split the company into three groups. Orson Pratt selected twenty-three wagons and forty-three men as an advance group to find the Reed road and with axes and spades hack it open for travel. The main company would follow them, and a few stayed behind to help the ailing Brigham, who could not keep up the pace.

The advance company under Pratt went down Echo Canyon, a narrow valley on whose sides red walls rose abruptly eight hundred to twelve hundred feet. When

Clayton came through, he would note the echo that gave the canyon its name: "The rattling of the wagons resembles carpenters hammering at boards inside the highest rocks."[53] From Echo Canyon the advance group went down the Weber Fork until it narrowed into an alley filled nearly wall to wall with river. Though it was possible to make it through, floundering among the water and boulders, the Donner party the year before had gone another way, picking a path through the mountains. It was this Reed trail that Pratt wanted to find, and when they did, Pratt marked the turnoff with a sign and went on.

As if Zion would not come without a heavy price, the last miles to the valley became even tougher, an ordeal of uphills and downhills, of chopping out willows that choked the way and left sharp stumps, like knives, to wound the feet of the next travelers. Progress seemed to be counted in inches, and the men fell into bed at night exhausted. With the road worked before them, the main camp made better time, but all were amazed at the intense challenge of the terrain.

On July 17, Orson Pratt wrote that he went out "alone and on foot, to examine the country back, to see if there was a more practicable route for the companies in the rear than the one we had come. I was soon satisfied that we had taken the best and only practicable route."[54] If it were best, one could hardly imagine what might have been worse. On the 20th, they made the grueling ascent up Big Mountain, and William Clayton, with the main party, was having an equally terrible time. He wrote, "The last three miles has been the worst road of the two, it being through willow bushes over twenty feet high, also rose and gooseberry bushes and birch timber. Although there has been a road cut through, it is yet scarcely possible to travel without tearing the wagon covers. We have crossed this creek which Elder Pratt names Canyon Creek eleven times during the day and the road is one of the most crooked I ever saw, many sharp turns in it and the willow stubs standing making it very severe on the wagons."[55]

*S*un rims Echo Canyon and sets the dried weeds
ablaze with light. Not far from here
Porter Rockwell found the cutoff that led away from
the Weber River toward the chosen valley.

L E F T *The company amused themselves here in
Echo Canyon (Utah) with shouting, shoot-
ing, and blowing band instruments to enjoy the
sound reverberating from the cliffs. Here
Brigham Young was deathly ill with mountain fever.*

Early morning light begins to fill Emigration Canyon just a few miles from the valley. Here hearts were pounding, less from the tremendous strain of the trail than from the hope and gratitude that welled in their bosoms as they viewed the landscape below. "We have come home," they thought. This photograph was taken July 24.

The next day, July 21, Erastus Snow caught up with the advance company, and he and Orson Pratt went down the canyon of Last Creek (which would later be named Emigration Canyon) to catch a glimpse of the broad valley below them. Their way led through a V-shaped canyon choked with willows and boulders, and the season before, fed up with hacking at trees, the Donner party had climbed a vertical wall to get out of the canyon. It had been another in a series of disastrous decisions, wearing down their animals, whose energy

scenery open before us, we could not refrain from a shout of joy which almost involuntarily escaped from our lips the moment this grand and lovely scenery was within our view."[56] Legend says they lingered long enough to wave their hats and cry "Hosannah, Hosannah, Hosannah" before they descended into the valley to make a twelve-mile circuitous tour. They found an expanse of land devoid of trees except for a few hardy willows that grew along creeks that pounded out of the mountains, black crickets that would later find their crops delicious, a few rattlesnakes, and fertile soil—a high mountain land on the shores of a sterile sea that to this point nobody else had wanted. It was perfect for a driven people. They and their grandchildren after them would look up at the Wasatch Mountains that separated them from all that had been so painful and sing:

> For the strength of the hills, we bless thee,
> Our God, our fathers' God.
> Thou hast made thy children mighty
> By the touch of the mountain sod.
> Thou hast led thy chosen Israel
> To freedom's last abode;
> For the strength of the hills we bless thee,
> Our God, our father's God.
> At the hands of foul oppressors,
> We've borne and suffered long;
> Thou hast been our help in weakness,
> And thy pow'r hath made us strong.
> Amid ruthless foes outnumbered,
> In weariness we trod.
> For the strength of the hills we bless thee,
> Our God, our fathers' God.[57]

That night back at camp, a messenger came with instructions from Brigham Young. It was not about the utter relief of finding their place to build Zion. It was instead about the urgency of a season already late to grow crops and the need to sow immediately: "The time for planting is fully come, and we feel anxious to make every move that would facilitate the potato crop, it matters not where it is. The president thinks the Utes may feel a little tenacious about their choice lands on the Utah Lake, and we had better keep further north towards the Salt Lake, . . . which is more of a warlike or neutral

could have carried them beyond the untimely snow storm. For now Pratt and Snow followed their route, but the pioneers behind them would take only four hours to cut their way through this part of the canyon.

At the top of the hill, Pratt and Snow could see the broad, golden valley below encircled by rugged, blue peaks and the gray blue of the shimmering salt lake to the north. Orson Pratt wrote, "After issuing from the mountains among which we had been shut up for many days, and beholding in a moment such an extensive

ground, and by so doing we should be less likely to be disturbed."[58] Thus when Brigham first looked out at the valley, the first soil had already been turned.

The sun was nearing the western mountains the next afternoon, July 22, when the main camp of pioneers finally cut their way through Emigration Canyon and came into the valley with untold sighs of relief. "I could not help shouting hurrah, hurrah, hurrah, there's my home at last," wrote Thomas Bullock. "The sky is very clear, the air delightful and all together looks glorious, the only drawback appearing to be the absence of timber. But there is an ocean of stone in the mountains to build stone houses and walls for fencing. If we can only find a bed of coal we can do well and be hidden up in mountains unto the Lord."[59]

They hardly took time for a breath, hardly stretched their strained and weary muscles before they were at it again. The morning of the 23rd, Orson Pratt led them in "prayer to Almighty God." Thomas Bullock wrote, "[We returned] thanks for the preservation of the Camp, [our] prosperity in the journey, safe arrival in this place, consecrated and dedicated the land to the Lord and entreated his blessings on the seeds about to be planted and on our labors in this valley."[60] Then they divided into committees, covering every aspect of plowing and planting. By noon the first furrow was turned; by nightfall three acres had been planted. By the next day they had dammed City Creek and brought water to the thirsty seeds.

*W*HAT DROVE THEM WAS A vision. The realists would come to the valley and complain that it was a wasteland. They would see that on the first day they broke several plows against the stony ground. Harriet Young was gloomy the entire journey about the dismal landscape, the treeless expanses. When she came to the valley she told her husband, Lorenzo, "We have traveled fifteen hundred miles to get here, and I would willingly travel a thousand miles farther."[61] But the visionaries saw more than a wasteland. They saw Zion, and they would take no time to rest when crops needed to be planted.

Brigham Young was a visionary. True, the mountain fever had ravaged him. There had even come a time when he seemed so close to death that several of the brethren held a special prayer circle in his behalf. But he was not to die somewhere along the trail; he had to live to fulfill the vision. On the same day the men were planting in the valley, Brigham, somewhat better but still drained physically from the ravages of the disease, was riding in a bed in the back of Wilford Woodruff's carriage when he arrived at a summit of Big Mountain and had a partial view of the valley. He later said, "I directed Elder Woodruff, who had kindly tendered me the use of his carriage to turn the same half way round so that I could have a view of a portion of Salt Lake Valley. The spirit of light rested upon me and hovered over the valley, and I felt that there the Saints would find protection and safety."[62] It may have been at this time, when the vision had passed, that Brigham said quietly, "It is enough. This is the right place. Drive on."[63] The next morning, on July 24, Brigham rolled into the valley, and with their prophet there, the Saints truly felt they had come home. The day would be marked for all generations that followed.

Within three days Brigham was laying out the city. On July 28, he walked with the Twelve, planted his cane in a certain spot, and said, "Here is the 40 acres for the Temple. The city can be laid out perfectly square, north and south, east and west."[64] With an eye to creating Zion and wasting no time about it, that day it was moved and carried that there be ten acres in each block and one and a quarter in each lot, "that each street be laid out eight rods wide, and that there be a sidewalk on each side, twenty feet wide, and that each house be built in the centre of the lot twenty feet from the front, that there might be uniformity throughout the city . . . that there be four public squares of ten acres each, to be laid out in various parts of the city for public grounds."[65] They had been trained to build the city of God. Joseph had taught them well.

*Sunset silhouettes the 60-foot-high This Is
the Place Monument at the mouth
of Emigration Canyon. Depicted on the top are
Brigham Young, Heber C. Kimball,
and Wilford Woodruff. The roadometer distance from Winter Quarters was 1,032
miles. Robert Sweeten, who would be the last
of the 1847 pioneers to pass away,
dedicated the first monument placed here.*

A survey of the new city began within a week. Men's hands and clothes became stained with clay as they made adobes for a fort. Acreage continued to be tilled and planted with corn, potatoes, and buckwheat. Yet it wasn't the efficiency of the group, the spirited verve with which they began the city of God that seems to speak beyond the years to their comfortable great-grandchildren. It was that having just made the hot, dusty, mosquito-ridden trip, so many of them unloaded their equipment, repaired their outfits, and turned around (the first group leaving within nine days) to go help their friends and families make the same journey. Where was rest, peace, perhaps a moment's ease? Those needs were swallowed up in a much greater need, a Zion kind of need, to give the pure love of Christ in service.

Many of them picked up and turned around. They would learn and forge into the blood of their children that *sacred* and *sacrifice* have the same root—that something is, in fact, made sacred by sacrifice. As Wallace Stegner wrote, "They went in groups of every size, Ezra Taft Benson and Porter Rockwell as messengers to the main emigration on August 2, Norton Jacob in charge of a group of hunters with a few wagons on August 11, William Clayton with eighteen ox teams and a new road-ometer on August 17, Brigham and the Twelve and a considerable party of horse and mule teams on August 25."[66]

Meanwhile, the Big Company, made up of more than two thousand Saints, were on their way from the Missouri

River to the valley. It was different than the vanguard company in that the women and children far outnumbered the men, a reality that put many women in the driver's seat. Women who had spent their days rocking babies in one arm while making bread and drying fruit with the other were now yoking up oxen, chasing stray cattle, and holding the reins over sometimes rough country. In fact, the entire migration and the gospel that motivated it had given Mormon women a kind of independence and rock sure competence that made them exceptional. They had become used to surviving in the most brutal conditions without their men. For instance, when it became apparent that the Saints must leave Nauvoo, Louisa Pratt's husband, Addison, was on a mission in the Society Islands, and she felt at a loss about how to pack up her life, abandon her home, and take her daughters alone into the wilderness. Then Almon Babbitt called to see her. She wrote, "I asked him if he could divine the reason why those who had sent my husband to the ends of the earth did not call to enquire whether I could prepare myself for such a perilous journey. His reply was, 'Sister Pratt, they expect you to be smart enough to go yourself without help, and even to assist others.' The remark wakened in me a spirit of self-reliance. I replied, Well, 'I will show them what I can do.'"[67]

She did show them, and so did her sisters who came along the trail in 1847. Charles Coulson Rich's plural wife Mary drove a team and felt better by the day for it. "I never had very good health, until I started on that trip," she later said. "And then I got to feeling so well that I felt it was a pleasure to take hold and do something." The only loss for Mary was modesty, as her dress, like those

of thousands of others who would march into the valley, became tattered over the long trail. "When we arrived in Emigration canyon," she said, "the longest place on my dress was just a little below my knees. I had walked over the brush, driving my teams, to keep them in the road, and could not stop to untangle my dress when it got fastened, but had to walk on, leaving part of my dress behind."[68]

Tattered or not, those who found the gospel wanted to gather. The migration of 1848 had as its major purpose the evacuation of Winter Quarters. Mary Fielding Smith, widow of the patriarch Hyrum, was one who in 1848 was still in Winter Quarters. She was eager to move West, but her situation was desperate. Determination and diligence did little to improve it. "Every nerve was strained and every available object was brought into requisition"[69] to gather the teams necessary for the trip. She even traded off the family's pet donkey, Jackie, much to her son Joseph F.'s dismay. The problem was that icy seasons at Winter Quarters had killed eleven of her thirteen

The upper plains of Wyoming Sarah Rich said the trail broke itself up into three parts— the buffalo, the prairie-dog, and the mountain region. She declared buffalo meat to be "the sweetest I ever tasted," but "it made the children fat."[4]

ABOVE Glow of first light touches thistle in Emigration Canyon. The Big Company of 1847, divided into three groups for ease of travel, began arriving August 29, 1847.

horror. Though she did all she could, her teams were comprised of wild steers, cows, and half-grown oxen that had not been well-broken and did not work together well in tandem.

Her predicament looked nearly hopeless that June 4 when they left Winter Quarters, and before she and her family had gone two miles, trouble seemed to be crashing in on them, "a series of most amazing and trying circumstances such as sticking in the mud, doubling up on all the little hills, and crashing at ungovernable speed down the opposite sides, breaking wagon tongues and reaches upsetting and vainly endeavoring to control wild steers and unbroken cows."[70] Arriving at camp that night, she had to endure the scowls of the company captain, Cornelius P. Lott, who sized up her situation without pity and told her it was folly for her to start in such conditions. Not only would she never make it, but she would also be a burden upon the whole company. He told her to go back to Winter Quarters and wait until she could find someone to help her. Lott had no idea of the strength of the woman he was belittling. Spunky and tireless, she had already been shoved from Kirtland to Far West to Nauvoo and then to Winter Quarters. She had stood by her husband's coffin after his assassination at Carthage and then without drooping turned to bring her family West. If these things had not stopped her, would the disdain of her company captain? She thought for a moment, then told him calmly that she would beat him to the valley and ask no help from him.

When Heber C. Kimball had left with empty pockets for his first mission to England, Mary had slipped five dollars into his hand. Now, back in Winter Quarters with Brigham Young to bring out the 1848 companies, he came forward to help her, sending her two yoke of oxen for the journey. This improved her situation, and she was able to join the company, but without the security of a reserve ox. Except for the badgering from Captain Lott, things went well until she was in the miserable no-man's land between the Platte and Sweetwater Rivers. At that point, her best ox suddenly lay down in the yoke. The ox was stiffening in death when Captain Lott approached, saying, "He is dead, there is no use working with him. We'll have to fix up some way to take the widow along. I told her she would be a burden on the company."[71]

Then, in a surprising move, Mary got a bottle of consecrated oil from the wagon, oil reserved for administering to the sick. James Lawson and Mary's brother Joseph laid their hands upon the ox, whose eyes were already fixed and staring. They blessed him, and in a moment the animal began to move. Then he lumbered to his feet and seemed as if nothing had ever been wrong. Motivated by this kind of faith, Mary did indeed beat Captain Lott to the valley.

All were not as eager. For some, leaving Iowa was a reluctant evacuation. Saints who had already been driven from their homes two or three times before had just begun to feel at home there when they had to pick up and leave again. Some left prospering farms to go to the valley and survive on sego lily bulbs. But they did have to leave. The Bureau of Indian Affairs did not want the Mormons on Pottawatamie lands, and for some it felt like another surrender.

Until 1852, the principal thrust would be gathering in the American Saints, who came as they could when enough money could be pinched together to buy a team. Then, after 1852, headquarters for the gathering was moved to Liverpool, England, as Saints who spoke in strange accents heard the gospel and abandoned all they had known to come and build Zion.

Each story of the thousands who came has its own drama, its own moment when the wilderness travelers had to square up their shoulders under loads that threatened to break them. In this hour, as they took their own measure, most were not found wanting. They put one foot in front of the other, sometimes through tears and loss, and came to Zion. The wilderness would play its part in purifying their souls, binding the generations that followed through the invincible power of love and sacrifice.

Fall colors in Fast Canyon, Utah. Joseph Fish described
the big company: "It presented a picturesque
appearance. Bare-footed children, here and there....
Women...traveling along...over the parched
plains. Men with their long whips walking beside the
lolling oxen...towards the setting sun." [5]

Five

WE KNEW
HIM IN OUR
EXTREMITIES

THE IDEA HAD BEEN RUM-
BLING IN THE BACK OF
Brigham Young's mind for years. In
the British Isles, the gospel had been
accepted by thousands of converts, many of
whom had the spirit of gathering but not the means.
These were proselytes who wearied themselves sometimes
with sixteen-hour days in the dank, drear coal mines of
Wales or the steaming factories of Manchester, whose
starvation wages were stretched so thin that scarcely a
shilling could be saved for the journey to Zion. They
included families who could only eke out enough savings
to send family members one at a time to Zion, or converts who had waited years since baptism to begin their
journey to the Salt Lake Valley.

To help these people, Brigham started the Perpetual
Emigration Fund in 1852. It was a compassionate and
efficient scheme, primarily funded by tithes and contributions, that helped poor but eager emigrants with the
costs of the journey. Once in Zion, they could repay the
debt and help others to come. For three years, Church
agents in Liverpool effectively extended the money to
bring 4,225 converts to America. But by 1855, costs of
emigrating were escalating. In addition, the grasshopper
plague in Utah had destroyed crops so that funds had
dwindled. Still, a swell of converts was waiting to come.
It was time for Brigham to resurrect his idea.

He presented it in a letter to European mission president Franklin D. Richards in September of 1855: "I have
been thinking how we should operate another year. We
cannot afford to purchase wagons and teams as in times
past. I am consequently thrown back upon my old
plan—*to make handcarts,* and let the emigration foot it, and
draw upon them the necessary supplies, having a cow or
two for every ten. They can come just as quick, if not
quicker, and much cheaper—can start earlier and escape
the prevailing sickness which annually lays so many of
brethren in the dust. . . . Fifteen miles a day will bring
them through in 70 days, and after they get accustomed
to it, they will travel 20, 25, and even 30 with all ease."[1]

The *Millennial Star* recounted the advantages to the
British Saints of this new experiment in a December edi-
torial: "It is only to those who have travelled the plains

with ox teams, that the advantages of doing without them
will appear in all their force. They alone can realize what
it is to get up on a sultry morning—spend an hour or two
in driving up and yoking unruly cattle, and while impatiently waiting to start on the dusty, wearisome road . . .
hear the word passed around that some brother has an ox
missing, then an hour, or perhaps half of the day, is wasted
. . . during which a company with handcarts would have
performed the greater part of an ordinary day's journey."[2]

What was probably most compelling to the anxious,
however, was the cost. Wilford Woodruff, who had
brought thousands into the Church in Britain and had
felt their Zion-longing, noted, "It would require more
gold than all the Saints possess upon the earth, to gather
the Saints unto Zion from all nations in the way they
have been gathering, but now the hand-cart operation has
been introduced to this people, it will bring five here to
where one has been brought heretofore."[3]

News of the handcart experiment came with great excitement to converts anxious to be brought to Zion. Franklin
D. Richards put it in understatement: "We have not had
much preaching to do to the people in the old countries
to get them started out with handcarts. . . . The hardest
part of my talking was to find the means to bring out
the many that were urgently teasing me to let them come."[4]

The handcart idea was certainly inviting to Isaac
Wardle. He had grown up without the sun in English coal
mines, his skin black with coal dust that seemed almost
permanent. At age seven he had been put to work as a
runner at the mines; at age nine he had gone under-
ground, training his eyes to darkness as he toiled from
seven in the morning until seven at night, perhaps
stripped to the waist like most boys and girls under the
age of thirteen who wore out their young bodies pulling
loads of coal. At day's end when his mother served him
supper, he was too tired to wash and often too tired to
eat, falling asleep between mouthfuls. Then, little boy that
he was, his mother washed him and put him to bed for
the night, which was never long enough. He had been
imprisoned by his social origins and lack of education,
and resistance to change was so powerful in England that
things would probably never be much different in his lifetime. So, when the missionaries found him, he responded

The skyline of Edinburgh, Scotland, has not changed much in 200 years. The message of the restored gospel would gather thousands out of Scotland, the rest of the British Isles, Scandinavia, and Europe. Nearly 3,000 of them would pull handcarts to the Great Salt Lake Valley.

PAGES 158–59 *The fourth and fifth handcart companies of 1856, under the direction of James Willie and Edward Martin respectively, left late, and snows came early in these Wyoming highlands. How they faced their challenges would affect generations to come.*

to the message of hope in this world and in a world to come. He was eighteen when he was baptized on September 23, 1853. He would join a handcart company.

In 1837 Margaret Perren Pusell had been one of the first women baptized in England, losing in her own race to the River Ribble just ten days after she heard the gospel preached in Preston at the Reverend James Fielding's church. Because great prejudice had developed against the Church, she hid the news from her husband,

Samuel, for three months, praying he would accept the gospel. But Samuel had his own secret; when he confessed to her that he had joined the Mormons, relief and joy swept over them both. Now they could share openly this gospel that had come to mean so much to them. Samuel worked in a factory, but there was never enough income for even the barest necessities. Their daughter Nellie remembered often going to bed without supper so the missionaries who chanced to call might be given

night during an especially important gathering when Wilford was going to speak, an angry, noisy mob gathered around their home. When William started for the door to quiet them, Ann begged him not to go, but he answered, "Why Ann, they are people I have known all my life. They are my neighbors and I'm sure they'll listen to reason."[5] He opened the door and was seized and beaten. With such opposition, the Rowleys' financial affairs soon faltered, and the humiliating day came when they auctioned off their house, their furniture, and all their featherbeds except Ann's.

As the years passed, the Rowleys dreamed of going to Zion, but they no longer had the money to do it. In fact, the heartbreak and disgrace of losing everything finally killed William, leaving Ann a widow with seven children under the age of twelve. The dream of Zion seemed further and further away. Samuel at seven and John at nine were hired to tramp mud in the brickyards, leaving home at daylight and meeting their mother at a narrow bridge again at night so she could help them across. They would join a handcart company.

Converts like these not only accepted the handcart proposal, but they also clamored for it. The fire of emigration blazed brightly as England's poor responded more dramatically than ever could have been imagined. If they could not afford wagons, they would walk to Zion; as it turned out, some of them would even crawl, bearing the scars from torn flesh until they died. The *Millennial Star* noted, "We do not doubt that a multitude of the faithful are ready to do anything, to gather to the mountains in any way that may be opened before them, and that will best subserve the interests of the work. The sacrifices and exertions they are willing to make

something to eat. Through the years, they watched, bound by their poverty, as others around them immigrated to Zion. They would join a handcart company.

Ann and William Rowley had been members of the United Brethren, that six-hundred-member splinter from the Wesleyan faith, who met in Herefordshire and prayed for knowledge. They had heard Wilford Woodruff preach and knew he offered a priceless treasure. They had opened their spacious home for meetings, and one

Reconstructed interior of a ship in Liverpool, England. A raging storm
tossed the Thornton, carrying the Willie company helplessly northward among
the icebergs. Later the ship caught fire, but
the sailors were able to put it out.

RIGHT *Belongings were few for members of the handcart companies. They
were to bring only one change of clothing and
dispense with heavy wooden chests.*

are the constant measure of their faith."[6]

They sold family furniture, discarded precious keep-sakes, and picked through possessions to take only the bare-bone necessities needed to join the 2,012 Perpetual Emigration Fund charges who were committed to hand-carts that spring of 1856. With nearly empty hands but with hearts full of the love of God, these Saints would leave on four ships. Because of a series of unfortunate delays, however, two ships would leave late, a reality some of them may have noticed like a chill wind in their hearts. The first, the *Enoch Train,* carrying 534 passengers, did not embark until March 23; the *S. Curling* departed on April 19. These departure dates would still ensure the passengers a safe passage to the valley, but the story would be tragically different for the third and fourth

ships. The *Thornton,* whose 764 passengers, mainly English and a few Scandinavian, left May 4; the *Horizon,* heavy with 856 passengers, was not on its way until May 25. The Saints on these last two ships would become the Willie and Martin handcart companies, and the passen-gers' stories would be written in their tardy departures and a series of devastating misfortunes. Ten-year-old Nellie Pusell, who bounded onto the ship with two healthy legs, would, after her handcart experience, waddle on painful stumps that would fester and bleed the rest of her life, and after all their years of waiting, her parents, Margaret and Samuel, would never see Zion. In June, when these handcart companies should have been setting out across the plains, they were still thousands of miles away on the high seas.

For six weeks on board ship, quarters were dark, cramped, and unventilated, the passengers crammed into tight bunks and sometimes separated from their families. Patience Loader, who would later join the Martin company, complained, "I began to think we would smother to death before morning, for there was not a breath of air. I made my bed on a large box, I had a big loaf of bread in a sack. This I used for my pillow to make sure of having bread for breakfast."[7] They were thrown about in storms, made anxious as they skirted icebergs, and felt the pangs of homesickness for the land most of them would never see again. They sweated with seasickness and fainted with malnutrition, but despite the miserable conditions, they were such a model of order and discipline that most crew members came to feel like Captain Collins of the *Thornton* that he had never seen a better lot of passengers. Once in America, the emigrants crammed into trains, watched the new country slide by through tiny windows, and arrived in Iowa City ready to walk to Zion.

Wallace Stegner describes them in this way: "In all its history, the American West never saw a more unlikely band of pioneers than the four hundred–odd who were camped on the bank of the Iowa River at Iowa City. . . . They were not colorful—only improbable. Looking for the brown and resolute and weather-seasoned among them, you would have seen instead starved cheeks, pale skins, bad teeth, thin chests, all the stigmata of

unhealthy work and inadequate diet. There were more women than men, more children under fifteen than either. . . . Most of them until they were herded from their crowded immigrant ship and loaded into the cars and rushed to the end of the Rock Island Line and dumped here at the brink of the West had never pitched a tent, slept on the ground, cooked outdoors, built a campfire. They had not even the rudimentary skills that make frontiersmen. But as it turned out, they had some of the stuff that makes heroes."[8]

THE WILLIE COMPANY ARRIVED in Iowa City on June 26, ready to thrust into the wilderness, but they were disappointed to learn their handcarts were not yet ready. Here, their efficient organization that had so perfectly shepherded them this far had faltered, unable to respond to their sheer numbers. Three handcart companies had left before them, depleting what few supplies of seasoned lumber had been available. They would wait another nineteen days while the men cobbled together carts and the women sewed tents and cart covers. They

One great advantage of handcarts was not having to constantly drive the trains in a wide and serpentine swath for the animals to find remaining forage along the well-used trail.

RIGHT *Representative handcart at Winter Quarters, Nebraska. Handcarts were three feet wide, four feet long, and one foot deep. Each weighed about 60 pounds and carried a load of just over 100 pounds.*

would wait in the sweltering heat and thundering downpours, their sallow English skin becoming burnt by the Midwestern sun. At first, without tents, they slept out at night, the mosquitoes swarming and biting; later they contended with tents that blew over in the blustery July downpours. They prayed and sang and raised the American flag for their first Fourth of July.

While they waited, they watched the number of handcarts grow almost daily, 120 for their five hundred people, as well as five wagons, twenty-four oxen, and forty-five beef cattle and cows. Ideally, their carts should have been made of well-seasoned hickory, elm, and white oak, but instead the flimsy contraptions were built with green lumber that would later dry out and shrink.

REAKING WITH COMPLAINT, THE carts would loosen and fall apart as the pioneers headed west to drier climes. Their wheels and axles, made with little iron, would wear down, grinding against the fine sand of the Platte River valley and the ruts of the Black Mountains ahead. Of the handcarts John Chislett, a sub-captain in the Willie company, noted in his journal, "The production was a fragile structure, with nothing to recommend it but lightness."[9]

Still the people were hopeful, brimming with faith that God, whom they loved, would be with them. They signed their carts with slogans like "The Merry Mormons," laughed together in the evenings around the campfire, and organized themselves according to a set of strict rules, not only because it was the Mormon way but also to safeguard against their own greenness. As Levi Savage, another sub-captain, noted in his journal, "Our teams were very awkward and the teamsters more awkward than the oxen."[10]

Of the five hundred members of the Willie company, the third hundred were principally Scotch, the fifth were Scandinavians, and the other hundreds were mostly English. Englishman James G. Willie was the company captain, and each hundred had a sub-captain. Each hundred also had five round tents, with twenty persons to a tent; twenty handcarts, one to every five persons, and one Chicago wagon, drawn by three yoke of oxen to haul provisions and tents. Each person was limited to seventeen pounds of luggage, which amounted to a scanty, shivering allowance of bedding and clothing. To this were added such cooking utensils as the five would need, bringing the total weight to about a hundred pounds, placed on a sixty-pound cart. The lightweight carts were so flimsy that even this load strained their seams. They couldn't have carried more, even if the people as they lumbered across the plains could have hauled more.

If the people were destitute before, paring down to seventeen pounds was harrowing as they sold off possessions no one would have considered "extra" or left their paltry goods in heaps along the way. "There were many keepsakes that I wanted to take," wrote Ann Rowley, "but I couldn't. But there was one thing I didn't consider a luxury and that was my feather bed. I had hung onto that beloved item from the time of the auction in England and now clearly there was no room for it. It wouldn't be bad to walk 1300 miles if one had a featherbed to sleep on at night, but no matter how I folded it, it was too bulky. . . . But a featherbed is a featherbed and when it came to choosing between Zion and a featherbed, well it was a little too late to turn my back on Zion, so I ripped it open and emptied the feathers on the ground and used the tick to cover the supplies on the handcart."[11]

On July 16, the Willie handcart company rolled out from Iowa City amid the cheers of friends. Oh, Zion, so much closer now. Yet Eliza Hurren would learn early on just how steep the price of Zion really was. In timing that was less than fortunate, she had just given birth the day before to a baby girl, Selena, who would bawl and then whimper and then die two weeks later.

The 277 miles from Iowa City to Florence, Nebraska, would be accomplished in less than four weeks. John Chislett noted, "As we traveled along, we presented a singular, and sometimes an affecting appearance. The young and strong went along gaily with their carts, but the old people and little children were to be seen straggling a long distance in the rear. Sometimes, when the little folks had walked as far as they could, their fathers would take

Crossing the Missouri River to the western shore put the Saints in Pottawatamie lands. Handcarts were out-fitted with covers and painted with such slogans as "Merry Mormons," "Zion's Express," and "Truth Will Prevail."

them on their carts, and thus increase the load that was already becoming too heavy as the day advanced."[12]

Yet green Iowa, with its ample grasses for livestock, its trees and bushes with fruits and berries, its abundant animal life to fill a gnawing stomach, would be the easiest part of the journey, though its inhabitants were mixed in their response to the weary walkers who strained against their carts. Some would come to the prayer meetings held each evening to listen with sympathy, but others were surly. On July 20 a man on the roadside said he would come and tear the Saints' tents down if it should take fifty to accomplish it. On July 25 a sheriff came to search the wagons for a woman supposedly kidnapped and hidden away. On July 28 the immigrants were told the natives were planning to mob them as they passed. The threats were empty but familiar. Even in Britain, from their day of baptism, they had known hostility. In response, the pioneers just told the leering gentiles it was

their "determination to carry out, or obey, the commandments of God regardless of the consequences."[13]

Willie's company crossed the Missouri and arrived in steaming Florence on August 11, facing a decision. Their ship had arrived late and they had waited wearily in Iowa City, but nothing but their own enthusiasm bound them to go forward to the valley that season. A mass meeting was held to determine what should be done, whether to stay and winter somewhere in Nebraska or against all odds to push on. Among those in the debate were Iowa City Church agents William H. Kimball and George D. Grant, who knew the high mountains and surely understood the early winter blasts that could chill late travelers. Yet they encouraged the fledglings who wanted to push through to Zion. Only one voice spoke against it—Levi Savage, a seasoned frontiersman who knew the mountains as well as anyone in the Church. With tears running down his cheeks, he pled for the Saints to reconsider. They could not possibly arrive before the end of October, and the hardships would be incalculable. With their numbers of children and elderly, many would starve and die. The risk was unthinkable.

He was not only voted down, but he was also repri-manded as one who denied the power of God to deliver his people. It was one of those moments when a soul reveals itself, and Levi proved himself well. Without the least hint of resentment, he pledged to go with them, saying, "Brethren and sisters, what I have said I know to be true; but seeing you are to go forward I will go with you, will help you all I can, will work with you, will rest with you, will suffer with you, and if necessary I will die with you."[14]

Thus, after repairing carts already wearing under the strain of travel, on August 18 Willie's handcart company rolled out of Florence; Martin's company would follow seven days later. As an added precaution, before they left, they added a ninety-eight pound bag of flour to each cart, a millstone that became heavier with each mile as the pioneers strained

and bowed under the weight. The weakest parties would be the first relieved of this burden, but for all, it taxed them to the limits of endurance. Savage noted, "The flour on some carts draws very hard."[15] As days passed, Levi Savage's warnings were forgotten, but misfortune would continue to dog the handcart company, edging their experience with apprehension, a darkness that rested just beyond the bright skies of summer.

Each day they made from ten to twenty miles, drawing ever farther away from civilization into a landscape more arid and strange to their eyes. Their shoes wore thin, their hands became blistered, and their muscles ached at the end of long days of exertion. More than they could ever have anticipated, their green-lumber carts were a plague that slowed them down. The extra weight of flour broke the axles at the shoulder as "dust picked up by the loose-fitting rims of the wheels would settle in the axles and grind out the wood. Some of the travelers cut up their boots and nailed the leather to the worn axles; others pounded their tinware flat and affixed that. They had no lubricant, so they dipped into their small supply of bacon and sop to grease their wheels."[16] This only served to worsen their situation, as the lubricant attracted more sand, which ground the wheels faster. John Chislett

noted, "When a cart collapsed it was difficult for the owner to see the long line move on without him while he remained behind with a few crude tools, struggling to repair the damage."[17]

Being left behind could have also been a sweating, heart-pounding experience for these tenderfeet, for they had heard much of the Indians in Britain, and word had spread that other wagon trains had been killed that summer by the Cheyenne. On August 29, near Wood River, the worry was made palpable as they passed the remains of the Almon Babbit party, which had been massacred just four days earlier, among them a woman and a child. It was a grim duty to rebury their mutilated dead, who had been uncovered by wolves, and to burn their tattered, pathetic belongings, leaving images in the pioneers' minds to haunt their nights. They doubled their guard duty and pushed on.

Four days later they had their own disaster as they looked up to see what appeared to be a storm coming from the southwest. Soon it was accompanied by the pounding of hooves as a herd of buffalo stampeded, turning just before it reached camp. However, it ignited some hidden, primordial wild streak in their oxen, and thirty head joined the stampede. Though the men tried

Western light glows upon the North Platte River
in Wyoming. Some women were carried
across streams. Others, in the words of John Jaques,
"through rivers and creeks . . . tied up their
skirts and waded . . . like the heroines that they were."
Wallace Stegner said many would have "waded
through fire to reach the sanctuary in the mountains
and some of them almost literally did."[1]

to follow them the next morning, their footprints had become obliterated in a rain storm. In a desperate, two-day search on foot for the cattle, they found nothing, heard nothing but the whistle of wind across the prairie. The company was left to regroup.

What they had lost were the oxen that pulled their supply wagons, and they had no choice but to yoke up their beef cattle and milk cows. These, unaccustomed to the harness, jerked and pulled wildly to free themselves. In one stroke of disaster they lost their milk and beef, and the remaining broken teams could not pull the hefty wagons. Levi Savage wrote, "The Saints, recognizing the need to get on, wearily accepted another sack of flour each for their handcarts, and the thin column again moved off across the sandy plain."[18]

Progress was slow, breakdowns were frequent and exasperating, and the pioneers were pushed beyond what strength could endure. As they bowed their heads, eyes fixed, they trudged across Nebraska's five hundred miles of vast, monotonous, prairie. On dry days, they could taste the dust thrown up from the carts before them; on rainy days, they could make little headway through the mud. The elderly began to feel the life draining from them, but the strong, like Eliza Hurren's husband, James, compensated by being willing to do more than their share. James put as many as five extra sacks of flour on his cart when the emigrants added to their loads, and he gave rides to two little girls who were not able to walk. At night he took more than his quota of guard duty, so that he often started his day bleary and fatigued from a night without sleep.

On September 12, near the North Bluff Fork of the Platte River, the Willie company was overtaken by fast-moving carriages containing President Franklin D. Richards and many of the missionaries who had converted them, including George Grant, William Kimball, and Joseph Young. They were returning to Utah from their missions abroad and stopped long enough to spend an evening of encouragement and counsel, a boost badly needed, and for many a sweet reunion. Captain Willie noted, "In the evening [President Richards] gave us a stirring address with a view to build up and encourage the people, and his sentiments were seconded by a hearty

amen from time to time."[19] Whether it was to cheer the flagging Saints or from undue optimism, President Richards encouraged them at their mass meeting. John Chislett recorded his promise: "Though it might storm on our right hand and on our left, the Lord would keep open the way before us and we should get to Zion in safety."[20] Since the date was already late and they were seven hundred miles from the valley, these words were probably more cheering than accurate, but he also promised that as soon as he got to the Salt Lake Valley, he would send back relief supplies. "It was indeed a time of refreshing with the presence of the spirit of the Lord,"[21] wrote Willie.

JUST A FEW DAYS LATER, WHILE still on the Platte, they felt their first frost, and a bitter, strong wind blew down from the northwest to eat at their souls. Levi Savage's journal through the rest of September reads like a compendium of misery. September 17: "The heavy sand made our progress very slow and extremely laborious. Several were obliged to leave their carts and they with the infirmed, could scarcely get into camp." September 18: "At dinner Sister Reade . . . was missing. . . . She is not in camp and no one knows where she is." September 21: "Sister Season's little boy, two years old, died at eleven o'clock last night." September 22: "Brother Empy departed this life at half past one P.M. . . . He has been having the ague for some time past, but no one thought him dangerous." September 23: "The Saints slow in rising and getting breakfast early, notwithstanding Brother Willey's repeated order to arise at the sound of the bugle (daylight). Apparently not realizing the necessity of our making as much distance as possible in order to reach the valley before too severe cold weather, some complain of hard treatment, because we urge them along. Many hang onto wagons." September 26: "Today we traveled fourteen miles without water. Sister Ann Briant, who had been ill for sometime, but not thought dangerous, was found dead in the wagon in a sitting posture, apparently asleep." September 27: "The old appear to be failing consistently."[22]

Hunger stalked them on the trail, their ration of a

pound of flour a day inadequate to fill their gnawing stomachs. Dysentery added to the ache and weakness. The longer they stayed on the plains, the more their energy flagged and the hungrier they grew. John Jaques wrote, "You felt as if you could almost eat a rusty nail or gnaw a file. You were ten times as hungry as a hunter, yea, as ten hunters, all the long day, and every time you woke up in the night. Eating was the grand passion of the pedestrian on the plains, an insatiable passion, for we never got enough to eat."[23]

For some, the weakness from hunger and exertion gradually overtook them. In the Martin handcart company, Patience Loader's father, James, came to the day when he collapsed as he pulled the cart. Patience said, "Father, you are not able to pull the cart. You had better not try to pull. We girls can do it this afternoon." "Oh," he said, "I must not give up. . . . I want to go to the valley to shake hands with Brigham Young."[24]

That day his daughters pulled the cart, and that night Patience's sister Zilpha groaned in childbirth, delivering an infant son while her sister Tamar was put to bed with Rocky Mountain spotted fever, her face hot with disease. The company moved on, while the Loaders stoked all-night fires, a glow against the prairie darkness, to protect themselves from the roving wolves.

Two miles west of Fort Laramie, eastbound Parley P. Pratt and companions met the Willie Company. Parley recorded, "Joy seemed to beam on every countenance. The company gathered around us and I tried to address them . . . but my utterance was choked and I had to make the third trial before I could overcome my emotions."[2] Parley would never return to the West as he was murdered May 13, 1857.

Not long after, James could pull no more. "One evening when we got to camp," wrote Patience, "he had walked seventeen miles with mother helping him. He said, 'My dear girls, I am not able to get any wood to make you a fire and I feel badly about it.' . . . We laid him down on some quilts until we could get the tent up, then he was unable to raise himself and had to be carried into the tent." The next day, realizing that he was dying, Patience's mother, three sisters, and brother gathered around James, who was now too weak to utter but one sentence. Patience wrote, "He looked at us all with tears in his eyes, then he said to mother with great difficulty,

'You know I love my children.' Then he closed his eyes. These were the last words he ever said."

The Loaders put their dying father onto a bed of quilts in their handcart. Patience wrote, "That day we had a very hard journey through the sandy bluffs. It was very hard pulling so much up hill and in deep sand. The sun was scorching hot. So bad for my dear father on the top of the hill and not the least shade for him. We had to stay there all day, with very little to eat until all the company got up the hill."[25] Of James's burial, she wrote, "We had to wrap my dear father in a quilt, all we had to wrap him in. No nice casket to lay him away in comfortable, but put into the grave and the earth thrown in upon his poor body. Oh that sounded so hard I will never forget the sound of that dirt being shoveled onto my poor father's body. It seemed to me that it would break every bone in his body. It did indeed seem a great trial to have to leave our dear father behind that morning, knowing we had looked upon his sweet, smiling face for the last time on earth; but not without a hope of meeting him again on the morning of the resurrection."[26]

The Willie handcart company reached the desolate Fort Laramie at the eastern edge of Wyoming on October 1, hoping to replenish their dwindling supplies.

They took their watches and rings, their precious keepsakes to the fort to buy provisions, but the fort had no flour to sell and only a barrel or two of crackers and a bit of bacon and rice. Until then, many of the handcart pioneers may have not realized how serious their condition was. Like Emma James, they "could look toward the west and see the snowcapped mountains in the distance" and feel cheered.[27] Yet Captain Willie and Levi Savage were not so naive. Considering the distance yet to be traveled, it was clear to them that their supplies would be exhausted when they were about 350 miles from their destination. With the willingness and unanimity of the Saints, it was resolved to reduce their allowance from a pound to twelve ounces of flour per day and to make every effort to travel faster.

Ironically, in some miserable law of diminishing returns, just as more was required of them, the way grew harder. Beyond Fort Laramie and into Wyoming's Black Hills, the road became steeper, rockier, and more rutted, wreaking havoc on their fragile carts. For many, the carts became so difficult to pull that they dumped articles of clothing and bedding to be burned along the way, a sacrifice that made carts lighter but left them shivering as the nights turned from chilly to freezing. Elder Richards had left them thirty-seven buffalo robes along the Platte, and even most of those had to be surrendered as too heavy to bear.

At Independence Rock, they received word that they would not receive any aid until at least South Pass, ninety-three rugged miles away. John Chislett wrote, "Our only alternative was to still further reduce our bill of fare"[28]—this time so that working men received twelve ounces of flour, women and old men nine ounces, and children from four to eight ounces, depending on their size. The distribution was left to the sub-captains, a thankless job when all were clamoring with hunger. Their paltry portion of flour was usually made into a gruel that hardly stalled the ravenous pains of hunger. Robert

came a time, when there seemed to be no food at all. . . . I asked God's help as I always did. I got on my knees, remembering two hard sea biscuits that were still in my trunk. They had been left over from the sea voyage, they were not large, and were so hard, they couldn't be broken. Surely, that was not enough to feed eight people, but five loaves and two fishes were not enough to feed 5,000 people either, but through a miracle, Jesus had done it. So, with God's help, nothing is impossible. I found the biscuits and put them in a dutch oven and covered them with water and asked for God's blessing, then I put the lid on the pan and set it on the coals. When I took off the lid a little later, I found the pan filled with food."[30]

As they traveled up the Sweetwater River, the severity of the cold nights increased. Eliza Hurren's seventeen-year-old sister, Caroline, traveled all day and, when the camp was made, took off her apron to gather some sagebrush for fires. Sitting down to rest, she leaned against her bundle, exhausted. They found her freezing and dying and carried her into camp. She never regained consciousness.

The mountains before them were "mantled nearly to their base in snow, and tokens of a coming storm were discernible in the clouds, which each day seemed to lower around us," wrote John Chislett. The Sweetwater in their frequent crossings "was beautiful to the eye, as it rolled over its rocky bed as clear as crystal; but when we waded it time after time at each ford to get the carts, the women and the children over the beautiful stream, with its romantic surroundings . . . lost to us its beauty, and the chill which it sent through our systems drove out from our minds all holy and devout aspirations, and left a void, a sadness. . . .

"Nearly all suffered more or less at night from cold. Instead of getting up in the morning strong, refreshed,

Hurren wrote of his diet, "Potato peelings and rawhide of old handcarts were good if we could get it. I, myself, set by the campfire . . . and scraped and singed the hair off a piece of hide, some that had been taken off discarded handcarts that had been pulled through the sands hundreds of miles. It was hard but we would boil and soften them and cut them up in small pieces and put in our pockets to chew on the road the next day."[29]

Ann Rowley noted, "It hurt me to see my children go hungry. I watched as they cut the loose rawhide from the cart wheels, roast off the hair and chew the hide. There

vigorous, and prepared for the hardships of another day of toil, the poor Saints were to be seen crawling out from their tents looking haggard, benumbed, and showing an utter lack of that vitality so necessary to our success.

"Cold weather, scarcity of food, lassitude and fatigue from over-exertion, soon produced their effects. Our  old and infirm people began to droop, and they no sooner lost spirit and courage than death's stamp could be traced upon their features. Life went out as smoothly as a lamp ceases to burn when the oil is gone. At first the deaths occurred slowly and irregularly, but in a few days at more frequent intervals, until we soon thought it unusual to leave a campground without burying one or more persons.

"Death was not long confined in its ravages to the old and infirm, but the young and naturally strong were among its victims. Men who were, so to speak, as strong as lions when we started on our journey, and who had been our best supports, were compelled to succumb to the grim monster. These men were worn down by hunger, scarcity of clothing and bedding, and too much labor in helping their families." John Chislett, who was single, continued, "It was surprising to an unmarried man to witness the devotion of men to their families and to their faith, under these trying circumstances. Many a father pulled his cart, with his little children on it, until the day preceding his death. I have seen some pull their carts in the morning, give out during the day, and die before next morning." While the Donner party, in a similar hour of desperation, had turned to cannibalism, John Chislett said, "These people died with the calm faith and fortitude of martyrs. Their greatest regret seemed to be leaving their families behind them, and their bodies on the plains or mountains instead of being laid in the consecrated ground of Zion. The sorrow and mourning of the bereaved, as they saw their husbands and fathers rudely interred, were affecting in the extreme."

"Each death weakened our forces," he wrote. "In my hundred I could not raise enough men to pitch a tent when we encamped. . . . When we pitched our camp in the evening of each day, I had to lift the sick from the wagon and carry them to the fire, and in the morning carry them again on my back to the wagon."[31] Their clothes were in rags; many of their shoes were worn out, replaced by strips of burlap or canvas about their feet.

Day after day through the high country of what would become Wyoming, they marched on in misery and sorrow, trudged like zombies as the shrill wind pierced their flesh and then their bones, and their exhaustion overtook them as the sea takes a drowning man. They sat down and died by the side of the road, died raising a spoon to the mouth, died not even realizing they were that close to death. For lack of food, their oxen died too. Levi Savage recorded the plight in his journal. October 8: "This morning when we arose, we found the best ox on our train dead. In the weak state of our teams, the loss impaired us much." October 10: "Our teams are very weak." October 11: "Three of our working cows gave out and one died. The remainder of our oxen were nearly overcome."[32]

"God only can understand and realize the torture and privation, exposure, and starvation we went through,"[33] wrote John Oborn. Eating like acid at the back of their minds must have been the fear they would all perish, be nothing but a frozen death camp before they were rescued.

Then came the bleak, October morning near the fifth crossing of the Sweetwater when the cutting wind held more than cold; it was snow that came in blustery torrents. This day, too, they were issued their last ration of flour. What was left were only six scrawny beef and four hundred pounds of biscuits to provision four hundred people, and the Salt Lake Valley was still three hundred miles away. Afraid to stop, they pushed on. At noon, pausing to rest, they looked up to see something coming toward them, a most joyous sight whose timing they took as the kindness of the Lord, who had seen them through it all. It was a light express wagon driven by, among others, Joseph A. Young and Stephen Taylor. These two had been in Elder Richards's party that had passed the immigrants just weeks before. Though they had been away from home for two years on their missions, they had neither stopped to rest nor linger with loved ones in the valley but had turned around after forty-eight hours to rescue the stranded Saints. These were their own converts; they had taught them and helped to outfit them, and they would be with them in this disastrous hour.

What they brought with them was more hope than provisions, staying only long enough to tell the frozen

*Sweetwater River passes beneath Split Rock Mountain here in Wyoming. Patience Loader recorded,
"I remember well poor Brother Blair. He . . . had been one of Queen Victoria's life guards in London. . . .
He . . . put his four children on the cart. He pulled his cart alone, his wife helped by pushing behind. The poor man was so weak and worn down that he fell several times . . . [and] instead of eating his morsel of food himself he would give it to his children. . . . He pulled the cart as long as he could, then he died." [4]*

Site of the Willie Company rescue just before the turn to climb Rocky Ridge. James Hurren recorded, "Each death weakened our forces. . . . I often help[ed] to dig the grave[s] myself. In performing these sad offices I always offered up a heartfelt prayer to that God who beheld our sufferings, and begged him to . . . send us help."[5]

immigrants that a more substantial wagon team was on its way. Then they sped off to find the Martin company still somewhere east of Fort Laramie. Captain Willie wrote, "We all felt rejoiced at our timely delivery."[34] To the Willie company, the rescuers seemed "like a thunderbolt out of the clear sky," its drivers like "messengers from the courts of glory."[35]

It was Brigham Young's boldness and compassion that brought the rescuers to the Willie people in their most desperate hour. Elder Franklin D. Richards and his party arrived in Salt Lake City on October 4, the very day the Willie company were cutting their rations a second time. Until Richards gave his report, Brigham assumed that the third handcart company that had arrived in Salt Lake City just two days earlier was the last of the season. Now he heard with great alarm that two more companies of nearly twelve hundred souls were still on the

that would be apt to perish, or suffer extremely, if we do not send them assistance.

"I shall call upon the Bishops this day, I shall not wait until tomorrow, nor until the next day, for sixty good mule teams and twelve or fifteen wagons. I do not want to send oxen. I want good horses and mules. They are in this Territory, and we must have them; also twelve tons of flour and forty good teamsters, besides those that drive the teams." To underscore the gravity of the situation, he repeated some of this three times. The people would find sixty spans of mules or horses, twelve tons of flour, and enough wagons to carry the supplies to the stricken. He said it forcibly: "Your faith, religion and profession of religion will never save one soul of you in the celestial kingdom of our God, unless you carry out just such principles as I am now teaching you. Go and bring in those people now on the Plains, and attend

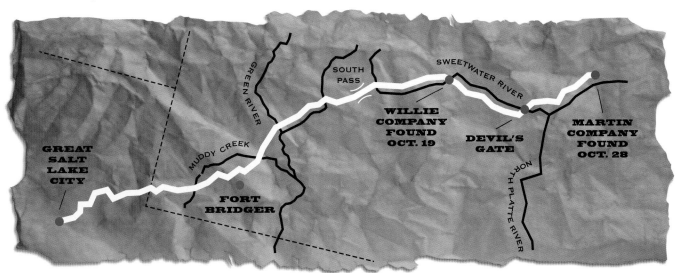

trail. Brigham called a meeting that very evening to begin rescue plans, and by the next day at that October 1856 general conference he was moved to urgency. Brigham told the Saints assembled in the Bowery, "I will now give this people the subject and the text . . . during the Conference, it is this: . . . Many of our brethren and sisters are on the Plains with handcarts, and probably many are now seven hundred miles from this place, and they must be brought here. We must send assistance to them. The text will be—to get them here!

"That is my religion: that is the dictation of the Holy Ghost that I possess, it is to save the people. . . . This is the salvation I am now seeking for, to save our brethren

strictly to those things which we call temporal, or temporal duties, otherwise your faith will be in vain."[36]

The Saints did not know the people on the plains; they had not felt their anguish or chewed on the bark of trees for relief from hunger. But they loved the Lord, and they understood something of sacrifice and compassion They, too, had dreamed of Zion and suffered for their religion, and they were bound to the handcart people in ways that went beyond mere acquaintance. Thus, their response to Brigham's call was immediate. Women stripped off their petticoats and stockings in the meeting and surrendered shawls to be packed into wagons. Even though it was time for the fall planting of the winter wheat crop and it had been a lean year in the valley, men stepped forward to the pulpit to volunteer for the mission. Among these was Ephraim Hanks, a frontiersman, who had been prepared for just such a moment. Two days before on the way back from a fishing trip, a man had appeared to him in the night and told him the handcart people were in trouble and that he needed to help.

The evening of October 6, the volunteers gathered in Brigham Young's office for counsel and priesthood blessings. The next day, the wagons were rolling out of town, already laden with provisions the bishops had collected, express wagons sent ahead to tell the Saints that help was coming. It was a remarkable feat to gather so much so quickly—twenty-five pounds from one family, ten from another, a team of horses from another—sacrifices these families would feel in the winter ahead. Not only did the people meet the subscriptions Brigham asked for the handcart pioneers, but they also beat them, and they would continue giving generously out of their own lean circumstances for the next three months as the heroic rescue effort grew in time and complexity.

THE ABILITY OF THE COMMUnity to respond with such heart and unanimity is a touching moment in Western history, but it is made even more noble when it is considered that the Saints in the valley had no idea of the extent of the immigrants' misery. The snow had not yet begun to fly, the plunging temperatures had not yet begun to freeze. No forecast could predict the violent and early winter in the high mountains, but a prophet with a gift for action could see the need and rally a people.

The rescue teams under the direction of George D. Grant and William H. Kimball made it to Fort Bridger in six days. There they stored some flour and picked up some beef. Another three days brought them to Green River, beyond where Franklin D. Richards guessed the Willie company should have been by that time. There was still no word or sign of the handcart company. No one had passed them on the trail. No one had even heard they were coming. Dan Jones wrote, "Our hearts began to ache when we reached Green River and yet no word of them."[37] Some supposed they must have stopped to winter some-

where and were ready to give up,[38] but Grant pushed on, lumbering over the South Pass, which they crossed in a snowstorm that finally stopped them on Willow Creek on October 19, the same day the advance scouts found the Willie company twenty-five miles farther.

Meanwhile, once the Willie company had been located by the advance scouts, John Chislett said, "We pursued our journey with renewed hope and after untold toil and fatigue, doubling teams frequently, going back to fetch up the straggling carts, and encouraging those who had dropped by the way to a little more exertion in

view of our soon-to-be improved condition, we finally, late at night, got all to camp—the wind howling frightfully and the snow eddying around us in fitful gusts. But we had found a good camp among the willows, and after warming and partially drying ourselves before good fires, we ate our scanty fare, paid our usual devotions to the Deity and retired to rest with hopes of coming aid."[39]

The next morning, the people awoke to a foot of snow, cattle that had widely strayed in the storm, and five more people dead. "The pitiless storm and the extra march of the previous day had been too much for their wasted

Dreary morning view into the Sweetwater valley where the Willie Company was rescued. Rocky Ridge lay before the company— five miles of lung-stinging ascent to the top. The company would hike for 25 hours before coming to relative relief at Rock Creek. Thirteen more would die there.

energies," wrote John Chislett. "We buried these five people in one grave, wrapped only in the clothing and bedding in which they died. We had no materials with which to make coffins, and even if we had, we could not have spared time to make them, for it required all the efforts of the healthy few who had remained to perform the ordinary camp duties and to look after the sick." In James Hurren's hundred, only he and one other man had enough strength to care for the rest. With these appalling conditions making travel nearly impossible, the camp decided to remain where they were and to send Captain Willie and Joseph Elder out into the whirling, biting snow to find the rescue teams.

It was a fortunate decision, for the rescue teams, still unaware how far away the immigrants were, would have stayed at Willow Creek to wait out the pounding storm. But on the evening of October 20, a frozen Captain Willie and Joseph Elder stumbled into camp on worn-out mules, having plodded through a blinding blizzard, with a grim announcement. The Willie company would perish in the snow if they did not receive help immediately.

Now the rescue teams were propelled to action, hitching up despite the snow to rescue their stranded friends. When they found the Willie company, they expected to find misery, but the cries of starving children and the gaunt desperation of parents who had no way to help them were more than they had conceived, enough to "stir the feelings of the hardest heart."[40] The relief for the handcart pioneers was described by John Chislett: "The news ran through the camp like wildfire, and all who were able to leave their beds turned out enmasse to see them. A few strong men wept till tears ran freely down their furrowed and sunburnt cheeks, and little children partook of the joy . . . and fairly danced around with gladness. Restraint was set aside in the general rejoicing, and as the brethren entered our camp the sisters fell upon them and deluged them with kisses. . . . That evening, for the first time in quite a period, the songs of Zion were to be heard in the camp, and peals of laughter issued from the little knots of people as they chatted around the fires. The change seemed almost miraculous, so sudden was it from grave to gay, from sorrow to gladness, from mourning to rejoicing. With the cravings of hunger satisfied, and with hearts filled with gratitude to God and our good brethren, we all united in prayer and then retired to rest."[41] Misery had not eaten away at their faith.

Had Lucy Ward known it, she would have had special reason to rejoice that night. She had come to New York City in the fall of 1855 and spent the winter working in a millinery shop, where she had obtained a green veil. James Barnett Cole, one of the rescuers, had had a dream he would meet his future wife with the stranded Saints and would know her because she would be wearing a fur cap tied with a green veil to keep it from blowing away. He told his dream to William Kimball, who scoffed, "We will see no beautiful girl with a fur cap and a green veil in these frozen Saints." The day of delivery, Kimball caught sight of Lucy and said to Cole, "Brother Jim, there is your dream girl." They were married at Fort Bridger before they ever reached the valley.[42]

However much excitement they caused, twenty or so wagons full of food and clothing and a refreshed group of young men did not mark the end of the ordeal.

Besides, more than half of them, led by George D. Grant, went on to help the Martin company, while William Kimball stayed behind to aid the Willie company. For one bright, freezing day, they moved on, camping at the Sweetwater bottoms; then, on October 23, they awoke to what many of them would later describe as the worst day of their lives. This was the ascent of the highest point on the Mormon Trail, at 7,300 feet, the killer known as Rocky Ridge. This windswept backbone of ragged rock was a rite of passage. Those who had the physical stamina to withstand the piercing wind, the jagged rocks hidden under snow, and the debility from weeks of malnutrition would probably make it all the way to the valley. But many would fall here.

They awoke on that fateful October 23 to another biting blizzard and two more dead: John James, who had left behind every member of his family in England to come to Zion, and Eliza Philpot, who had lost her husband a few days before and now left two little girls to go on by themselves. Every death had its own story, its own wake of tragedy that would wash over the lives of those left behind, its own children who would call, "Mother, Father" to no answer.

Large rocks marred the landscape; snow drifted, hiding the trail; and the wind was pitiless, so severe it froze on contact. It was a ragtag group with thin clothes and worn shoes that started that five-mile climb, shoving, pushing their

*I*n the last mile up Rocky Ridge, the clouds and rocks seem to reflect each other in unpredictable patterns of challenge and surprise. A remnant of the original trail can still be seen here. It seemed that those who survived the ordeal of Rocky Ridge generally could make it the final 300 miles to the Great Salt Lake Valley.

carts. Many finally sat down by the side of the road, unable to push any farther through the knee-deep snow. In all it would be a seventeen-mile, twenty-five-hour, nonstop, killing journey to Rock Creek. John Chislett was assigned to bring up the rear to help the stragglers. He said, "By all hands getting to one cart we could travel; so we moved one of the carts a few rods, and then went back and brought up the other. They worked this way, until we had six carts, not one of which could be moved by the parties owning it."[43] The wagons were so overloaded with the sick and debilitated that Levi Savage "was fearful some would smother."[44]

The leaders warned the weary to keep moving, to get up when they'd fallen, to never rest. Levi Savage found one man in a heap by the side of the road and slapped him hard in the face, a plot to keep him alive. It so infuriated the man that he got up and chased Levi up the trail and was thus spared freezing to death.

Beyond the summit was Strawberry Creek, which was frozen over. John Chislett, who had the supply wagons with the tents, said, "We started one team to cross, but the oxen broke through the ice and would not go over. No amount of shouting and whipping would induce them to stir an inch. We were afraid to try the other teams for even should they cross we could not leave the one in the creek and go on." Chislett went on foot to get help, finally seeing the fires of the camp about 11:00 P.M., and by midnight he was joined by some boys from the valley to go back to rescue the many who had fallen by the wayside and to retrieve the supply wagon stuck in the creek.

In those trying hours when minds and hearts were pushed to the limits of endurance, the immigrants showed staggering amounts of courage and compassion. Considered social outcasts in class-conscious Britain, they now showed themselves as the truly noble and great. They were children of a God who loved them, knew them, and endowed them with his attributes in embryo, and in this very worst of circumstances they did not disappoint Him.

Eleven-year-old James Kirkwood was responsible for getting his four-year-old brother Joseph to Rock Creek that night, carrying the boy on his back as he slogged through the snow on frozen feet. His widowed mother

could not help, for she, with his brother Robert, were pulling their crippled, nineteen-year-old brother Thomas and their meager belongings on a cart that barely budged. Faithful to his charge and dutiful to the end, James staggered into camp with his precious load, put Joseph down by the fire, and then died of exposure and overexertion.

Archibald McPhail was the captain of a tent whose responsibility included two older women who often lagged behind the rest of the group. When one of them did not arrive soon after the other, he went to search for her and finally found her sitting on the other side of the frozen Strawberry Creek, refusing to cross, saying she would stay there and die. She had given up, but he wouldn't. He crossed the creek, picked her up, and carried her back across. Unfortunately, their combined weight broke the ice, and he sank to his waist in the shockingly icy water. By the time they had made it to camp, his clothing was frozen, and he was shaking with chills. The tent he lay down in was only a handcart cover, which he gave up trying to keep in place after the gale had blown it down three times. Having saved the life of his charge, he would die in Echo Canyon.

Else Nielsen could not care for her six-year-old son Niels because she had to pull her husband, whose feet were badly frozen. Instead, nine-year-old Bodil Mortensen, a Danish child who was planning to meet her older sister in the valley, was put in charge. She labored to get Niels to camp, then began gathering sagebrush to build a fire. Exhausted and frozen, she leaned against a cart wheel and died with the sagebrush still in hand.

It was an hour when sacrifice was called for and sacrifice was delivered, when the basest in human nature could have triumphed as each person scrambled for survival. Instead, at the peril of life, the handcart pioneers considered their fellows. As the blizzard raged that night, John Linford's wife took off her own flannel petticoat and tucked it around him. It was not enough to save him, and he died before morning.

Young Elizabeth Cunningham collapsed before reaching camp, and the stricken family, believing she had died, wrapped her in a blanket and left her by the side of the road, thinking to come back to bury her. Yet that night her frantic mother could not rest with her child out in the cold and, despite the protests of friends, decided to go back for her. When her body was brought in, some hot water spilled on her foot, and it quivered. Life! They worked on her until she revived.

For all it was an intolerable night; many of the tents were not even pitched because they were in wagons stuck along the trail. Levi Savage spoke for many who spent the night working to save others: "By the time I got them as comfortably situated as circumstances would admit (which was not very comfortable), day was dawning. I had not shut my eyes for sleep, nor lain down."[45]

That morning John Chislett had the

unhappy task of gathering the dead, "thirteen corpses, all stiffly frozen." They were buried in the clothes they had died in, laid in a shallow, common grave. James Hurren held out his eight-year-old Mary to see her playmate in the arms of death. The bodies were covered with willows, then earth and rocks to keep the wolves from disturbing them. Two who helped dig the graves died that day and were buried nearby.

From Willow Creek (or Rock Creek, as it is now called), the way was easier. On October 25 they approached South Pass, where they met Reddick Allred, who had seven fresh teams and provision wagons. At Green River, ten more wagons came to rescue them. By the time they had left Fort Bridger, about fifty wagons were assisting them, and they were able to discard their handcarts and ride. They arrived in Salt Lake City on a sunny November 9, a different group than had left England, marked and transformed by suffering. Franklin D. Richards, who in his absence during his three missions to England had lost all three of his children and knew something of suffering himself, met them at the mouth of the canyon with open arms.

Without ever knowing firsthand of the violence of the

The men with supply wagons were cautioned not to pass out the provisions too freely, as gorging with food would be unhealthy for those of the company who had been starving.

LEFT *When the rescuers arrived, Little Mary Hurren later wrote, "I could hear the squeaking of the wagons as they came through the snow before I could see them."[6] Even the men wept.*

storms that racked the souls of the handcart Saints, Brigham Young had organized a monumental rescue. We learn something of his feelings in a speech he made in the Tabernacle on November 2: "We can return home and sit down and warm our feet before the fire, and can eat our bread and butter, etc., but my mind is yonder in the snow, where those immigrating Saints are, and my mind has been with them ever since I had the report of their start from Winter Quarters. . . . I cannot talk about anything, I cannot go out or come in, but what in every minute or two minutes my mind reverts to them; and the questions—whereabouts are my brethren and sisters who are on the plains, and what is their condition, force themselves upon me and annoy my feelings all the time."[46]

So it was that by that first Sunday in November, express horsemen were hurrying between Fort Bridger and the valley to apprise the Brethren of the handcart pioneers' condition. More than two hundred wagons loaded with provisions and medical supplies were on the road, and each Sunday since he had learned the handcart companies were en route, Brigham had called for more volunteers, whose wagons would be on the road east the next day. The prophet would shortly write to Amasa Lyman, mission president in England, "Those who are yet out, we hope and expect at this time are all this side of the South Pass but do not certainly know."[47]

Yet the Martin handcart company was not yet "this side" of South Pass—not even close. On that October 19 when the Willie company had first felt the flakes of snow, so had the Martin company, only they were just at the last crossing of the Platte, some hundred miles east of the Willie company and still four hundred miles from the valley. "The river was wide," said John Jaques, "the current was strong, the water was exceedingly cold and up to the wagon bed in the deepest parts, and the bed of the river was covered with cobble stones."[48] In the icy current that came to her armpits, Patience Loader drifted and nearly drowned, while her mother on shore was shouting, "For God's sake, some of you men help my poor girls."[49] Aaron Jackson had gone only a short way before he sank onto a sandbar in utter exhaustion.

Jackson's sister-in-law and an elder were able to get him across, but it was the last he would walk. Once the company had come to the other side, they were pelted with an angry storm of snow, hail, sand, and fierce winds, and in wet clothes they struggled to camp. Just two days earlier they had gratefully reduced their luggage allowance to ten pounds per adult and five pounds per child, burning the excess by the roadside. Now they wished they had the things they had burned.

Patience Loader recorded, "After we got out of the water we had to travel in our wet clothes . . . and our clothing was frozen on us. When we got to camp we had but very little dry clothing to put on. We had to make the best of our poor circumstances and put our trust in God our Father that we take no harm. . . . It was too late to go for wood and water. The wood was too far away. That night the ground was frozen so hard we were unable to drive any tent pins in. As the tent was wet, when we had taken it down in the morning it was somewhat frozen. So we stretched it open the best we could and got in under it."[50]

In their sorry camp Aaron Jackson could no longer swallow the scant dinner his Elizabeth had prepared. At midnight when Josiah Rogerson went to stand guard, he stumbled over Jackson's stiff legs and stooped down to touch his face. He later wrote, "I found that he was dead with his exhausted wife and little ones by his side all sound asleep. . . . I did not wake his wife."[51] But Elizabeth awoke later, reached over to touch Aaron, and realized he was dead. She called out but no one heard, and she stayed by his frozen corpse through the tedious hours of that endless night. "There was nothing with which to produce a light or kindle a fire," she wrote, "Of

Devil's Gate, with the bright, cold Sweetwater flowing through it, was a major landmark on the trail west. Here, just after the Martin Company had decided to try to move on, a blizzard loaded 18 inches of snow on the ground, and the temperature plunged to 11 degrees below zero.

course I could not sleep. I could only watch, wait and pray for the dawn."[52] Because the ground was too frozen to dig, he was laid that morning in the snow with twelve others.

The next day they wallowed in snow, but they dared not stop. Three more days of snow brought them to a halt. Here, with their flour rations falling to four ounces a day, they stopped with the futile hope that the snow had been only the foretaste of winter and would soon stop. By this point those who remained were so emaciated, their strength spent, that no one was left to raise the poles and pitch the tents. "We camped out with nothing but the vault of heaven for a roof, and the stars for companions," remembered Elizabeth. "The snow lay several inches deep upon the ground. The night was bitterly cold. I sat down on a rock with one child in my lap and one on each side of me. In that condition I remained until morning."

The conditions had acted like a corrosive upon her soul. "It will be readily perceived," she said, "that under such adverse circumstances I had become despondent. I was six or seven thousand miles from my native land in a wild, rocky mountain country, in a destitute condition, the ground covered with snow, the waters covered with ice, and I with three fatherless children with scarcely nothing to protect them from the merciless storms." That night, at the end of her strength and will, she had what she called a "stunning revelation." "In my dream," she wrote, "my husband stood by me

and said—'Cheer up, Elizabeth, deliverance is at hand.'"[53] The next day, October 28, the express team found them.

It was at this Spartan, snow-encrusted Red Buttes camp that a sister happened to look westward and screamed, "I see them coming. I see them coming. Surely they are angels from heaven!"[54] It was Joseph A. Young, Abel Garr, and Dan Jones[55] who had been sent on from Devil's Gate, where Grant's rescue team, running out of feed for their horses, was holed up and awaiting further news about the Martin company.

"We are saved," the first woman to see the express team shouted, waving her shawl. For their part, the express riders felt overcome by helplessness. Jones lamented,

Leaving Devil's Gate, the Martin company had to cross the bitterly cold, ice-choked Sweetwater and move their camp three miles away to Martin's Cove. When Patience Loader saw the river with its ice, she said, "I could not keep my tears back."

"There were two of us and hundreds needing help. What could we do?"[56] Between the Martin handcart company and the nearby Hodgett wagon train, fifty-six had died since the faithful immigrants had crossed the Platte, and more would die that very evening.

Patience Loader remembered tears streaming down Joseph Young's face as he came to her fire and asked, "How many are dead and how many are still living?"[57] Since provisions were coming, the job for now was to give everyone a pound of flour, kill any remaining cattle for food, and get the camp, almost overcome with despondency, moving. Brigham Young had sent counsel that their only salvation was to come toward the valley, if

only a few miles a day. So they began, plodding like sleepwalkers in a nightmare, their company spread out for three or four miles as they inched toward help. Jones and Garr rode another fifteen miles east to alert the Hunt wagon train that relief was close, then rode like the wind for Devil's Gate and the rescue team.

It was the last day of October when Grant's rescue team finally met the Martin company at Greasewood Creek. Grant would never forget the sight: "You can imagine between 500 and 600 men, women and children, worn down by drawing handcarts through snow and mud, fainting by the wayside; falling chilled by the cold; children crying, their limbs stiffened by the cold, their feet

bleeding, and some of them bare to snow and frost. The sight is almost too much for the stoutest of us. Our company is too small to help much. It is only a drop in a bucket, as it were in comparison with what is needed. I think not over one third of Martin's company is able to walk. . . . Some of them have good courage and are in good spirits, but a great many are like little children, and do not help themselves much more, nor realize what is before them. Brother Charles Decker has now traveled this road the forty-ninth time and he says he has never before seen so much snow on the Sweetwater at any season of the year."[58]

The Martin company along with the Hunt and Hodgett wagon trains arrived at Devil's Gate on November 2, about twelve hundred people hoping to find shelter in three or four trader's cabins and a log stockade. The next day they held a council to discuss whether to winter there or push on to Salt Lake City. Both choices were formidable. Feeding a small city of people in the wolf-haunted, wild mountains was impossible, but, to many, going on seemed worse. They decided to move on, just as another northern blizzard lashed

the country. As the gale blew, temperatures plunged to eleven degrees below zero, snow piled in some places to eighteen inches, and fewer than a third of the people could crowd into the stockade.

Puzzled about why no help had yet arrived from the valley, Captain Grant sent the unflagging Joseph A. Young and Abel Garr back as couriers to Salt Lake City. After several days of waiting for help, living on the hide from dead cattle or broth made from boiled wagon-tongue cover, the company decided to move their camp three miles away into a cove for better shelter from the relentless storms. Yet this entailed crossing the Sweetwater, at this point only about two feet deep but excruciating in its bitter temperatures, pain slicing

through the body on contact. Ice choked the water, the bottom of the river was muddy, and the river was an appalling 90 to 120 feet across.

Patience Loader, describing her feelings when she saw the river that must be crossed, wrote, "I could not keep my tears back."[60] She also noted, "When the handcart arrived at the bank of the river, one of these men who was much worn down, asked in a plaintive tone, Have we got to go through there? On being answered yes, he was so much affected that he was completely overcome. That was the last strain. His fortitude and manhood gave way. He exclaimed, 'Oh dear! I can't go through that,' and he burst into tears. His wife, who was by his side, had the stouter heart of the two at that juncture, and she said soothingly, 'Don't cry, Jimmy. I'll pull the cart for you.'"[60]

In the end, few of the wearied immigrants pulled their carts that day. Four young men of the rescue party, C. Allen Huntington, George W. Grant, David P. Kimball, and Stephen W. Taylor spent their day in the freezing water, carrying people and hauling carts across. Coming to the shore on one side of the river meant only that they would turn around and plunge in again, endlessly crossing the pitiless water to spare the others.

Historians claim that these boys (three of whom were still in their teens) suffered ever after from the effects of their heroism, and all died young.

At Martin's Cove, the company lingered five hungry days, looking anxiously every evening for help from the valley. When the weather broke, they moved on, still waiting. Where were the backup rescue teams?

John Jaques wrote, "Now people hesitated when the morning bugle blew. It would be better, they said to stay here and die comfortably than push forward into the ice-bound mountains. Brigham Young had never heard of their plight and even God was far away.

"So the company moved slowly, not all together as they had at first, but strung out in a long line that made . . . a trailing black line in the snow. No one sang, no one

talked. Folks just pushed along at their own pace and tried not to think of how the days and nights stretched into weeks and months before the last of them found a long sleep in a trench of snow.

"And one evening, just before sunset, a strange quiver like a thrill of hopefulness was communicated down the wavering line. Coming toward the train was a lone man leading two horses with great pieces of buffalo hung on each side of the animals." This was the dogged Ephraim Hanks, on the Lord's errand to save the handcart pioneers. He passed out hunks of buffalo to the ravenous, explaining, "I wouldn't ever have expected to meet a buffalo. But you folks needed meat, and he was put in my way." He went on, "I do know when a body needs the Lord, needs something the Lord can do for him so bad that there isn't any other out—that is the time the Lord will show His face or His voice."[61] In addition to feeding the famished, Eph became their rough, frontier surgeon, for many of the Saints were carrying frozen limbs that endangered their lives.

He wrote, "Many such I washed with water and castile soap, until the frozen parts would fall off, after which I would sever the shreds of flesh

from the remaining portions of the limbs with my scissors. Some of the emigrants lost toes, others fingers, and again others whole hands and feet."[62]

TWO MORE DAYS OF TRAVEL brought them to the much-delayed wagon teams, and later they came upon reinforcements. Wallace Stegner notes, "A hundred years away in time, and from a position of soft contemporary ease, it is hard to imagine that road and the emotions of rescue, the dazed joy of being snatched from the very edge of a snowdrift grave, and then the agony of being forced to put out more effort when the whole spirit cries to give up and be taken care of. It is hard to feel how hope that has been crushed little by little, day by day, can come back like feeling returning to a numbed limb. It is hard even to imagine the hardship that rescue entailed—the jolting, racking, freezing, grief, numbed, drained and exhausted three hundred miles through the snow to sanctuary."[63]

On November 30, three weeks after the Willie company had arrived, the Martin company finally entered the Salt Lake Valley, rolling past a throng of Saints and stopping at the tithing offices. Between the Willie and Martin handcart companies, some two hundred people lay dead along the trail, their bones scattered by wolves before spring.

Some years later in a Sunday School class, "the subject under discussion was the ill-fated handcart company that had suffered so terribly in the snow of 1856. Some sharp criticism of the church and its leaders was being indulged in for permitting any company of converts to venture across the plains with no more supplies or protection than a handcart caravan afforded.

"One old man in the corner sat silent and listened as long as he could stand it, then he arose and said things that no person who heard him will ever forget. His face was white with emotion, yet he spoke calmly, deliberately, but with great earnestness and sincerity. He said in substance, I ask you to stop this criticism. You are discussing a matter you know nothing about. Cold historic facts mean nothing here for they give no proper interpretation of the questions involved. Mistake to send the handcart company out so late in the season? Yes! But I was in that company and my wife was in it, and Sister Nellie Unthank whom you have cited here was there too. We suffered beyond anything you can imagine and many died of exposure and starvation, but did you ever hear a survivor of that company utter a word of criticism? No one of that company ever apostatized or left the church because every one of us came through with the absolute knowledge that God lives for we became acquainted with Him in our extremities.

"I have pulled my handcart when I was so weak and weary from illness and lack of food that I could hardly put one foot ahead of the other. I have looked ahead and seen a patch of sand or a hill slope and I have said, 'I can go only that far and there I must give up, for I cannot pull the load through it.' I have gone on to that sand and when I reached it the cart began pushing me! I have looked back many times to see who was pushing my cart, but my eyes saw no one. I knew then that the Angels of God were there.

"Was I sorry that I chose to come by handcart? No! Neither then nor any minute of my life since. The price we paid to become acquainted with God was a privilege to pay and I am thankful that I was privileged to come in the Martin Handcart Company."[64]

Trail remnant in Wyoming highlands. The Martin
Company's desperate trek ended on a
hopeful note as an infant was born to a weary mother
in Echo Canyon. A member of the rescue
party gave his temple garments for the baby to be wrapped
in against the cold, and the infant was giv-
en the name "Echo." Both mother and child survived.
Despite the Willie and Martin disaster, some
pioneers continued to come in handcarts until 1860.

Six

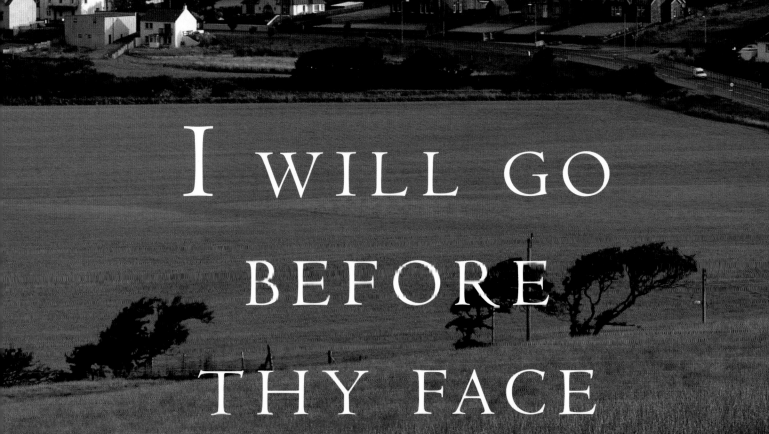

I WILL GO
BEFORE
THY FACE

HE PICTURE COULDN'T BE MORE TYPICALLY AMERICAN, a scene right off a movie set. Women in gingham dresses with their curls hidden under sunbonnets. Wagons rolling west toward a new home, their drivers scanning the horizon for Indians. Barefoot children scrambling to keep up after they'd fallen behind while picking currants. Only, for thousands of pioneers, walking that golden trail to Zion from 1847 to 1869, America was a wild, strange place, and they babbled at each other in accents decidedly foreign. Augusta Stevens of Copenhagen, walking on aching feet across the wilderness, thought how her elderly parents could never endure such a journey, and she would never see them again. "I had my sobs and cries and pangs of sorrow," she later said. "What comfort it would have been to me if I could have been able to speak or understand the American language in this new land of America."[1]

They were coming to Zion because missionaries had come to them, fanning across Europe to find the pure in heart. In 1849 Erastus Snow had left his family in Utah in two rude huts, one of adobe, the other of logs, with wagon-boxes drawn up alongside for sleeping, to open a mission in Denmark. He had found a land lulled to apathy, numbed by the established religion. Church-going had gone out of style. In the city, the ministers preached to scant audiences of eight to ten in the most popular churches, and Sunday had become the day for brilliant

balls and crowded theaters. In the villages, where cobblers and weavers labored under thatched roofs, the church was eager to accept their required tithes. Indeed, in Sweden, "everyone was born a legal member of the state church, paid it an automatic tithe, and could separate from it only by formal application."[2] Even the distribution of scriptures was under the thumb of the clergy. "We sometimes may hunt whole neighborhoods over and not find a copy of the Scriptures, except, perhaps, in church, or with a priest,"[3] the missionaries reported.

A natural hunger in the people for spiritual things had gone too long unfilled, and when Erastus Snow and his three companions came to Scandinavia, they found

*S*torm gathers around small church on the Benbane Head of the northern coast of Ireland. The preaching of Mormon missionaries in Europe raised the ministers' ire. One in Denmark asked the king to take steps to stop "that awful delusion, Mormonism." The king answered that he would consider the matter for "it had been upon his mind a long time."[1]

PAGES 198–99 *Ailsa Craig rises like a giant tooth in the ocean beyond the village of Ballantrae, Scotland. Saints who lived in charming towns like this across Britain and Scandinavia could think only of a valley far away in the American West—their Zion. For most, when they left home, they would never see it again.*

an eager audience—and the opposition to match it. Elder John Forsgren was banished from Sweden complete with a fully-paid, one-way ticket to America on a steamer. In Norway, the entire missionary force was sent to prison and subsisted for months on bread and water. In Denmark it became a common saying that to join the Mormon Church was to have one's windows broken. Hans Peter Jensen had to flee from a mob that stormed his cottage, ripped the tiles from his roof, and tore up the place. Peasant girls held stones in their skirts to pelt the elders, chanting, "Call on your God now and see if he will help you."[4]

Stones or not, the gospel spread like a fire on a field of dry brush through the country, even though at no time were there more than four American-born missionaries in the work. Ardent young men were baptized one day and left on missions the next, stumping the countryside, meeting around warm fires to give the good news. Hans Christensen, who herded sheep and courted his employer's daughter, lost both his job and his sweetheart in one day when at twenty-one he joined the Mormons. Although, forced to leave home in disgrace, he sold his ewe lamb and clothes chest and became a missionary, confident the Lord would provide.[5]

The ministers and local officials sometimes conspired to stop the "Mormon plague." Yet "if standing up was

construed as preaching, they preached sitting down; if religious services were forbidden in homes, they held 'conversations'; if after imprisonment or court examination in one place they agreed not to proselyte, they went on to another and sent fresh laymen in their stead who had made no such promise. . . . A shoemaker stuffed Mormon tracts into his customers' shoes; a tailor sermonized as he sewed. They baptized by night along river banks and on the seashore."[6]

To be baptized was also to catch the fever of emigration, the Zion longing. "Everywhere among the Saints," wrote Christian A. Madsen in 1862, "the next year's emigration is almost their every thought. This circumscribes their prayers, their anxieties, and their exertions."[7] Some could afford the $75 to $100 it cost to emigrate; others sold everything they had to make the journey. "Anna Widtsoe, widow of a school master in Trondhjem, Norway auctioned the family library . . . ; Hans Zobell, weaver, sold his Danish cottage for 400 *kroner* [$100] . . . and Andrew M. Israelsen, as a boy of seven, remembered the heavy red box of silver coins his parents received when they sold their little farm in Norway."[8]

Selling every trifle still did not raise enough money for the emigration of many. As lush fruit may sometimes grow from dry ground, this financial need nurtured one of the most remarkable and ennobling features of the gathering. People reached into the corners of their pockets and paid for each other to go to Zion, even if it meant giving up all they had. Before Hans Rasmussen emigrated in 1856, he paid a tithe of 700 *rigsdaler*, contributed 1,400 *rigsdaler* to the emigration fund, and paid the passage for another thirty converts. Then, caught in early snowstorms in Wyoming, he lost everything but his life and arrived in the Salt Lake

Valley penniless. Jens Andersen of Veddum, Aalborg, helped at least sixty of his fellow Saints emigrate but never made it to Zion himself, meeting death on the North Sea in 1862. J. C. Nielsen, writing from St. Louis in 1855, urged would-be emigrants not to take so many chests of clothing, most of which would have to be discarded at Mormon Grove anyway. Far better, he said, to use that money to pay the passage for another soul. The emigrants would need more patience than baggage.[9]

The Perpetual Emigration Fund, which loaned money to the Zion-bound convert, was fueled by the contributions of Church members, the prepayment of fares by emigrants, and the prepayment of fares by relatives and friends already in Utah. So the fund would not be exhausted, loans had to be repaid and contributions had to be constant. Thus, one of the callings of the missionaries in Scandinavia and throughout Europe was to collect for the PEF. And if giving in their homeland hadn't been enough, even after the emigrants arrived in Utah, they continued to sacrifice their financial resources for those who had not yet come.

Once in Utah, for instance, Hans Zobell could not trade his wheat and molasses for money for a ticket from Sweden for his mother-in-law, so he went to work for the winter on the railroad to earn the fare. Every town had a fund to help bring the European Saints to Zion; such funds were known as the "Ephraim Fund," the "Provo Fund," or the "Moroni Fund." In Ephraim, Utah, Sarah Ann Peterson urged the Women's Relief Society to donate the eggs their hens laid on Sunday, and thereafter everyone claimed that their hens laid more eggs on Sunday than on other days.

From these tangible sacrifices, the gathering became the heartfelt effort of Saints on either side of the ocean. The journey to build Zion was not taken only once in walking the trail; it was also a journey of the heart that continued through a lifetime, felt with every consecrated effort. The coming to Zion was not just a physical effort but also a spiritual one in which the souls of the Saints were transformed through sacrifice. Their hearts became altars upon which was laid their most precious possessions, even their lives.

The sacrifice of one often became the blessing of

*S*tain-glassed window glows with rich light in the interior of the Music Hall in Liverpool, England. The Church often rented this hall, and nearly every member of the Twelve preached here to eager congregations.

RIGHT *Liverpool's Music Hall was a six-story building that lodged the entire Welsh company leaving on the* Buena Vista. *They stayed here five nights, and when they left, one wrote, "it was the biggest sight that the Liverpool people ever seen by the way they were looking at us."[2]*

another. "Well do I remember the day," John Nielsen recalled, "when the missionaries brought us the welcome news that my parents had been hoping and praying for, for eleven years. . . . It is possible that you will emigrate to Zion this year," they said. It seems that a wealthy Brother Gregerson had sold out to emigrate and was offering to pay the fare of others. When John's mother returned from the bakery he ran to tell her the news. "She uttered the word 'Really?' and with a loud and joyous scream ran to the house. I say ran, if I would say flew it would be nearer right. I remember how surprised I was to see my mother run so fast. She was 44 years old and carrying a 12–pound loaf of rye bread."[10]

The Saints' feelings were a poignant mix of anticipation and nostalgia as the converts from Scandinavia, the British Isles, and other parts of Europe made their way to Liverpool to launch into an unknown sea and a new life. Some would be leaving behind family who would never speak to them again. English Saint Eliza Goodson Jex had been told by her father, "Your death would have been preferable to your having been deceived by that wicked people."[11] Others would be sailing away from children or a wife whom they hoped to be able to send for soon. For most it would be the last time their eyes would pass over the familiar scenes of home.

Hannah T. King, who had been reared amid the antique towers of Cambridge and had learned about the gospel from her dressmaker, faced all the antagonism that flying in the face of a closely held tradition always means: "I, a member of the Church of England. My grandfather a rector in the same, my father and my mother, my family and friends. All had to be met. Could I bring the grey hairs of my parents in sorrow to the grave? Could I so lay my all upon the Altar of my God? Could I, like Abraham of old arise and go to a far country—even the wilds of America?" She went, she said, because God gave her strength, but as she stood on the deck of the *Golconda* , she said, surely with a catch in her throat, "My native land, good night."[12]

The Saints leaving Liverpool for America were usually much better off than other emigrants in every aspect of their journey—their supplies and equipment, their route, the logistics of travel—all were carefully orchestrated by a savvy and practiced Church leadership. The Saints would be accompanied on their journey by those who had taken it several times before. The organization of the gathering simply amazed observers. One of these was Charles Dickens, who climbed on board a Mormon emigrant ship, the *Amazon*, in 1863 and left this observation: "My Emigrant Ship lies broadside-on to the wharf. Two great gangways made of spars and planks connect her with the wharf; and up and down these gangways perpetually crowding to and fro and in and out like ants, are the Emigrants who are going to sail in my Emigrant Ship. Some with cabbages, some with loaves of bread, some with cheese and butter, some with milk and beer, some with boxes, beds and bundles, some with babies—nearly all with children   nearly all with brand-new tin cans for their daily allowance of water, uncomfortably suggestive of a tin flavor in the drink. To and fro, up and down, aboard and ashore, swarming here and there and everywhere, my Emigrants. . . .

"Now I have seen emigrant ships before this day in June. And these people are so strikingly different from all other people in like circumstances whom I have ever seen, that I wonder aloud, 'What would a stranger suppose these emigrants to be!'

"The vigilant bright face of the weather-browned captain of the *Amazon* is at my shoulder, and he says, 'What indeed! The most of these came aboard yesterday evening. They came from various parts of England in small parties that had never seen one another before. Yet they had not been a couple of hours on board, when they established their own police, made their own

regulations, and set their own watches [guards] at all the hatchways. Before nine o'clock, the ship was as orderly and as quiet as a man-of-war.'

"... I went between-decks, where the families with children swarmed in the dark, where unavoidable confusion had been caused by the last arrivals, and where the confusion was increased by the little preparations for dinner that were going on in each group. A few women here and there, had got lost, and were laughing at it, and asking their way to their own people, or out on deck again. A few of the poor children were crying; but otherwise the universal cheerfulness was amazing. 'We shall shake down by tomorrow.' 'We shall come all right in a day or so.' 'We shall have more light at sea.' Such phrases I heard everywhere, as I groped my way among chests and barrels and beams and unstowed cargo."[13]

Despite the order and camaraderie that made the passage on a Mormon emigrant ship bearable, the sea was unsteady, and the nausea worse than could have been foreseen. Singing on deck was interspersed with white-fingered clutching at the beams for support. Jean Rio Griffiths Baker recorded her experience: "Jan. 12. Sunday. Meeting on deck in the afternoon, spent the evening in singing. Jan. 13. Provisions served out for a week. Laughed heartily at our supply of oatmeal, 70 pounds! Jan. 15. The wind has been very high the last four days but against us. The ship rolls as badly as if she were off the North Finland in a gale and that is no joke, as I well know. Jan. 23. Shift of wind in our favor. At 10: A.M. The tug hauled us out of the Mersey river into the Irish Sea. At 6 P.M. The wind turned dead against us. More than half of the passengers sick, and we who have escaped are obliged to hold onto anything that comes in our way in order to keep on our feet.... Jan. 25. We have had a dreadful night; the ship has seemed as if she really

Light bursts for a moment through a storm at the Albert Docks on the River Mersey at Liverpool Harbor in England. From this place nearly all of the converts from the British Isles and Europe sailed to the United States. The trail to Zion, like the crossing of the Sinai, would be a crucible of refinement for the Lord's people.

must turn over several times. Some of the passengers terribly frightened, but as for myself, the sea has never had any terror for me at any time. One of the sisters delivered of a fine healthy boy this A.M. Jan. 30. . . . The wind has not advanced us twenty miles for the past six days. Jan. 31. . . . My dear little Josiah continues very weak, but is not, I think, any worse than when we left home. Oh how I pray that the sea may return his health."

WHILE SHE PRAYED, THE ship pulled out of the Irish Sea and into the Atlantic. "Feb. 2. . . . Cooked our last piece of fresh meat this day. . . . Feb. 6 Almost a dead calm the last two days. The folks at home, I suppose, are sitting by a good fire while we are on the deck enjoying the view of a smooth sea in warm sunshine. Feb. 14. . . . I can hardly describe the beauty of this night—the moon nearly full, with the deep blue sky studded with stars, the reflection of which makes the sea appear like an immense sea of diamonds. And here we are walking the deck at nine o'clock in the evening without shawls or bonnets. What a contrast from this day three weeks ago when we were shivering between decks and not able to keep on our feet without holding fast to something or other. If we managed to get on the upper deck the first salute we got was a great lump of water in the face.

Well, I have seen the mighty deep in its anger with our ship nearly on its beam end, and I have seen it as now, under a cloudless sky and scarcely a ripple on its surface. I know not which I admire most."

Placid days for Jean were not to last on board the ship: "Feb. 22. At half past 5 P.M. my little Josiah breathed his last. He had sank rapidly since last Tuesday, when he practically lost his speech. I did not think his death was so near, though when witnessing his sufferings, I prayed that the Lord would shorten them. He has done so, and my much beloved child is in the land of the spirits awaiting the morning of Resurrection. . . . The Captain has given me permission to retain his little body until tomorrow, when it will be committed to the deep nearly one thousand miles from land, there to remain until the word goes forth for the sea to give up its dead. Then shall I have my child again, and with those others who have gone before him, to present before the Lord, never again to be separated. I do feel this trial to be a severe one. I had hoped to be able to take all my family safely through to the city atop the mountains. . . . Feb. 23. Sunday. The body of my dear little boy is removed to a snug little cabin under the forecastle, where the male adults of my family have watched it all night. The second mate with the assistance of Uncle Bateman have sewn up the body of the dear little fellow ready for burial. At eleven o'clock the tolling of the ship's bell told us that the time had come that the mortal part of my dear child was to be committed to the deep. . . . But the Lord has answered my prayer in one thing—that if it was not His will to spare my boy to reach his destined land with us, that He would take him while at sea, for I would much rather leave him at sea than alone in a strange land."

As if nature mourned with Jean, a storm began crashing upon the boat with a fury that again terrorized the emigrants and sent them nauseated to dark, tight beds below. "March 2. Sunday. The last three days have been a succession of exceedingly heavy squalls. . . . It was awful, yet grand to look at the sea. I could only compare it to an immense cauldron, covered with white foam, while the roaring of the wind and waves was like the bellowing of thousands of wild bulls."[14]

As unnerving as the storms at sea were for the emigrants, it was the silent, deadly creeping of disease through their ranks that truly endangered them. If a ship didn't get struck with cholera or smallpox, most of the Saints made it safely to America's shores. But some entire groups had cholera run among them, decimating their numbers like an invisible angel of death.

Cholera is a highly infectious bacterial disease carried in polluted food or water, but its cause was not known in the nineteenth century, and speculation on how to prevent and cure it ran wild. Some thought it was carried in the fumes of the air, so cities waged great campaigns to burn sulfur for purification. Lime was spread on the streets to disinfect them. Doctors tried bloodletting or burning the soles of the sufferers' feet as possible cures, remedies that usually sent the victims sooner to their deaths.

A common destination for the emigrant ship was New Orleans, where a boat would carry the passengers up the Mississippi River to St. Louis. Orson Spencer, who arrived in New Orleans as president of a company of Saints, said, "It was confidently said by officers of this steam boat, that at least fifty of so large a company would die on our passage to St. Louis"[15] of the dreaded cholera. And for some boatloads of emigrants, the grim statistics were true. In a twenty-three-day period between April 28 and May 21, 1849, 44 of the original 249 Welsh Saints from the *Buena Vista* collapsed and

died. It must have been with horror that David and Mary Phillips, who had started their journey with four children, buried three of them in three days on the Missouri River. And Margaret Francis, who was widowed on April 30, had buried her three children in as many days by May 8. "Samuel Leigh, whose wife had presented him with a new son just before reaching St. Louis, looked on helpless nine days later as both were taken from him."[16]

William Appleby, on the Missouri River at the same time as these Saints, left this all-too-vivid description of a cholera epidemic: "To add to the horrid spectacle were the graves, side by side—beds and pillows half burned up—pieces of tents, broken cups, bowls, pillows, mattresses, etc., lined as it were the banks of the river near the boat; while blankets, mattresses, beds, etc., on which

On August 13, 1852, Rebecca Winters died of cholera on Nebraska's dreary plains. William Reynolds supported that an old wagon rim he used to mark her grave. By candlelight he etched the inscription, "Rebecca Winters, aged 50 years." Of the 6,000 graves along the trail, it is one of a handful remaining.

LEFT *Rebecca's grave was forgotten until, in 1899, the Burlington Railroad was constructing a line and found the wagon rim right where the railroad was to go. In respect for the grave, they reengineered the line, making it swerve imperceptibly for miles to barely miss the grave.*

the sick had died came floating down the river."[17] During a cholera epidemic, townsfolk along the river shut up their houses and fled into the countryside, while the boat stopped daily on its journey to unload the dead.

Once the Welsh Saints from the *Buena Vista* reached Council Bluffs, as Isaac Nash said, "Nobody would come near us. We were put out on the banks of the river with our dead and suffering. Apostle George A. Smith, hearing of our arrival and of the sad condition we were in, came down to the river banks. . . . Brother Smith sent word to the people that if they would not take us in and give us shelter, the Lord would turn a scourge upon them. It was not long before teams and wagons came down and all were taken care of."[18]

Once in America, some Saints hunkered down for months or even years, working in cities or frontier towns to raise the rest of the money to continue their journey to Zion. "Next year in the valley" was their phrase of hope, their rallying cry. William and Mary Hibbert Smith and their extremely sick baby arrived penniless in New York in 1856 and secured an upstairs room in the poorest part of town. They bought a little milk for the baby and rationed it out to make it last as long as possible.

Their baby was seriously ill, and they were strangers in a strange land, friendless and without means. Day after day the father tramped the city, starting at daybreak, looking for work, and he came home at night to the bleak flat hungry and exhausted. The baby grew worse and finally refused food. Then, one night, William came home, empty-handed but with word that he had found a few days' work at the dock on the early morning shift.

That evening in their dark room, the baby was near death, and the Smiths had only a stub of a candle left. In the flickering light, they wondered whether the child or the candle would go first. They prayed that the candle would last long enough to see them through to the end. Soon they could see that the baby would outlast the candle, so they blew out the light and sat in the shadows, holding the tiny hand and listening to the breath coming shorter and shorter.

Sometime after midnight the mother said, "Now is the time." The father lit the flame, and the sad watch began again, the parents still wondering, "Would the candle outlast the baby? It was such an even race." But the quiet of the breathing became quieter still until there was only silence. The little one passed away just a few minutes before the candle flickered out. Because the job was so desperately needed, the father felt around in the room, gathered his things, and stumbled out into the night air to start on the long walk to the docks, saying he would send someone to take care of the baby.

Mary sat alone with her dead child until the light of morning began to creep across the sky. She scrubbed the room, then got out the baby's clothes—poor little things but the best she had, and clean. She washed and dressed the baby for burial. Then, spreading a diaper on the clean floor, she laid the baby on it, covered it with another diaper, and sat down to wait. "Weak from hunger and emotion, weary almost beyond endurance from the long nights and days before," the mother was swept with a wave of despair. "'Never,' she said afterward, 'in all the long years of hardship and trouble either before or after that day, have I ever been so near to desperation.'"

LATER THAT MORNING A KNOCK came on the door. Opening it, she saw two men with a little wooden box. "We have come for your dead baby," they said. They brought the plain wood box in and laid it on the floor beside the child, a box "without soft pillows, padded lining or ruffled lace to give it the softened appearance of comfort.

"The mother knelt on the floor, picked up the tiny form, held it to her heart a minute, kissed it and laid it in the box. Then the men put the lid on and nailed it down. One man picked it up and lifted it to his shoulder and started for the street. The mother reached for her bonnet and shawl intending to go along and see her child buried, but the men stopped her, not unkindly, and said, 'Oh, you can't go with us. It's a long way and we are busy and must hurry. You couldn't keep up with us, and even if you could walk that far you could never find your way back, and we couldn't bring you home.' So the mother stood in the door and watched the two men go down the street carrying the tiny box on their shoulders, until they turned the corner and were lost in the crowd. And that was the last that mother ever saw or heard of her baby."[19]

*S*ometimes the trail divided familes. Celia Taylor's
husband apostatized and took her five-year-
old Sarah to live with his mother while, heartbroken, she
prepared to go west with her handicapped
three year old son. Just before leaving, she learned that
her Sarah had been placed in a home with
strangers, and she rode 200 miles to find her. Celia
was able to bring both children to Zion.

Pioneer wagon at Scott's Bluff, Nebraska. To
add to their rather drab diets, the inventive
pioneers picked berries, wild currants, native black
currants, bullberries, and wild gooseberries
from the bushes that grew along the streams. Out of
some of these they made pies, though one
child said it would take more sugar than they had
in camp to sweeten a buffaloberry pie.

Mary Walker lived in St. Louis three years, hiring out here and there, to raise money for the journey west. "One day," she said, "I came home with about fourteen dollars which I gave to our father to help get our outfit. We always had this object in view, and I remember whenever we were tempted to make some little expenditure, father would always say, 'Remember the wagon wheels.'"[20]

THOSE WHEELS WEST TOWARD a distant mountain valley and a dream called Zion were so much a part of the thinking of the early Saints that even the separation of family members, sending one at a time as the means could manage, was common. Just to set your foot there, for a son or brother to plant a crop and call it home, for a baby bearing your name to catch its first breath in the mountain air, this ensured your family's inheritance in Zion. It was a prize worth any sacrifice. "I can die quietly without any complaint," thought the old and weak ones, "if my grandchildren and their children will grow up there." Thus trail stories abound of children traveling only with an older sibling, of fathers sent ahead willing to do anything to find a way to bring a waiting wife and children, of teenagers left to come alone when orphaned by their parents' deaths along the way. The trail sometimes made children old before their years.

B. H. Roberts, who would become president of the First Council of Seventy, was nine years old when he came with only his sixteen-year-old sister, Polly, in 1866. Their father was in England, and their mother had come to the Salt Lake Valley four years earlier, counting the days until she could see them again. For him the trail was high adventure, an unsupervised lark, dimmed only because the shoes and heavy bedding his mother had sent with a teamster from Bountiful never made it to them, and he shivered through the nights with only his sister's petticoat for a covering. Still, what a boy can make of the trail, its wildness matching an untamed wildness inside him. He lingered behind to pick yellow currants along stream banks while the wagons rolled on without him; he watched Indians from a secret place, awed and trembling with "magnificent terror" at their "immobile and solemn" faces, and with other boys he searched among the willows for swimming holes.

He later wrote, "On one occasion a night drive was necessary, and a young man was entrusted with the freight wagon team. The young teamster was unusually devoted to helping the young ladies, especially on this night, so I ran in behind the ox on the near side and climbed up on the seat that had been arranged in the front of the wagon by the regular teamsters. This seat consisted of a broad plank placed across the open head of a large barrel. The day had been hot and the hours of the journey long, and I was decidedly tired, nearly unto exhaustion. Fearing that my riding, which was 'agin' the law,' would be discovered, I slipped the broad board from the barrel head and conceived the idea of dropping down in the barrel, secure from the eyes of those who might oust me from my seat in the wagon if I were found. To my surprise, if not amazement, I discovered when I let myself down in the barrel that my feet went into about three or four inches of a sticky liquid substance which turned out to be molasses. The smarting of my chapped feet almost made me scream with pain, but I stifled it. Too tired to attempt to climb out, I remained and gradually slipped down and went to sleep doubled up in the bottom of the barrel, with such results as can well be imagined. It was daylight when I woke up and there began to be the usual camp noises of teamsters shouting to each other to be prepared to receive the incoming team driven from the prairie by night herdsmen. As I crawled out of the uncomfortable position, and with molasses dripping from my trousers, I was greeted with yells and laughter by some of the teamsters and emigrants who caught sight of me. I crept away as fast as I could to scrape off the syrup, which added to the weight and thickness of shirt and trousers, for there was no change of clothing for me, and so bedaubed I had to pass on until dusk and drying somewhat obliterated the discomfort."[21]

Falling asleep at the wrong place had greater hazards for six-year-old Arthur Parker. He had crept into the shade to rest during a morning break on a sultry June day in 1856 and had been left behind. His parents, Robert and Ann Parker, had assumed he was playing along the way with other children and did not miss him

The presence of the federal troops in the West was diminished during the Civil War, and consequently the pioneers experienced more hostility from the Indians. In September 1865, the Indians swooped into camp, wounded several pioneers, and carried away a Sister Gruntvig, her long hair flowing in the breeze. She was never found again.

If you find him alive, use this as a flag to signal us." Then, with a sinking heart, she and their other children struggled on. Out on the trail each night Ann scanned the horizon for her husband, eyes straining for the sign. Day after frightening day—nothing. Then, just at sundown on July 5, she saw a figure approaching from the east. In the last light of the setting sun she saw the glimmer of the bright, red shawl.

One of the diaries records: "Ann Parker fell in a pitiful heap upon the sand, and that night, for the first time in six nights, she slept." On July 5, Archer Walters recorded, "Brother Parker came into camp with a little boy that had been lost. Great joy through the camp. The mother's joy I cannot describe."[22] It seems the little boy, sick with illness and terror, had been found by a woodcutter who had cared for him until his father had found him.

until they stopped that afternoon to make camp in the face of a sudden thunderstorm. It was then they realized Arthur was not with them.

Who can imagine the rising panic these parents felt in the next two days as the company remained while the men searched for their son? Finally, on July 2, with no alternative, the company was ordered west. Robert Parker went back alone to continue searching for his missing child. As he was leaving, his wife pinned a red shawl around his shoulders and said words such as these: "If you find him dead, wrap him in the shawl to bury him.

Fourteen-year-old George Staples was not found nearly so soon. He had been the only one of his family to leave England, sent ahead while his parents lingered to raise money for themselves and the rest of the children. They knew it would be a long time before they could join him and that the boy would have to fend for himself, but a chance to send one of their family was not to be missed. He left in 1848 with a company of Saints and made it as far as the Sioux country, where, delirious and tormented by mountain fever, he could travel no farther. The company was perplexed about what to do for him.

Endangered by warring Sioux, they dared not tarry, but it was clear the lurching of the wagon was unbearable to the boy, who seemed only hours from death. It was the kind of dilemma faced by many during the gathering—impossible to stop and just as impossible to leave him behind. Finally, they determined that the kindest thing to do was leave him with a trapper with whom he could spend his last few hours in peace and comfort. The trapper agreed to care for him and then bury him, marking the spot with a permanent identification.

That afternoon a friendly band of Sioux greeted the trapper and noticed the sick boy. A squaw, looking at the tormented young man with tenderness, asked if she could take him. In the days that followed, she and the tribal doctor nursed him with Indian remedies, for this mountain fever that was so strange to the settlers was more common to them. The delirious boy rose in and out of consciousness, but finally the searing pain in his head and the wild expression in his eyes settled down, and he realized with some delight where he was. His loneliness and sickness were replaced by the mothering of a squaw and the attentions of a friendly people who seemed delighted to have him among them. They didn't seem to understand when he told them he had to find the white people; they simply broke camp and moved on.

As the months passed and turned into years, George enjoyed his life among the Sioux. His Indian mother made him beautiful buckskin clothing, and when the braves went on the warpath, they left him behind with the women and children, telling him to take care of the camp. He thought less and less about any other life. Then one day a group of pioneers saw him with the Sioux and carried word to the Salt Lake Valley. Not long after, a group from the valley came looking for him. Among them was a familiar and beloved face. With a wild whoop, he fell into his father's arms. James Staples had received word in England that his son had died two years before, but when he brought the family to Salt Lake he heard the story about the spotting of the white boy among the Indians and, grasping at a straw, came looking for him. "Could this be my son? Please let this be my son." It was a sweet reunion for an emotional father and son, but George's Indian mother was devastated, weeping inconsolably at the loss of her adopted boy. James took him with the promise that he would be back to visit, and four years later the promise was kept. The Indian mother greeted George with all the emotion of a mother who had been deprived of a dear sight for too long.

The European emigrants who had come from a world long civilized and tame heard sometimes exaggerated stories about the dangers of Indians along the trail. For

The prairies were gay with flowers, and one diary tells of the women gathering them and fashioning them into wreaths to decorate the lonely graves along the plains. Joseph Fish said, "My father walked counting the graves as we passed along, getting up to a little over a thousand when he gave it up."[3]

them the Indians with their feathers and war paint were the most exotic feature of an already exotic experience. William Morgan, a Welsh emigrant, riding ahead of his company to find a suitable camp, was aghast to suddenly find himself in the midst of several hundred Sioux. But the chief greeted him with "How do, Mormon good" and took him to a spot a mile and a half away to smoke a "pipe of peace."

Other encounters were not so benign. A Danish woman of thirty-five had fallen behind the last wagon with a young boy because they were driving an old, lame cow. Seeing them, an Indian warrior came along, swooped her off the ground, and started to carry her away on a white horse. She fought him desperately and managed to dismount several times until finally he dragged her along behind the horse. The struggle allowed just enough time for the boy to run, frantically, and muster help. Five armed men went to rescue the woman against the strength of eighteen hundred Sioux. With the help of an Indian interpreter, they brought the Danish woman back, but she was so terrorized that she hid for several days in the wagon under a feather bed and would not come out.

WHILE MARY MORRIS'S company were traveling along the Platte at a time when the Pawnee and Sioux were warring, they suddenly found themselves in the midst of hundreds of painted Pawnee. "I was not afraid for something seemed to testify they would not hurt us," Mary said. She gave them the little blue jacket she was wearing, and the company did not travel any farther. That night after the fires were lit, much to Mary's surprise, the Pawnee chief himself came to patrol the camp to protect them from his own band of warriors. "I sat and looked at the chief with pride and pleasure, he seemed so noble and grand," she said. "I could feel a protective power over us.

. . . We were permitted to continue our journey unmolested and unharmed and filled with gratitude to our Heavenly Father for his merciful protection."[23]

The more immediate, day-by-day hazard for the European emigrants was their own inexperience, especially with the cattle. Most of the Europeans had never seen an ox before, let alone managed one, and at the beginning of the journey the practiced captains had to go from one team to another yoking cattle for the sometimes nervous and skittish emigrants. They got hasty lessons in "geeing" and "hawing," which served well enough when the way was easy. When there was danger of running against a rock, however, or of getting a wheel locked in a tree, panic might enter the teamster's voice, and an entire wagon train would be a cacophony of "gees" and "haws" in foreign, trembling accents.

One day a partially broken steer sulked and lay down in the road, unwilling to move any farther. This was just at the summit of a steep ridge, which merged on the other side into a narrow flat. Beyond that was a twelve-foot-deep ravine with vertical sides. The father in the next wagon handed the whip to his little boy, who was dressed in a calico shirt and overalls, and left him in charge of the wagon, which contained two little sisters. The company captain, William G. Young, cracked a whip to persuade the steer to rise, and with a frantic bellow it sprang to its feet and dashed down the road. The team on the children's wagon suddenly followed, rushing in a frenzied, wild panic down the road. The boy's desperate efforts were hopeless, and things became worse when the stubborn steer suddenly lay down in the road again. In an instant, the children's oxen swerved toward the murderous-looking ravine. Every heart stopped in helpless horror as the wagon neared the plunge. One man was close enough to make a last-ditch effort. Snatching his cloak from his shoulders, he leaped in front of the team and waved it. The maneuver worked. The leaders reared

One of the delights of the trail for weary pioneers sick of dust in their mouths and hot, dry roads was found here at the ice slough. Digging just below the deep, insulating turf, even in the summer, they found ice.

and fell, and the wagon came to a standstill. The children were shaken but saved.

Despite such mishaps, the pioneers often sang at night, particularly the Welsh, whose vocal cords seemed to be a national inheritance. A Welsh Saint remembered, "As we sang the first part of the verse . . . we saw the English and the Norwegians and everyone . . . with their heads out of their wagons. With the second part the wagons were empty in an instant and their inhabitants running toward us as if they were charmed. . . . Some asked me where they had learned and who was their teacher? I said that the hills of Wales were the schoolhouse, and the Spirit of God was the teacher."[24] Along with their singing, they sometimes pulled out fiddles and danced around the fire at night, some of them barefoot, having worn out their shoes or maybe saving them for another day. "I remember in walking," said Mary Morris, "I was so anxious to save the soles of my shoes that I walked in the grass wherever possible, so the uppers wore out first."[25]

Tragedy and hardship they may have known, but faith often gave a lightness to their step. They were Zion's children, and every earthly experience was endowed with spiritual significance. If their clothes wore thin, they were still wearing the whole armor of God. If they went without shoes, so did Moses when he approached the burning bush. Their world was not drab or colorless but everywhere endowed with light, the vision that transforms. Because of this, even if their possessions were reduced to nothing, they were rich. Their sacrifices were laid upon God's altar, their experiences made holy there. As Mary Ann Winters was nearing the valley, she described one of the last Sabbaths on the trail: "The sun arose on a scene of calmness and beauty. After a quiet breakfast and at a given signal all repaired to the grove with happy hearts to listen to the words of inspiration that might be given there. The men in their clean hickory shirts and the women and children in their clean starched sunbonnets and dresses looked pure and neat though humble and primitive."[26]

Their first glimpse of Zion brought mixed responses— sometimes a sigh of disappointment. Swedish-born John Lingren admitted, "The picture in our minds of the city, and the real city, failed to have any resemblance."[27]

But every company that wound down Emigration Canyon, footsore, weary, and hungry, were met with open arms by Saints from the valley, who were anxious to welcome them. "I was most forcibly struck with the neat, clean and fair appearance of the people as they came up to us," said Mary Morris of her first meeting with the valley Saints. "We did not realize that as they looked fair and clean to us, we looked correspondingly brown and grim to them."[28]

Sarah Laub Perkins remembered going as a six-year-old to meet the string of wagons jolting down Emigration Canyon. "Word had been given out to meet them with food and all due necessities for their comfort," she said. They would take flour, a pound of butter, a few potatoes, and a can of molasses to greet the weary travelers, and her father would bow his head and say,

Ruts reminiscent of the trail can be seen on the distant hill in this Emigration Canyon scene. As if they were a final test, a last rite of passage, the steep mountains just before entering the valley held one of the most grueling parts of the trail.

"Oh God, we thank thee for these dear ones who have withstood the test."

"Then came the joy of meeting, clasping hands while tears of gratitude were exchanged; for some of these pioneers were without shoes, some wore sandals crudely made from buffalo skins obtained along the way. As they left their offerings of food and clothing, a large bonfire was made in the circle, and the food was prepared to eat. Everyone knelt and thanked God for his protecting care and for their arrival under the shadow of the everlasting hills with its streams of clear, pure water. . . . Mother said she would look up into her father's face and see tears falling. Someone in charge suggested that they sing, 'All is Well.' It was dark when they took their father's hand and returned home full of joy and thanksgiving."[29]

B. H. Roberts' first impression as he entered the valley

as a nine-year-old was a flush of embarrassment about how unkempt he looked. He later wrote, "Along the road . . . I saw a bright-colored, dainty, charming little girl approaching in the middle of the street. . . . My hair stuck out in all directions; the freckles seemed deeper and more plentiful and the features less attractive than when the journey began. Shirt and trousers barely clung to my sturdy form, and my feet were black and cracked. . . . No wonder the dainty little lady was somewhat timid in approaching me." Yet all emotions were overcome by one. Harry and his older sister Mary had not seen their mother for four years. "Presently, however, approaching from the west gate, I saw a woman in a red and white plaid shawl slowly moving among the hillocks of fertilizer that had been raked from the sheds and the yard. She seemed to be daintily picking her way, and there was something in the movement of her head as she looked to the right and to the left that seemed familiar to me. The woman was moving in my direction, and the closer she came the stronger the conviction grew upon me that there was my mother, I would have known her from the dainty cleanliness of everything about her.

"I stood until she came nearly parallel to where I sat; then sliding from the tongue of the wagon, I said, 'Hey Mother,' and she looked upon my upturned face. Without moving she gazed upon me for some time and at last said, 'Is this you, Harry?' . . . It seemed difficult for our mother to realize that we at last were her children after more than four years of separation, but once in a while, a smile would break through the tears and she seemed to be extremely happy."[30]

In 1860 Brigham Young, whose mind was bounteous and whose leadership was bold, came up with yet another idea to bring in the anxious Saints to Zion. In lieu of having Saints raise the money for their own wagons and teams, Church trains would be sent from Salt

Removed in time and circumstance, we can only imagine the sweet relief pioneers must have felt wending
their way down Emigration Canyon and being met by open
arms and wagons full of watermelons, mushmelons,
potatoes, cucumbers, and grapes. They had come home at last.

Lake City to the Missouri River to pick up waiting converts and then return to the valley in the same season. It was a sweeping solution, once thought to be impossible. How could a wagon train, laden with goods and people, make the trip twice in one year? But a better method of immigration was needed, and there was a surfeit of oxen in the territory. They would try it. The foundation for the system was true to the Saints' way of doing things—based on cooperation. Every ward was asked to provide a specific number of men and wagons, flour and provisions, according to their ability to give. It was an efficient system that during the 1860s would bring twenty thousand converts safely to Zion and, more important, give a sense of love and social cohesion to the communities they were building.

By 1866 Church trains were taking the trip east and back on the average of 120 days, and with the Civil War ended, work was resumed with renewed energy on the Union Pacific Railroad. The rattle of train wheels would gradually change the journey, the clank of metal on rails transform the trail of tears into a routine trip. As the train pushed farther and farther west, the Saints began their wagon journey closer to the valley, starting at points in Nebraska, moving their starting point to Wyoming, and at last in 1869 coming all the way by train.

Covered wagons would be retired and oxen turned to other work. The graves of the six thousand dead who had dreamed of Zion would mostly be lost, their markers eroded into the earth, following the path of all nature. The trail itself, in most places, would become obliterated by time and wind.

But the trail had always been more than a road, and even though its physical tracings began to disappear, it was indelibly etched into the souls of a people, and, like a stubborn, dominant gene that shows up in every generation after, the trail would mark the pioneers' descendants, a part of their very marrow that says, "We have given our all for what we believe. You must never take it lightly."

The time for Zion, that city of exquisite beauty and peace that waits to receive the Lord, had not yet come. It would. The Lord first had to build a Zion people whose faith was more precious than gold seven times purified. The trail to Zion was strewn with this kind of gold.

Notes

NOTE: Some of the quotations in this book have been edited for clarity.

ONE

I REMEMBER THOSE WHO ARE UPON THE ISLES OF THE SEA

1. George Cannon, Life History, typescript, in private possession.

2. Hugh Nibley, *Approaching Zion* (Salt Lake City and Provo, Utah: Deseret Book Company and Foundation for Ancient Research and Mormon Studies, 1989), p. 22.

3. JST Luke 17:38.

4. Matthew 6:10.

5. Doctrine & Covenants of The Church of Jesus Christ of Latter-day Saints 133:5, 14 (hereinafter referred to as D&C).

6. D&C 115:6.

7. D&C 101:64.

8. D&C 29:8.

9. Nibley, *Approaching Zion*, p. 28.

10. *Journal of Discourses*, 26 vols. (Liverpool: Latter-day Saints' Book Depot, 1853–1886) 25:179–80 (hereinafter referred to as *JD*).

11. JD 7:16–17, 10:245–46.

12. JD 25:179–80.

13. Joseph Fielding Smith, *Doctrines of Salvation*, 3 vols., comp. Bruce R. McConkie (Salt Lake City: Bookcraft, 1954–1956) 3:256.

14. John Taylor, *The Gospel Kingdom* (Salt Lake City: Bookcraft, 1987), p. 122.

15. JD 4:11.

16. JD 9:170.

17. JD 4:32.

18. Parley P. Pratt, *The Autobiography of Parley P. Pratt* (Salt Lake City: Deseret Book Co., 1985), p. 110.

19. JD 23:31.

20. Joseph Fielding, Journal, typescript, LDS Church Archives.

21. Orson F. Whitney, *Life of Heber C. Kimball* (Salt Lake City: Bookcraft, 1978), p. 104.

22. Ibid.

23. Ibid., p. 109.

24. Ibid., p. 119.

25. Heber C. Kimball to Vilate Kimball, May 27, 1840, Heber C. Kimball Collection, LDS Church Archives.

26. Report to the First Presidency from Brigham Young and Willard Richards, September 5, 1840, Brigham Young Papers, LDS Church Archives.

27. Whitney, *Life of Heber C. Kimball*, p. 122.

28. Ibid., p. 125.

29. Fielding, Journal.

30. Ibid.

31. Whitney, *Life of Heber C. Kimball*, p. 133.

32. Ibid., p. 135.

33. James Fielding to Joseph Fielding, August 27, 1838, Joseph Fielding Collection, LDS Church Archives.

34. Whitney, *Life of Heber C. Kimball*, p. 130.

35. Ibid., p. 132.

36. Ibid., p. 156.

37. JD 4:305.

38. Willard Richards, "History of Willard Richards," *Millennial Star* 27:118–52.

39. The Elders' Journal of the Church of Latter day Saints, October 1, 1837, p. 5.

40. Ibid.

41. JD 12:256.

42. Fielding, Journal.

43. Heber C. Kimball to Vilate Kimball, November 12, 1837, Heber C. Kimball Collection, LDS Church Archives.

44. Whitney, *Life of Heber C. Kimball*, p. 171.

45. Ibid., p. 172.

46. Ibid.

47. D&C 118:4, 5.

48. Matthias F. Cowley, *Wilford Woodruff, History of His Life and Labors* (Salt Lake City: Bookcraft. 1964), p. 100.

49. Ibid., p. 109.

50. *Times and Seasons* 2:311.

51. Ibid., 2:313.

52. Ibid.

53. Cowley, *Wilford Woodruff*, p. 116.

54. *Times and Seasons* 2:328.

55. Ibid.

56. Ibid.

57. Ibid.

58. Ibid.

59. Wilford Woodruff, *Collected Discourses*, vol. 5, October 6, 1895 (Woodland Hills, Utah: B.H.S. Publishing).

60. Ibid.

61. *Times and Seasons* 2:331.

62. Brigham Young to Joseph Smith, May 7, 1840, Joseph Smith Papers, LDS Church Archives.

63. In *Ensign*, April 1987, p. 53.

64. Journal History, June 21, 1847.

65. Rex LeRoy Christensen, *The Life and Contributions of Captain Dan Jones*, master's thesis, Utah State University, 1977, p. 17.

66. Ibid.

67. Ibid., p. 27.

68. *Millennial Star* 7:187.

69. Christensen, *Dan Jones*, p. 28.

70. Ibid.

71. Ibid., p. 29.

72. Dan Jones, *The Guide to Zion*, trans. Ronald D. Dennis (Swansea, Wales: Dan Jones, 1855), p. 1.

TWO

MY PEOPLE MUST BE TRIED IN ALL THINGS

1. George Q. Cannon, *The Life of Joseph Smith* (Salt Lake City: Deseret Book, 1986), p. xxvii.

2. *Young Woman's Journal* 16:554.

3. "Eliza R. Snow's Nauvoo Journal," *BYU Studies* 15, Summer 1975.

4. Autobiography of Electa C. Williams, typescript, LDS Church Archives.

5. In William Mulder and Russell A. Mortensen, comp., *Among the Mormons* (Lincoln: University of Nebraska Press, 1973), p. 171.

6. John Henry Evans, *Joseph Smith, An American Prophet* (Salt Lake City: Deseret Book), p. 9.

7. D&C 128:22.

8. In B. H. Roberts, *A Comprehensive History of The Church of Jesus Christ of Latter-day Saints*, 6 vols. (Salt Lake City: The Church of Jesus Christ of Latter-day Saints, 1930) 2:352; hereinafter cited as *CHC*.

9. *Warsaw Signal*, June 12, 1844.

10. Joseph Smith, *History of the Church of Jesus Christ of Latter-day Saints, Period 1*, 7 vols. (Salt Lake City: The Church of Jesus Christ of Latter-day Saints, 1932–1951) 6:558; hereinafter cited as *HC*.

11. Lewis Barney, typescript, Brigham Young University Archives (hereinafter cited as BYU Archives).

12. HC 6:621–22.

13. Ibid.

14. HC 6:626.

15. Maureen Ursenbach Beecher, ed., "All Things Move in Order in the City: The Nauvoo Diary of Zina Diantha Jacobs," *BYU Studies*, Spring 1979.

16. In Carol Cornwall Madsen, *In Their Own Words: Women and the Story of Nauvoo* (Salt Lake City: Deseret Book), p. 221.

17. Jane Richards Papers, typescript, Richards Family Collection, LDS Church Archives.

18. Vilate Kimball to Heber C. Kimball, June 30, 1844, LDS Church Archives.

19. Pratt, *Autobiography*, p. 294.

20. Wilford Woodruff, Journal, Aug. 6, 7, 1844, LDS Church Archives.

21. Ibid.

22. *Millennial Star* 24:211, 213, 216.

23. Edward Tullidge, *Life of Brigham Young* (New York: [n.p.] 1877), pp. 115–16.

24. *Millennial Star*, May 5, 1845, p. 198.

25. Wallace Stegner, *The Gathering of Zion: The Story of the Mormon Trail* (Lincoln and London: University of Nebraska Press, 1964), p. 35.

26. HC 7:431.

27. HC 6:552.

28. HC 6:222.

29. Louisa Decker, "Reminiscences of Nauvoo," *Woman's Exponent* 37:41–42).

30. Elizabeth Terry Kirby Heward, typescript, LDS Church Archives.

31. Charles Lambert, History, typescript, BYU Archives.

32. Wilford Woodruff Journals, Feb. 8, 1857, LDS Church Archives.

33. Nancy Naomi Alexander Tracy, *Life History of Nancy Naomi Alexander Tracy Written by Herself*, typescript, BYU Library.

34. *Times and Seasons* , January 15, 1845.

35. *CHC* 2:473.

36. In Madsen, *In Their Own Words*, p. 211.

37. Autobiography of Mary Bigelow, June 26, 1809–April 10, 1888, typescript, LDS Church Archives.

38. Lewis Barney, typescript, BYU Archives.

39. John Taylor, Journal, Sept. 13, 1845, p. 123, typescript, LDS Church Archives.

40. *CHC* 2:477.

41. *Quincy Whig*, Sept. 1845.

42. *Nauvoo Neighbor*, Oct. 29, 1845.

43. Joseph Fielding Smith, *Essentials in Church History* (Salt Lake City: Deseret Book, 1979), p. 326.

44. *CHC* 2:538.

45. Mulder and Mortensen, *Among the Mormons*, p. 175.

46. Ibid.

47. Ibid.

48. Ibid.

49. In Madsen, *In Their Own Words*, p. 221.

50. Mulder and Mortensen, *Among the Mormons*, p. 171.

51. In James A. Little, *From Kirtland to Salt Lake* (Salt Lake City: The Juvenile Instructor Office, 1890), p. 46.

52. HC 7:547–48.

53. Madsen, *In Their Own Words*, p. 213.

54. In Preston Nibley, *Exodus to Greatness: The Story of the Mormon Migration* (Salt Lake City: Deseret News Press, 1947), p. 111.

55. HC 7:582.

56. In Little, *From Kirtland to Salt Lake*, p. 46.

57. Psalm 137:1.

THREE

HOW SHALL WE SING THE LORD'S SONG IN A STRANGE LAND?

1. Gilbert Belnap, Autobiography, typescript, BYU Archives.

2. In Nibley, *Exodus to Greatness*, p. 115.

3. Edward Tullidge, *Women of Mormondom* (New York: Tullidge and Crandall, 1877), pp. 307–8.

4. In Nibley, *Exodus to Greatness*, p. 114.

5. Ibid., p.116.

6. Ibid., p.117.

7. Ibid., p.119.

8. Eldon J. Watson, *Manuscript History of Brigham Young, 1846–1847* (Salt Lake City: Eldon Jay Watson, 1971), pp. 150–51.

9. In Nibley, *Exodus to Greatness*, p. 128.

10. Ibid., p. 116.

11. Ibid, p. 125.

12. Orson Pratt, *The Orson Pratt Journals*, Elden J. Watson, ed. (Salt Lake City: Elden J. Watson, 1975), p. 321.

13. Eliza R. Snow, Journal, LDS Church Archives.

14. In Nibley, *Exodus to Greatness*, p. 131.

15. Lorenzo Young, Journal, March 23, 1846, LDS Church Archives.

16. In Tullidge, *Women of Mormondom*, pp. 311–13.

17. Watson, *Manuscript History of Brigham Young*, p. 106.

18. In Tullidge, *Women of Mormondom*, pp. 311–13.

19. In Nibley, *Exodus to Greatness*, p. 139.

20. Ibid.

21. Ibid, p. 142.

22. Ibid, pp. 133–34.

23. Ruth 1:16.

24. In Richard E. Bennett, *Mormons at the Missouri, 1846–1852* (Norman, Oklahoma and London: University of Oklahoma Press, 1987), p. 37.

25. In Bennett, *Mormons at the Missouri*, p. 248.

26. *Hymns* (Salt Lake City: The Church of Jesus Christ of Latter-day Saints, 1985), no. 30.

27. In J. Spencer Cornwall, *Stories of Our Mormon Hymns* (Salt Lake City: Deseret Book, 1975), p. 18.

28. *Women's Exponent*, 12:135–36.

29. In Nibley, *Exodus to Greatness*, p. 162.

30. Pratt, *Autobiography*, pp. 307–8.

31. In Nibley, *Exodus to Greatness*, p. 172.

32. Mina Scovil Wignal, The Life of Lucius Nelson Scovil, typescript, Nauvoo Visitors' Center.

33. Jane Richards Papers, LDS Church Archives.

34. Lucius N. Scovil to Brigham Young, April 14, 1846, Brigham Young Papers, LDS Church Archives.

35. Juanita Brooks, ed., *On the Mormon Frontier: The Diary of Hosea Stout, 1844–1861* (Salt Lake City: University of Utah Press, 1964), p. 172.

36. Journal History, July 13, 1846.

37. *Millennial Star* 13:133.

38. In Nibley, *Exodus to Greatness*, p. 204.

39. William Draper, Autobiography, typescript, BYU Archives.

40. In Daniel Tyler, *A Concise History of the Mormon Battalion in the Mexican War, 1846–1848* (Chicago: Rio Grande Press, 1964), p. 94.

41. Ibid.

42. *Millennial Star*, 10:28.

43. In Little, *From Kirtland to Salt Lake*, pp. 67–74.

44. Ibid., p. 75.

45. In Tullidge, *Women of Mormondom*, pp. 316–17.

46. Journal History, February 26, 1847.

47. Journal History, August 23, 1846.

48. Benjamin Brown, typescript, BYU Archives.

49. Charles Kelly, ed., *Journals of John D. Lee*, Feb. 28, 1847 (Salt Lake City: University of Utah Press, 1984), pp. 104–5.

50. In Bennett, *Mormons at the Missouri*, p. 135.

51. Ibid.

52. Jane Richards typescript, LDS Church Archives.

53. D&C 136:17–18.

FOUR

WE'LL FIND THE PLACE WHICH GOD FOR US PREPARED

1. Stegner, *The Gathering of Zion*, p. 114.

2. In Nibley, *Exodus to Greatness*, p. 345.

3. Wilford Woodruff, *Wilford Woodruff's Journal, 1833–1898 Typescript*, Vol. 3, April 18, 1847 (Salt Lake City: Signature Books, 1983), p. 157.

4. Woodruff, *Journal*, April 23, 1847, p. 157.

5. In Nibley, *Exodus to Greatness*, p. 377.

6. In Leonard Arrington, *Brigham Young, American Moses* (New York: Alfred A. Knopf, 1985), p. 136.

7. In Nibley, *Exodus to Greatness*, p. 380.

8. Ibid.

9. Woodruff, *Journal*, May 8, 1847, p. 171.

10. In Nibley, *Exodus to Greatness*, p. 382.

11. Joseph E. Brown, *The Mormon Trek West* (New York: Doubleday & Company, 1980), p. 93.

12. Appleton M. Harmon, Journal, May 7, 1847, typescript, LDS Church Archives.

13. Brigham Young to Mary Ann Angell, April 20/May 4, 1847, typescript, LDS Church Archives.

14. Woodruff, *Journal*, May 11, 1847, p. 173.

15. Pratt, *The Orson Pratt Journals*, p. 395.

16. Woodruff, *Journal*, May 22, 1847, p. 181.

17. John H. Krenkel, *The Life and Times of Joseph Fish, Mormon Pioneer* (Danvale, Illinois: Interstate Printers and Publishers, 1970), p. 27.

18. Pratt, *Journal*, p. 319.

19. Journal History, May 29, 1847.

20. William Clayton, *An Intimate Chronicle: The Journals of William Clayton*, George Smith, ed. (Salt Lake City: Signature Books, 1991), p. 334.

21. Ibid., May 29, 1847, p. 333.

22. Woodruff, *Journal*, May 29, 1847, p. 189.

23. Brown, *The Mormon Trek West*, p. 114.

24. Ibid.

25. Ibid., p. 114.

26. Woodruff, *Journal*, June 17, 1847, p. 203.

27. Pratt, *Journal*, June 5, p. 418.

28. Woodruff, *Journal*, June 13, 1847, p. 204.

29. In Brown, *The Mormon Trek West*, p. 121.

30. Krenkel, *The Life and Times of Joseph Fish*, p.28.

31. Woodruff, *Journal*, June 19, 1847, p. 298.

32. Heber C. Kimball, Journal, June 19, 1847.

33. In Brown, *The Mormon Trek West*, p. 126.

34. Clayton, *Journal*, June 20, 1847.

35. Woodruff, *Journal*, June 20, 1847, p. 210.

36. Ibid., June 21, 1847, p. 211.

37. Clayton, *Journal*, June 23, 1847, p. 316.

38. In Brown, *The Mormon Trek West*, p. 126.

39. Ibid.

40. Clayton, *Journal*, June 23, 1847, p. 345.

41. Woodruff, *Journal*, June 26, p. 216.

42. Clayton, *Journal*, June 27, 1847, p. 347.

43. Woodruff, *Journal*, June 28, 1847, p. 219.

44. Ibid., June 28, 1847, p. 219.

45. In Brown, *The Mormon Trek West*, p. 130.

46. Woodruff, *Journal*, June 29, 1847, p. 220.

47. In Brown, *The Mormon Trek West*, p. 313.

48. Woodruff, *Journal*, July 4, 1847, p. 223.

49. Ibid., July 8, 1847, p. 225.

50. Thomas Bullock, Journal, July 10, 1847, LDS Church Archives.

51. Clayton, *Journal*, July 11, 1847, p. 356.

52. In Arrington, *Brigham Young*, p. 145.

53. Clayton, *Journal*, July 16, 1847, pp. 357–58.

54. Pratt, *Journals*, July 17, 1847, p. 449.

55. Ibid., July 20, 1847, p. 452.

56. Ibid., July 21, 1847, p. 453.

57. *Hymns*, p. 35.

58. Arrington, *Brigham Young*, p. 144.

59. Bullock, Journal, July 22, 1847.

60. Ibid., July 23, 1847.

61. In Arrington, *Brigham Young*, p. 159.

62. Watson, *Manuscript History*, p. 145.

63. A discrepancy exists between Brigham Young's account and Wilford Woodruff's account of the date and place of this vision.

64. Woodruff, *Journal*, July 28, 1847, p. 239.

65. Ibid.

66. Stegner, *The Gathering of Zion*, p. 173.

67. In Maureen Ursenbach Beecher, *Eliza and Her Sisters* (Salt Lake City: Aspen Books, 1991), p. 78.

68. John Henry Evans, *Charles Coulson Rich, Pioneer Builder of the West* (New York: Macmillan, 1936), p.138.

69. In Don Cecil Corbett, *Mary Fielding Smith, Daughter of Britain* (Salt Lake City: Deseret Book), p. 226.

70. Ibid., p. 228.

71. Ibid., p. 237.

FIVE

WE KNEW HIM IN OUR EXTREMITIES

1. Brigham Young to Franklin D. Richards, Sept. 1855, LDS Church Archives.

2. *The Millennial Star*, Dec. 22, 1855.

3. In Andrew Love Neff, *History of Utah, 1847 to 1869* (Salt Lake City: Deseret News Press, 1940), p. 591.

4. Ibid.

5. Ann Jewell Rowley, Autobiography typescript, Riverton Stake Library, Riverton, Wyoming.

6. *Millennial Star*, Dec. 22, 1855.

7. Diary of Patience Loader Rozsa Archer, typescript, Harold B. Lee Library Special Collections, Brigham Young University; hereinafter cited as Loader, Diary.

8. Stegner, *The Gathering of Zion*, p. 221.

9. John Chislett, Journal, typescript, Riverton Stake Library.

10. Levi Savage, Journal, typescript, Riverton Stake Library, typescript p. 62.

11. Rowley, typescript.

12. Chislett, Journal.

13. Savage, Journal, p. 62.

14. Stegner, *The Gathering of Zion*, p. 140.

15. Savage, Journal, p. 69.

16. Chislett, Journal.

17. Ibid.

18. Savage, Journal.

19. James G. Willie, typescript, Riverton Stake Library.

20. Chislett, Journal.

21. Willie, typescript.

22. Savage, Journal, p. 71.

23. Stella Jaques Bell, ed., *Life History and Writings of John Jaques, including a Diary of the Martin Handcart Company* (Rexburg, Idaho: Ricks College Press, 1978), p. 142.

24. Loader, Diary, pp. 59–60.

25. Ibid., pp. 68–69.

26. Ibid., p. 71.

27. Rebecca Bartholomew and Leonard J. Arrington, *Rescue of the 1856 Handcart Companies* (Provo, Utah: Brigham Young University, Charles Redd Center for Western Studies, 1993), p. 3.

28. Chislett, Journal.

29. In Myrtle Stevens Hyde, comp., James Hurren and Eliza Reeder, typescript, Riverton Stake Library.

30. Rowley, typescript, Riverton Stake Library.

31. John Chislett, Journal.

32. Levi Savage, Journal, pp. 72–73.

33. In Kate B. Carter, *Heart Throbs of the West* (Salt Lake City: Daughters of Utah Pioneers, 1951), 6:364–66.

34. Willie, typescript.

35. In Carter, *Heart Throbs of the West*, 6:364–66.

36. JD 4:113.

37. Daniel W. Jones, *Forty Years Among the Indians* (Salt Lake City: Juvenile Instructor's Office, 1890), p. 60.

38. Chislett, Journal.

39. Ibid.

40. Jones, *Forty Years Among the Indians*, p. 65.

41. Chislett, Journal.

42. Ruby M. F. Hall, Story of Lucy Ward, typescript, Riverton Stake Library.

43. Chislett, Journal.

44. Savage, Journal.

45. Ibid.

46. Brigham Young, speech of November 4, 1856, recorded in *Deseret News*, November 12, 1856.

47. Brigham Young to Amasa Lyman, November 4, 1856, LDS Church Archives.

48. Bell, John Jaques, p. 144.

49. Ibid., p. 145.

50. Ibid., p. 146.

51. Stegner, *Gathering*, p. 248.

52. Elizabeth Kingsford, *Leaves from the Life of Elizabeth Horrocks Jackson Kingsford* (Ogden, Utah: 1908).

53. Ibid.

54. Stegner, *The Gathering of Zion*, p. 252.

55. This is not the same Dan Jones who was a Welsh missionary.

56. Jones, *Forty Years Among the Indians*, p. 66.

57. Loader, Diary, p. 91.

58. From letter by G. D. Grant *Daily Herald*, 1878–1879.

59. Bartholomew and Arrington, *Rescue of the 1856 Handcart Companies*, p. 27.

60. Ibid.

61. Bell, *John Jaques*, p. 168.

62. In Stegner, *The Gathering of Zion*, p. 254.

63. Ibid., p. 255.

64. In William Palmer, She Stood Tall on Her Knees, The Story of Nellie Unthank, typescript, Riverton Stake Library.

SIX

I WILL GO BEFORE THY FACE

1. In Kate B. Carter., comp., *Treasures of Pioneer History* (Salt Lake City: Daughters of Utah Pioneers, 1952), p. 468.

2. William Mulder, *Homeward to Zion: The Mormon Migration from Scandinavia* (Minneapolis: University of Minnesota Press, 1957), p. 43.

3. Ibid., p. 40.

4. Ibid., p. 47.

5. Ibid., p. 48.

6. Ibid., p 51.

7. Ibid., p. 146.

8. Ibid., p. 147.

9. Ibid., p. 149.

10. Ibid., p. 51.

11. In Carter, *Treasures of Pioneer History*, 1955, p. 42.

12. In Carter, *Treasures of Pioneer History*, 1954, pp. 46–47.

13. In Mulder and Mortensen, *Among the Mormons*, pp. 334–44.

14. Jean Rio Griffiths Baker, Diary, typescript, LDS Church Archives.

15. *Millennial Star*, June 15, 1849, p. 184.

16. Ronald D. Dennis. *The Call of Zion: The Story of the First Welsh Emigration* (Salt Lake City: Bookcraft, 1987), p.44.

17. Ibid., p. 46.

18. Ibid.

19. In Carter, *Heart Throbs of the West*, pp. 107–9.

20. In Carter, *Treasures of Pioneer History*, 1954, p. 38.

21. B. H. Roberts, *The Autobiography of B. H. Roberts*, ed. Gary Bergera (Salt Lake City: Signature Books, 1990), pp. 25–44.

22. LeRoy Hafen and Ann Hafen, *Handcarts to Zion* (Glendale, California: Arthur H. Clark, 1960), p. 61.

23. In Carter, *Treasures of Pioneer History*, 1954, p. 39.

24. In Dennis, *The Call of Zion*, p. 60.

25. In Carter, *Treasures of Pioneer History*, 1954, p. 39.

26. In Carter, *Treasures of Pioneer History*, 1952, p. 485.

27. Ibid., p. 240.

28. In Carter, *Treasures of Pioneer History*, 1954, p. 41.

29. In Carter, *Heart Throbs of the West*, 1951, p. 113.

30. Roberts, *Autobiography*, pp. 37–11.

PHOTO CAPTIONS

— Section 1 —

1. Matthew 9:37.

2. Whitney, *Heber C. Kimball*, pp. 89, 881.

3. Ibid., p. 171.

— Section 2 —

1. Cowley, *Wilford Woodruff*, p. 152.

2. Photograph courtesy Missouri Historical Society, St. Louis. Thomas M. Easterly, photographer.

3. *Nauvoo Neighbor*, September 6, 1843.

4. HC 7:479.

5. HC 7:480.

6. George Whitaker, Life of George Whitaker, a Utah Pioneer, 1820–1907, Typescript, LDS Church Archives, p. 12.

— Section 3 —

1. In Nibley, *Exodus to Greatness*, p. 145.

2. Stegner, *The Gathering of Zion*, p. 107.

— Section 4 —

1. "Sites on the Trail West," *Ensign*, January 1980, p. 37.

2. Robert Sweeten, Journal, December 14, 1840–January 19, 1936), Typescript, authors' possession, p. 9.

3. Stegner, *The Gathering of Zion*, p. 151.

4. John Henry Evans, *Charles Coulson Rich, Pioneer Builder of the West* (New York: Macmillan, 1936), pp. 135–36.

5. Krenkel, *Joseph Fish*, p. 26.

— Section 5 —

1. Wallace Stegner, *Mormon Country* (New York: Bonanza Books, 1942), p. 73.

2. Pratt, *Autobiography*, pp. 400–401.

3. Elizabeth Horrocks Jackson, *Leaves from the Life of Elizabeth Horrocks Jackson Kingsford* (Ogden, Utah, 1908), p. 8.

4. Loader, Diary, p. 86.

5. James Hurren and Eliza Reeder, Typescript, Riverton Stake Library, p. 13.

6. Mary Hurren Wight Biography, in Journal History, November 8, 1856, LDS Church Archives.

7. Loader, Diary, p. 86.

8. Elizabeth Green, Typescript, Riverton Stake Library.

— Section 6 —

1. Mulder, *Homeward to Zion*, p. 42.

2. Dennis, *The Call of Zion*, p. 10.

3. Krenkel, *Joseph Fish*, p. 30.

I want to tell one secret. . . . The Spirit of the
Lord was all the time prompting the
[people] . . . to do as they did; they could not do
anything else, because God would not
let them do anything else. The brethren and sisters
came across the Plains because they
could not stay; that is the secret of the movement."

—Brigham Young, November 9, 1856

At the first ringing of the bell, I was ready for breakfast.

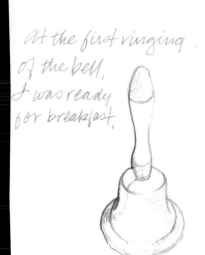

I laid there in the dark and thought that home was far away.

The women gathered prairie flowers and fashioned them into wreathes to place beside lonely trailside graves.

Because the earth was frozen, many of the dead were buried in a shallow grave, covered with willows and then earth and rocks to keep the wolves away.

We took our tools with us for we were determined to build another city to our God.

When the indians got too close, we fired the cannon as a warning.

The bugle sounded at 5:00 each morning, a signal for everyone to arise and see to prayers.

Oct. 9, 1846 — The quails descend. The sick knock them down with sticks and the little children catch them alive with their hands! God remembered us.

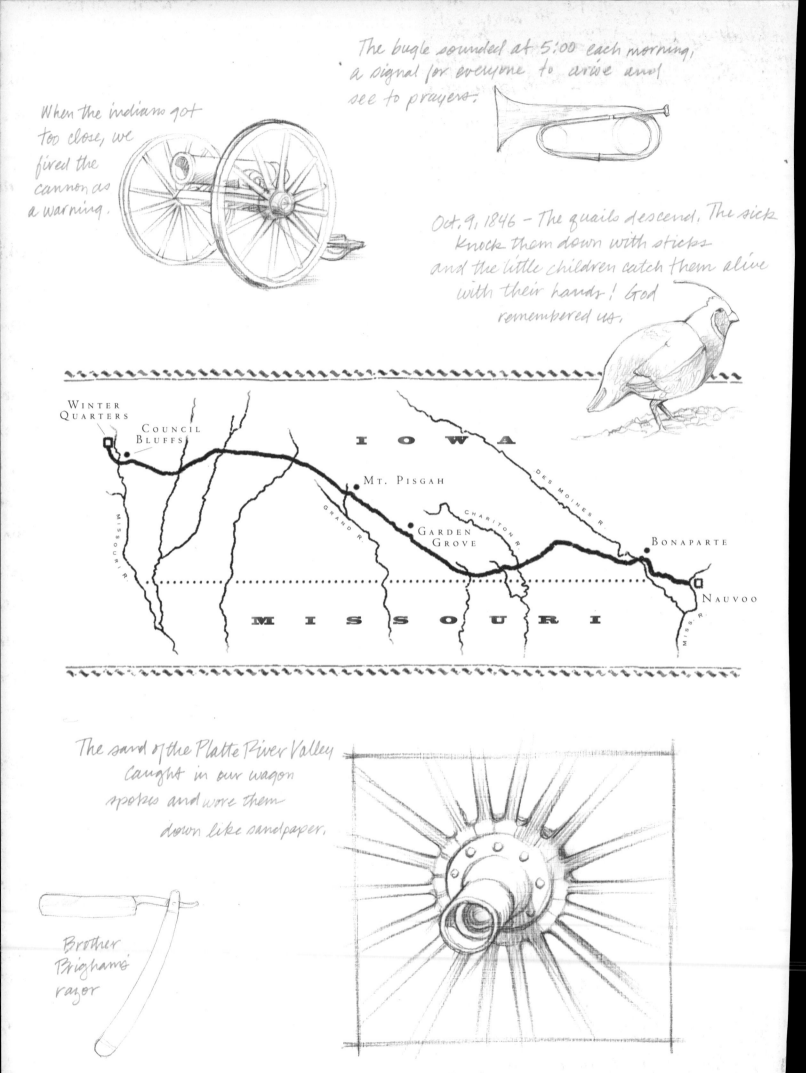

WINTER QUARTERS
COUNCIL BLUFFS
I O W A
DES MOINES R.
MT. PISGAH
GRAND R.
CHARITON R.
GARDEN GROVE
BONAPARTE
MISSOURI R.
NAUVOO
MISS R.
M I S S O U R I

The sand of the Platte River Valley caught in our wagon spokes and wore them down like sandpaper.

Brother Brigham's razor